D0152959

BR
936
.P64   Powell   cop.1
              Antireligious
        propaganda in
        the Soviet Union.

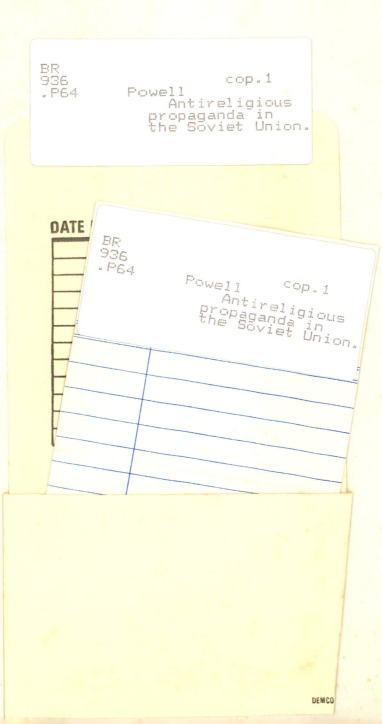

BR
936
.P64
          Powell   cop.1
                Antireligious
        propaganda in
        the Soviet Union.

DATE

DEMCO

Donated by

DR. JAMES HUNT
FEBRUARY 9, 1994

© DEMCO, INC. 1990 PRINTED IN U.S.A.

Antireligious Propaganda in the Soviet Union

**Antireligious Propaganda in the Soviet Union:
A Study of Mass Persuasion**

David E. Powell

The MIT Press
Cambridge, Massachusetts, and London, England

BR
936
.P64

Copyright © 1975 by
The Massachusetts Institute of Technology

All rights reserved. No part of this book may be reproduced in any form or by any means, electronic or mechanical, including photocopying, recording, or by any information storage and retrieval system, without permission in writing from the publisher.

This book was set in CRT Times Roman,
printed on Mohawk Neotext Offset,
and bound in Roxite B 51501 Vellum (Red),
by The Colonial Press, Inc.,
in the United States of America.

Library of Congress Cataloging in Publication Data

Powell, David E
  Antireligious propaganda in the Soviet Union.
  Bibliography: p.
  Includes index.
  1. Russia—Religion. 2. Communism and Christianity—Russia. 3. Propaganda, Russian.
I. Title.
BR936.P64   301.15′4   74-34127
ISBN 0-262-16061-7

for my elizabeth anne
b. 2.12.68   d. 5.6.72

Contents

Acknowledgments

Any book, including this one, is the product of many people's efforts. My own task has been made significantly easier by the existence of a rich body of literature on both propaganda and the status of religion in the USSR, and even more so by the support of numerous friends and colleagues.

I am indebted to several institutions, each of which provided assistance at one or another stage in this project. The University of Virginia was most generous in its support, especially by awarding me a Sesquicentennial Associateship for the 1972–73 academic year. The American Philosophical Society also granted me financial assistance in 1972–73, enabling me to complete this manuscript during a leave of absence from Virginia. Perhaps most important, the Russian Research Center at Harvard University has provided me with an environment conducive to serious and productive scholarship. I would like to express my gratitude to the Center's past Director, Richard Pipes, and to its present Director, Adam B. Ulam, for helping to make the Center such a special place. My experience at the Center has been an exhilarating one. I am profoundly grateful to my colleagues here, as well as to the Center's staff and students, for making me feel at home.

Portions of Chapters 3 and 4 appeared in Bohdan R. Bociurkiw and J. W. Strong (eds.), *Religion and Atheism in the USSR and Eastern Europe* (Macmillan & Co. of London and the University of Toronto Press, 1975). An earlier version of Chapter 8 appeared in *The Public Opinion Quarterly*, Vol. XXXI, No. 3 (Fall 1967). I should like to thank the editors of these publications for allowing me to use this material. St. Martin's Press kindly granted me permission to reprint the maps in Appendix 1. These maps originally appeared in Walter Kolarz, *Religion in the Soviet Union* (1961).

I would also like to thank several individuals who gave generously of their time, interest, and concern. In particular, I would like to thank Frederick C. Barghoorn, Bohdan R. Bociurkiw, Walter D. Connor, Erich Goldhagen, John Hodgson, Norman Naimark, Marshall Shatz, Gregory Shesko, and the anonymous reviewers of The MIT Press. Without their frequent criticism and occasional enthusiasm, this book would not have seen the light of day.

I would like to express special thanks to my closest friends, Helen Desfosses and Susan and Michael Mezey. I have gained immeasurably from their friendship, affection, and love.

My father, Professor Norman J. Powell, was a very special source of personal and scholarly support. I found his enthusiasm for this project, and his critical reading of what must have seemed like endless drafts of the manuscript, invaluable. It is a matter of great sorrow to me that he did not live to see the final product.

Finally, I have been motivated—even driven—to complete this work as an expression of love for my little girl, Elizabeth Anne, who died in 1972. This book is lovingly dedicated to her.

David E. Powell
Cambridge, Massachusetts
March 1975

A Note on Transliteration

The transliteration system employed in this book is essentially the system used by the Library of Congress. There are, however, two basic differences. I have used "ya" rather than "ia," for the Russian letter "Я." In addition, I have not transliterated soft or hard signs which appeared in the original Russian. My purpose has been to ease the task of readers who are unfamiliar with the Russian language.

1 Modernization, Secularization, and Socialization

The struggle against religion is not a campaign, not an isolated phenomenon, not a self-contained entity; it is an inseparable component part of the entire ideological activity of Party organizations, an essential link and necessary element in the complex of communist education.

Pravda, January 12, 1967

The political function of communism is not to overthrow authority but to fill the vacuum of authority.

Samuel P. Huntington,
Political Order in Changing Societies
(1968), p. 335

This is a study of mass persuasion. It is concerned with the effort of the Communist Party of the Soviet Union (CPSU) to refashion the political culture of an entire people. For more than half a century, the Party has sought and effected radical change. It has created new political, economic, and social institutions and has transformed Russia from a relatively backward state into one of the world's great powers. It has brought industrialization, urbanization, and improved standards of living and education to the people. But the Soviet leaders, unlike other modernizing elites, have sought to go beyond institutional change in their quest for modernity. They have attempted to change the people themselves. The Party has invested, and continues to invest, vast resources in an effort to remold the values, attitudes, and expectations of individual citizens.

Although they have always believed that social change would itself alter people's views and behavior, the Soviet authorities have attempted to guide this process toward a particular objective. Institutional change has been channeled toward "social mobilization," as "major clusters of old social, economic, and psychological commitments have been eroded or broken and people have become available for new patterns of socialization and behavior." [1] The Party has tried to break down traditional authority patterns and relationships that it considers inappropriate to the modern world, and to develop in their place a new set of attachments. It has chosen to shape the values of an entire people through a massive program of education and indoctrination—the "communist upbringing *(kommunist-icheskoye vospitaniye)* of the populace." It has tried to change the views of adults and to inculcate into younger people, who have fewer and less firmly held preconceptions and attitudes, views that it deems correct. Perhaps no other ruling elite in all of history has attempted so strenuously to implement

Aristotle's dictum: "The citizen should be molded to suit the form of government under which he lives." [2]

The Party's ultimate objective is to rear a "New Soviet Man," whose noble character and varied talents will be worthy of the ultimate communist society. In the first years after the Revolution, official theorists spoke rhapsodically about the New Man. For example, Trotsky wrote in 1924:

Man will become immeasurably stronger, wiser and subtler; his body will become more harmonized, his movements more rhythmic, his voice more musical. The forms of life will become dynamically dramatic. The average human type will rise to the heights of an Aristotle, a Goethe or a Marx. And above this ridge new peaks will rise. [3]

Inflated rhetoric of this kind became much less fashionable during the Stalin years, when revolutionary élan of any kind was discredited. After the dictator's death, however, Party ideologists once again addressed themselves to the theme of the New Man. The man of communist society, it was said, would be "cultured and well-rounded, possessing a strongly developed sense of collectivism and public duty"; he would be "distinguished by the clarity of his outlook, by the richness of his intellectual life and physical perfection." [4]

Official promises today are no less effusive. As two Soviet ideologists have written: "We have in our hands a truly miraculous method of transformation, our 'philosopher's stone'—the philosophy of Marxism-Leninism." With it, "Soviet society is rearing a man whose spiritual and moral qualities are worth more than any treasures in the world. . . ." [5] With the aid of this "philosopher's stone," such negative traits as individualism, "bourgeois nationalism," chauvinism, indolence, and "religious prejudices" will be eradicated. The New Man will be intelligent, creative, and humane, imbued with feelings of collectivism, proletarian internationalism, socialist patriotism, love of labor, and militant atheism.

The task of developing citizens with these characteristics has obviously been a difficult one. When the Bolsheviks assumed power, they were faced with a population that was largely preindustrial in outlook. [6] They were also confronted with two powerful institutions that protected and transmitted nonsocialist attitudes—the family and the church. The Bolsheviks' program made a clash with these two institutions inevitable.

Early efforts to destroy the family as an institution have been abandoned, or at least put aside for the foreseeable future. The government now pursues a policy of supporting and strengthening the family. This has led some Western scholars to conclude that "the orientations contained within the family are now congruent with the political order," and that the family now transmits political values "that are appropriate for the Soviet state." [7] This interpretation, although plausible, cannot yet be documented, because very little empirical evidence on the subject is available. In fact, whether the family actually facilitates or hinders official socialization efforts today is not altogether clear.[8] Despite this uncertainty, the Party continues to support the family as an institution.

In contrast, the Party has continued its early efforts to undermine the influence of the church. The Soviet leaders have always viewed secularization as basic to their political program. As Marxists, they expected secularization to follow from scientific progress and socioeconomic change. But as Leninists, they decided to accelerate this process by pursuing an active *policy* of secularization. While they were confident that religion would eventually die out (its disappearance was said to be "demanded by history"), they sought to hasten this inevitable process. Over the half century that they have been in power, they have utilized a wide range of measures—from education and propaganda to legal restrictions, extralegal pressure, and outright terror—in their effort to achieve a secular society.

Lenin and his followers regarded religion as a major barrier to their program of modernization. Their rejection of the church derived both from ideological conviction and from the special character of Orthodox Church power. On the one hand, the Bolsheviks saw religious belief as an "opiate," used by exploiting groups to deceive the masses and by the masses themselves to escape from intolerable realities.[9] On the other, Russia in the period before the Bolshevik coup was, to use Donald Smith's term, an "integrated religiopolitical system," [10] one that was highly resistant to change. Church and state were linked in a conservative alliance, and both profited from the arrangement.

The Orthodox Church helped to sustain the autocracy, operating in a very real sense as part of the tsar's control system. It was virtually a subdivision of state power, helping to ensure social stability. The Church encouraged allegiance to the tsar and to the Russian fatherland, and it blessed personal sacrifice for the glory of the state. It urged obedience to authority and acceptance of a rigid and unequal social order, while nourishing dreams of a beautiful afterlife for the poor and docile. The Orthodox Church, in turn, derived benefits from the secular authorities. It had little competition for the souls of the Russian people, and its officials were men of prominence, wealth, and power. Other religious denominations were subjected to various pressures, and this helped to reinforce the authority of the Orthodox faith. During the reactionary reigns of Alexander III (1881–1894) and Nicholas II (1894–1917), these discriminatory measures became more pervasive, and the primacy of the Orthodox Church was elevated to a major principle of Imperial Rule.[11]

In 1917, organized religion, especially the Orthodox Church, was a formidable power in temporal affairs, and the overwhelming majority of the population were believers. The Communist Party sought to destroy the political and economic might of the church and, at the same time, to induce people to renounce their religious beliefs. As we shall see, the second task has proved far more difficult than the first.

Modernization and Secularization

The sources of religion, Marx once suggested, "are found not in heaven but on earth."[12] Religion, that is, is man's invention: it is "the sigh of an oppressed creature . . . , the opium of the people."[13] But if people invent God or gods in order to rationalize their unhappy lot on earth, improving their lives should lead them to abandon their religious beliefs. As Marx put it, "As man affects and changes Nature, he simultaneously changes his own nature."[14]

While the evidence is far from conclusive, there does seem to be a relationship between economic conditions and religion. Throughout the world, higher living standards, improved education, urbanization, industrialization, and scientific progress are associated with a lower incidence of religious belief.[15] In the USSR, too, sweeping changes in the polity, economy, and society have had a substantial impact on religious beliefs and practices. To quote a leading Soviet philosopher, the erosion of religious belief has been "closely and inseparably linked with the resolution of general economic, social and cultural problems in the building of communism."[16] "From their own personal experience," another authority has argued, "people are convinced of the real possibility of creating a 'paradise' on earth and disregarding the 'heavenly Garden of Eden.' "[17]

Although the Soviet system has been termed "the best atheist agitator of all,"[18] broad social change only provides the preconditions needed to fulfill history's mandate. Even Marx, who predicted that religion would inevitably disappear with the consolidation of the socialist order, expected education to play an important role in this development.[19] For more than fifty years, the CPSU, as history's agent and interpreter, has pursued a policy of secularization. Indeed, according to one Soviet commentator, without the "tremendous educational and organizational work" of professional atheists, "the successes which have been achieved [thus far] in forming a materialist world-view among the people would have been impossible."[20]

This linking of an ultimate goal that is allegedly inevitable with conscious, purposive activity to achieve it is a basic feature of Soviet political life, as it was for the Bolsheviks before they assumed power. Impatience with the slow pace of history is fundamental to the Leninist version of Marxism; it is considered expedient and right to accelerate the pace of history. To be sure, there is a logical contradiction between a determinist philosophy of history and aggressive political action. But, as Robert V. Daniels has pointed out, this contradiction makes a great deal of sense in *psychological* terms. The man who is convinced of the inevitability of his cause "strives all the more vigorously to make sure it succeeds." [21] Soviet antireligious efforts should be understood in this context.

Although Marx and Engels were atheists—their uncompromising denial of the existence of a divine being is one of the essential features of their weltanschauung—both saw direct attacks on religion as useless and misplaced. Such measures, they argued, were useless, because religion "cannot be abolished as long as the world is not put straight," and were misplaced, "because the real enemy is the perverted social order of which . . . religion is only the 'spiritual aroma.' " [22] Lenin, on the other hand, was extremely impatient with history and with religious beliefs and practices. He considered it appropriate and even necessary to combat religion actively. Once he and his Party assumed power, Lenin's approach, especially his call for militant antireligious propaganda, became official policy.[23]

More generally, the Party's program of secularization has involved four basic objectives: (1) the separation of the political system from religious ideologies and ecclesiastical structures, (2) the performance by political authorities of socioeconomic functions formerly carried out by organized religion, (3) the restructuring of the political culture to emphasize temporal goals and rational, pragmatic means to achieve them, and (4) the elimination of any vestige of religious belief or practice and the creation of a completely atheist society.[24] While the first two objectives were achieved fairly quickly through the application of terror and highly restrictive laws, the latter two have yet to be achieved. To reach these goals, the Party has developed an elaborate program of political socialization.

Socialization

"Political socialization" is the process by which people acquire their political standards and beliefs.[25] It involves a wide range of institutions and individuals, from parents and teachers to the press, the courts, and the military. Through contact with these socializing agents, people modify or discard old values, acquire new ones, or reinforce their preexisting notions.

The end product of the socialization process is "a set of attitudes—cognitions, value standards, and feelings—toward the political system, its various roles and role incumbents." [26]

In every society, individuals are exposed to countless socializing experiences. But different socializing agents are apt to transmit different viewpoints. Some lead to support of the official value system, while others stimulate or reinforce alternative sets of values. What distinguishes the Soviet system is the vast and overt character of the official program—the "communist upbringing" of the population. The Party systematically, directly, and repeatedly communicates its political messages. The approach is simple and direct. Its principal theoretical underpinning is expressed in a favorite saying of Nikita Khrushchev, *povtoreniye mat' ucheniya* (repetition is the mother of learning)." [27] Moreover, Soviet ideologists apparently agree with Herbert Hyman's contention that, to promote political stability, people "must learn their political behavior early and well and persist in it." [28] Political lessons taught in the USSR as early as the preschool years are reinforced through constant repetition. But whether the symbols and values presented by the regime are in fact internalized by the masses is another matter.

In their effort to restructure the political culture and transform a religious people into atheists, the Soviet leaders have tried to socialize and resocialize the entire population. They have been working at this task since 1917. Their first efforts were clumsy and often vicious, serving only to offend and alienate believers. Most of the tactics used in the early years have since been criticized as excessively provocative and counterproductive. Nonetheless, they seem to have left a lasting imprint on the atheist movement. While atheist propaganda today is somewhat more sophisticated than it was half a century ago, it still is based essentially on the repetition of outdated formulas, still offends believers, and still helps to create a climate that encourages antireligious excesses.

Since Stalin's death, the Soviet authorities have expanded their indoctrination and socialization programs. In particular, they have renewed their drive to eradicate religious beliefs and practices from the USSR. In the past two decades, antireligious propaganda has been the subject of three Central Committee resolutions, thousands of articles and books and millions of lectures. Indeed, as the Soviet Union, according to the official rhetoric, draws closer to communism, defects in the system become matters of increasing concern and the target of more intense and energetic propaganda.[29]

The Underlying Rationale

When the Bolshevik regime was established half a century ago, organized religion, especially the Russian Orthodox Church, represented a threat. Its political and economic power were vast, and many leading church officials were active and outspoken in their hostility to the new government. Lenin and his followers viewed the church as a danger to the very existence of the new order, as well as an obstacle to the future reconstruction of society. Given their understanding of politics and their ambitions for Russia, their policies toward the church are understandable.

The wisdom of current policies toward religion, however, is less clear. The church can no longer be scorned as an ally and prop of the ruling class, although, ironically, there is more than a little truth to the charge that it continues to play this role. The church's hold over the citizenry has been severely eroded. Its wealth has been expropriated, its doctrines have been revised to conform more closely to the contemporary world, its political pronouncements are invariably supportive of Soviet domestic and foreign policies, it has been infiltrated by the security police, and it is now a rather docile creature of the political authorities.

Why, then, does the Party continue to combat religion? The logic and expediency of such a policy are far from clear. Indeed, its costs may well outweigh any benefits that have been or could be achieved. As we shall see, continued antireligious efforts have led to the erosion of traditional social control mechanisms, as well as to personal alienation and diminished support for the regime. In fact, official antireligious policies have, to some extent, stimulated and reinforced the very practices and beliefs they were designed to eradicate.

The rationale underlying Soviet policy toward religion involves three factors:

1. The Party objects to religion on power-political grounds: it is determined not to share its power with any other organization. The regime, as Jeremy Azrael has pointed out, is "committed to the destruction of all autonomous social institutions and groups—that is, to the eradication of all focal points for alternative loyalties." [30] It cannot accept the notion that other doctrines or institutions have the right to remain independent, with a dignity and a validity of their own.[31] The political authorities are concerned that religious loyalties might conflict with those they consider more suitable. Ironically, though, the Party is so preoccupied with "enemies," "opponents," and "rivals" that it sometimes exaggerates the threat of religion, adopting policies that sometimes make believers hostile to the political regime.

2. Political concern about establishing the full internal sovereignty of the state is reinforced by the desire to mobilize the citizens' energies for radical social change. Despite considerable evidence that religious believers are as loyal and hardworking as nonbelievers,[32] stereotyped views of the influence of religion are still widespread. In fact, these outdated conceptions of religious belief and believers dominate the entire atheist movement. Religion, it is said, "sows illusions . . . and acts as a . . . serious obstacle on the path to social progress." [33] It encourages humility and submissiveness to fate, attitudes that "disarm people spiritually, hinder their creative powers and public activity." [34] Religion keeps people weak and downtrodden and tells them that they are impotent. It urges them to resign themselves to fate, requiring that they patiently endure "all ills and misfortunes, persecution and oppression." [35] It demands that people become "slaves by conviction . . . , hoping only for the mercy of the Almighty." [36]

Religion also draws people away from concern with the real world, preventing them from "fully displaying their creative forces in work and social life." [37] "By the whole of its ideas, [religion] distracts people from labor . . . and leads believers away from participation in the life of society." [38] It "shuts [them] off from the seething life of the people, making them indifferent to the interests of society." [39] Its focus is otherworldly; it deludes believers, compelling them to devote time to prayer and to sacrifice their lives on earth in order to prepare for an illusory life after death. According to the official ideology, the earthly life is a matter of secondary importance to believers: "the purpose of this life is to prepare for death," or, more properly, for life after death.[40]

3. It is not simply the general thrust of religious doctrine, i.e., its unscientific character and its focus on otherworldly matters, that is considered inimical to the regime's goals. Certain teachings and practices, characteristic of one or another church, are regarded as especially undesirable.

a. Perhaps most important, the Christian concept of individual salvation is said to impede the development of a spirit of collectivism. Fidelity to church doctrine promotes individualism, a "private-property psychology," and a "petty, egotistical concern about 'saving one's soul.' " [41] It creates a world "whose center is man's personal 'I' and . . . concern for 'personal salvation' and 'entry into the Kingdom of Heaven.' " [42]

b. Religious differences allegedly breed hostility among individuals and groups. The principle of "religious exclusiveness" promotes contempt for, and conflict with, those of other faiths.[43]

c. In some regions of the USSR, especially Central Asia and the Baltic States, religious differences become intertwined with national differences, thereby nourishing "bourgeois nationalist" tendencies.[44]

d. Religious teachings, especially in the Moslem and Jewish faiths, are said to propagate male chauvinism, relegating women to an inferior position in the conduct of religious rituals and in society as well.[45]

e. Certain religious practices are seen as directly endangering the health of parishioners, e.g., prolonged fasting, frenzied prayer, baptism by immersion, overindulgence at religious celebrations, or contact with stagnant holy water.[46]

f. Members of some of the fundamentalist sects refuse to work on Saturday or Sunday, refuse to serve in the military, refuse to take part in elections or trade union activities, and sometimes prohibit their children from joining the Pioneers, taking part in sports activities, or attending the theater.[47] The regime feels so strongly about these practices that it has prosecuted both clergymen and ordinary believers and has even banned a number of religious groups.

While there is a good deal of truth in many of these allegations, they are on the whole oversimplified, misleading, and outdated. Most churches in the USSR have revised their attitudes toward social, political, economic, and scientific questions.[48] Some religious groups, most notably the Baptists, have done away with elaborate rituals and have placed relationships between clergy and laymen on a more democratic basis.[49] But the authorities are not impressed by these changes. Revisions in religious doctrine, no matter how significantly they depart from traditional teachings, are dismissed as superficial and limited in scope. Modern versions of religious doctrine, Soviet ideologists argue, are "rational in form and in details, but dogmatic in content." [50] The changes involve minor issues, whereas the essence of religion—belief in God—remains intact.[51] And, if most believers today are sometimes acknowledged to be "honest workers who conscientiously fulfill their obligations to society and march side by side with atheists," they are said to do so despite, not because of, their religious convictions.[52]

Who Is Religious?

Soviet scholars, like their Western counterparts, have found it difficult to define "religiousness." According to a Soviet handbook, religion is "belief in a nonexistent, supernatural world, supposedly inhabited by gods, spirits, angels, saints, the souls of the dead or other supernatural beings." [53] This formulation fails to distinguish between religious beliefs and religious practices, and it does not discriminate among religious, quasi-religious, and ethical beliefs. Belief in a Supreme Being, church attendance, the performance of certain rituals, the acceptance of certain ethical norms, identification of oneself as religious—all can signify religiousness. But some who believe in God may not attend church; others who claim not to believe in God may baptize their children; still others who belong to no church may adhere to a moral code usually associated with one of the major religions. Who is religious and who is not often cannot be determined with any degree of precision.

This difficulty is seen most clearly in the area of religious ceremonies and rituals. It is not only religious persons who take part in these rites; many nonbelievers engage in them as well. Some observe church holidays, others baptize their children, while still others arrange church marriages and funerals. According to Soviet specialists, the overwhelming majority of parents who participate in baptismal rites do *not* consider themselves believers and do not take part in the ceremony for religious reasons. (This is somewhat less true in rural than in urban areas.) A study done in the city of Gorky, for example, revealed that only 5.5 percent of parents taking part in baptismal ceremonies were impelled to do so by religious convictions. Most said they were influenced by their belief that baptism is "an old Russian rite, a national custom and a tradition which ought to be preserved," or else attributed their participation to pressure from grandparents.[54] (Some grandparents get their way by threatening not to look after an unchristened infant.)[55] On the other hand, many people who consider themselves to be believers do not engage in religious rituals. A study of Moslems in Kazan, for example, showed that approximately half of the believers did not fast during Ramadan and did not take part in other rites basic to Islam.[56]

Because only some citizens readily identify themselves as believers, Soviet social scientists have had to devise more sophisticated classification schemes to deal with people who are reticent and with situations that are ambiguous. Some researchers count as religious only those who are members of, or who actively participate in the life of, an organized church group. Others see as religious anyone who believes in God or other supernatural forces. Still others consider self-designation the only valid criterion of religiousness. Although leading academic specialists have increasingly come to appreciate the rich and varied nature of religion, the problem of definition remains troublesome.

In the years since Stalin's death, Soviet scholars have attempted to discover precisely who is, and who is not, a believer. Research teams of sociologists, anthropologists, ethnographers, and historians have conducted numerous surveys of religious communities and individuals. The results of these investigations indicate quite clearly that, regardless of the criterion or criteria used, religious people are apt to be elderly, female, rural dwellers, and people with little formal education. (Not all are, of course. Some young, well-educated urbanites, even Party members and Komsomols, believe in God.)[57] Studies have shown that two-thirds of believers live in rural areas.[58] Perhaps 75 to 80 percent of those who are religious are women, and the overwhelming majority are over fifty years of age.[59] The following tables (Tables 1.1, 1.2, 1.3, and 1.4) provide survey data on the religious populations of several areas of the USSR.

The findings cited in Tables 1.1, 1.2, 1.3, and 1.4 allow us to construct an image of the typical religious believer: an elderly woman with little education who is very likely a collective farmer or pensioner residing in a remote provincial village. The model is not a very attractive one; it is unlikely to stimulate efforts at emulation. Indeed, the image is itself

Table 1.1 Attitudes Toward Religions in Voronezh Province, 1966 (in percentages)

Group	Among Men	Among Women	Of Total
Atheists	60.7	47.4	53.4
Nonreligious	25.5	18.2	21.5
Waverers	8.3	15.9	12.5
Convinced believers	5.5	18.5	12.6

Source: M. K. Tepliakov, "Pobeda ateizma v razlichnykh sotsialnykh sloyakh sovetskogo obshchestva," in A. F. Okulov et al. (eds.), *Voprosy nauchnogo ateizma*, Vol. 4 (Moscow, 1967), p. 137.

Table 1.2 Nonreligious Belief among Citizens of Voronezh Province, 1966 (in percentages)

Age Group	Of Men and Women	Of Men	Of Women
18–25	94.5	95.9	93.3
26–30	86.6	92.1	81.0
31–40	83.9	90.6	76.5
41–50	77.1	89.6	67.6
51–60	56.2	76.4	43.4
61–65	44.3	60.5	36.2
66 and over	34.6	52.4	23.5
All age groups	74.9	86.2	65.6

Source: M. K. Tepliakov, "Pobeda ateizma v razlichnykh sotsialnykh sloyakh sovetskogo obshchestva," in A. F. Okulov et al. (eds.), *Voprosy nauchnogo ateizma*, Vol. 4 (Moscow, 1967), p. 138.

antireligious propaganda: it helps to derogate religion by painting an unattractive, even ridiculous, picture of the typical believer.

The Soviet population can be subdivided into categories according to the intensity of their religious convictions. The most widely accepted classification scheme involves five subgroups: (1) atheists; (2) the nonreligious (who, while not believers, are indifferent toward both atheism and religion); (3) waverers (who express doubts about the existence of God and other supernatural forces and who perhaps observe certain religious rites); (4) convinced believers; and (5) fanatics (who are distinguished by "blind, reckless belief in God," and who actively disseminate religious views).[60] Each of these people feels and acts as he does for a variety of reasons,

Table 1.3   Sect Membership in the Byelorussian SSR, 1961–1963 (in percentages)

| Group | Brest Province | Eastern Provinces of the BSSR | | |
		Mogilev	Gomel	Vitebsk
Men	33.6	13.0	25.0	23.0
Women	66.4	87.0	75.0	77.0
Nonworking	10.3	47.0	53.0	60.0
20–40 years	26.4	12.0	15.3	7.2
40–50 years	13.5	—	—	—
40–60 years	—	45.0	40.7	34.5
50 years and older	60.1	—	—	—
60 years and older	—	43.0	44.0	58.3
Illiterate and semiliterate	71.4	65.0	55.0	35.3

Source: A. I. Klibanov, *Religioznoye sektanstvo i sovremennost* (Moscow, 1969), p. 82.

Table 1.4   Parishioners at Sakona Church, Gorky Region, 1965 (in percentages)

Occupation	Percentage of All Parishioners	Men	Women
Skilled workers in industry, transport	2.6	53.8	46.2
Unskilled workers in industry, transport	7.8	30.8	69.2
Agricultural specialists	0.2	100.0	0.0
Teachers, doctors, workers in children's institutions	1.2	16.7	83.3
Workers in cultural-enlightenment institutions	1.4	57.1	42.9
Skilled collective farm workers	7.0	22.9	77.1
Other collective farm workers	18.8	21.3	78.7
Pensioners	35.6	21.9	78.1
Housewives	20.2	0.0	100.0
Others	5.2	25.0	75.0

Source: V. G. Pivovarov and A. S. Seregin, "Opyt primeneniya kolichestvennykh metodov k issledovaniyu religioznykh yavlenii," in A. F. Okulov et al. (eds.), *Voprosy nauchnogo ateizma*, Vol. 5 (Moscow, 1968), p. 78.

depending on his experience, needs, and perceptions. As a Soviet philosopher has written,

Belief in God has different meanings and values for different believers. For many . . . religion is not the decisive element in their life. . . . Quite often it is merely a traditional custom learned in the family, where the dying faith still clings. For others, religious beliefs represent a world of special experiences and feelings that . . . is to some extent separate from the milieu in which this person lives and works. And sometimes this world is opposed to the social relations, requirements, criteria, procedures and principles of our society. In the latter case, we are dealing with fanatics, with clerics of the most reactionary stripe.[61]

Those of different age groups seek and find in religion the answers to different kinds of questions. Elderly people are particularly concerned about death and "life beyond the grave." Middle-aged people are more interested in problems of morality, while young people appear to be attracted primarily by the beauty of religious rituals. Education also makes a difference: people of little education, particularly in rural areas, are more apt to believe in miracles, make offerings and sacrifices, and even pray for rain or a good harvest.[62] Finally, the character and intensity of religious belief vary from denomination to denomination. Religious views tend to be far less intense and relevant to members of the Russian Orthodox Church than to members of the various Protestant denominations.[63]

Religion in a Socialist Society
Marxists view religion as the product of a society beset with antagonisms and contradictions. Why, then, should a country whose means of production were nationalized in 1917, which "built socialism" in 1936, and which claims to be virtually free of internal contradictions have more than a handful of religious citizens?

The Soviets acknowledge that the "social and economic roots" of religion were long ago destroyed. Industrialization, the collectivization of agriculture, the nationalization of land, and the elimination of "exploiting classes" are said to have severely undermined belief in God.[64] But the early expectation that religion would disappear quickly without the proper economic base to sustain it has not been fulfilled. Investigators now understand that, in addition to economic factors, emotional, social, and political phenomena contribute to the maintenance of religious beliefs and practices in the USSR.

According to the official view, Soviet society has inherited religion along with a number of other views, customs, and traditions that were originally formed in pre-Revolutionary Russia. Religion, thus, is not an expression or a product of Soviet conditions, but rather a carry-over from Tsarist times. The argument, while imaginative, is not very plausible.

In general, Soviet philosophy argues that material being is primary; individual consciousness merely reflects objective reality. But changes that occur in social life are not immediately reflected in human consciousness, and, for an indefinite period of time, people's minds may not accurately reflect the changed environment. Thus, religious beliefs, nourished by the political, economic, and social conditions that prevailed in pre-1917 Russia, linger on in people's minds today, even though conditions are no longer "appropriate" for the development of religion. In the Soviet phrase, religion is a "survival of the past" *(perezhitok proshlogo),* for which there is no longer any social base.[65]

This line of reasoning presents two basic problems. First, it does not come to grips with the existence of religious views among citizens born long after the Revolution, who have had no exposure whatsoever to the old order. To be sure, Marx did argue that the post-Revolutionary period would be "stamped with the birthmarks of the old society from whose womb it emerges." [66] But Soviet ideologists have extended the notion of "birthmarks of the old society" or "vestiges of the past" to explain the behavior of second- and even third-generation citizens of the USSR.

Second, and probably more important, the explanation that consciousness lags behind reality is a prescription for passivity. As one Soviet ideologist has argued, "This explanation cannot satisfy us today if we wish to have an active influence on social processes." [67] That is to say, analysis of defects in the social order must point out how such defects are to be eradicated. The notion that religion represents a vestige of the past, while placing the "blame" on non-Soviet causes, in no way helps the authorities to deal with the problem.

What Is to Be Done?

If religion is a survival of the past in people's minds, then the struggle with religion becomes "a struggle to cleanse the minds of a section of the people of wrong notions about reality, i.e., an ideological struggle." [68] If social consciousness lags behind social reality, the Party must take steps to compensate for this. Although the decline and fall of religion are viewed as inevitable and irreversible, the Party seeks to accelerate the pace of its demise. If man cannot alter the laws of nature or social development, he can act as an agent of the historical process, and thus bring about the results that the laws of history themselves require.

The very fact that religious belief has been partially eroded may make the task of fully eradicating it more difficult. It is sometimes argued, much as Stalin did with respect to other class enemies, that the religious "enemy" becomes more and more resourceful with each victory on the atheist front. "Religion is on the run," a *Komsomolskaya pravda* editorial argued, "but its adherents try all the harder to maintain their influence on young minds." [69]

Soviet ideologists have tended to blur the differences among various religions, regarding all as equally undesirable. Lenin himself argued that "Every religious idea, every idea of God, even flirting with the idea of God, is unutterable vileness . . . vileness of the most dangerous kind, 'contagion' of the most abominable kind." [70] Official practice since the Revolution has been, by and large, faithful to this point of view. The Party has been almost uniformly antireligious in the broadest sense—equally critical of all churches and equally ready to ignore distinctions among them. (See Appendix 1.)

Some groups have been treated differently, however. The Jews, the Catholics, and some of the smaller Protestant sects have been subjected to harsher treatment than other denominations. They have been singled out for special treatment because their doctrines are thought to threaten the security of the Soviet state, because they reside in strategic areas of the country, or because their practices are considered dangerous to people's health.

The Jews have been subjected to a wide range of discriminatory practices in economic and cultural affairs, and they have suffered more than any other group from Soviet restrictions on emigration.[71] (In the recent past, of course, they have *benefited* more than any other groups from the regime's liberalized emigration policy.) Anti-Jewish propaganda has also tended to be more aggressive and crude than propaganda directed at other faiths. Trofim Kichko's *Judaism Without Embellishment* (1963), for example, declared that "Jewish ideology is impregnated . . . with greed, love of money, and the spirit of egoism," while Jewish religious leaders were alleged to engage in "speculation . . . , thievery, deception and debauchery." [72] Another publication refers to the Jewish God as a "blood-sucker" and racist, and says that Judaism preaches "intolerance and the bloody extermination of people of other faiths . . . ." [73]

The Catholic Church, too, has suffered heavily. The Catholics, who have shared most of the tribulations of Russian Orthodoxy, have never been allowed to benefit from the 1943 church-state concordat. Because so many Soviet Catholics live in the Western border areas, the regime has tended to view them as a security risk. Soviet nationalities policy has reinforced this bias, because almost all Catholics belong to one or another of the national minorities and are thus assumed to be threatened by "bourgeois nationalism." [74]

Moreover, Jewish, Catholic, Lutheran, and several other religious groups have not been allowed to establish any kind of central administrative apparatus, while the Orthodox, Baptists, and other faiths have been permitted to do so. Jehovah's Witnesses, Pentecostalists, and dissident Baptists and Russian Orthodox (i.e., people who have broken with the officially recognized churches) have been treated especially harshly. They object to many Party and government programs and often refuse to cooperate with the authorities. As a result, they have been subjected to harassment and even persecution.[75] The Russian Orthodox Church, too, has generally been treated badly. While it has at times "benefited from special tolerance," it has more often been "singled out for special martyrdom." [76]

On the other hand, the authorities have dealt with certain denominations in a relatively mild manner. The Old Believers, for example, "who worship God quietly and unobtrusively . . . and (who) do not go out to make new converts," have been treated leniently.[77] Similarly, Islam has fared relatively well, especially in the period since Stalin's death. Soviet foreign policy objectives in the Middle East have overridden concern about the Moslems as a religious and/or nationality problem. The regime apparently views Islam as a bridge to the Middle East, rather than simply as a barrier to domestic socioeconomic change.[78]

In its attempt to eradicate religion, the regime has utilized a variety of weapons:

1. It has sought to provide a social and economic environment that guarantees all citizens equal opportunity to develop—under the Party's close supervision and control. "Religion will disappear," Marx once said, "to the extent that socialism develops. It must disappear as a result of social development . . . ." [79] Today, it is said, people's value systems have been refashioned "by the whole tenor of Soviet life . . . by the revolutionary transformation of society." [80] The Party has eliminated the most blatant forms of social and economic inequality. It has changed the role of women in family and society, eliminated illiteracy, and expanded all levels of education. Much effort has gone into building schools and clubs, raising rural standards of living, and providing for the leisure time of the population. The authorities have sought to insulate and mobilize the population, to draw all citizens into officially sponsored social and political activities, and to control the people's access to foreign media, foreign citizens, and Soviet citizens anxious to win religious converts.

2. The government has harassed, intimidated, threatened, and punished clergymen and ordinary believers. It has erected an elaborate network of legal and quasi-legal barriers to the expression of religious views. Throughout most of Soviet history, the authorities have interpreted these laws very strictly, and at certain times they have ignored the law and resorted instead to naked force or terror.

3. It has initiated a program of scholarly research into the causes and character of religious belief in the USSR. These investigations are designed to achieve an instrumental aim. As one of the leading Soviet authorities has put it, "Religious prejudices can be overcome only if we know the concrete forms in which religion exists today, the [present] state of religious consciousness, and the tendencies toward change in it." [81] An atheist propagandist from Tadzhikistan has made the same point more vividly: "Here, as in war, before advancing, it is essential to study the enemy defenses well. Only then can one count on a positive result." [82] The argument is clear: knowledge of contemporary religious beliefs and practices will help the Party to subvert them. The establishment of special research institutions, the training of social scientists, and the carrying out of field research all contribute to this goal.

4. The authorities have devised a set of secular holidays and ceremonies, to compete with and supplant religious holy days and rituals. These are designed primarily to satisfy the citizen's desire to mark significant events in his or her life, but without resort to religious rites.

5. Finally, these programs have been supplemented by a vast propaganda effort aimed at refashioning human consciousness, "improving" the belief systems of Soviet citizens, raising their ideological level to such a degree that religion will not merely become superfluous but will actually disappear.

At the outset of Soviet rule, the Bolsheviks apparently expected their radical socioeconomic changes to produce immediate and radical changes in the human personality. As Robert C. Tucker has pointed out, they sought "not to remold man by a long process of training into a new kind of being, but simply to liberate him to become for the first time himself . . . ." [83] Even now, the Soviet authorities regard social and economic development as the foundation on which changes in "human nature" can be erected. But "building socialism" or "building communism," eradicating the differences between mental and physical labor or between city and countryside, raising educational and cultural levels or the standard of living will not automatically cause religion to die out. Atheist propaganda is needed. Religion cannot be abolished; nor will it wither away. It must be systematically attacked to be destroyed.

Unresolved Problems

The Party's approach to religion has undergone frequent and sometimes radical change during the half century of Soviet power. Periods of repression have alternated with periods of relaxation as the Party's priorities have shifted and shifted again. What is more, official pronouncements on religion tend to be ambiguous, and policies that are publicly condemned are sometimes secretly encouraged. As a consequence, neither church officials nor ordinary believers can ever be quite certain of official policy, and they are likely to have reservations about expressing their religious convictions.

From the Party's point of view, this circumstance is of course welcome. But if ambiguously worded pronouncements and constantly changing priorities have perplexed the religious community, they have had the same effect on atheist cadres. Indeed, there is a great deal of confusion among Party officials, including those responsible for ideological matters, on the very nature and purpose of atheist work. There is substantial disagreement on the most basic of questions: (1) Should the Party make an active effort to combat religious views and practices? (2) How much emphasis should be placed on persuasive techniques, and how much on coercion? (3) At which individuals or groups should official efforts be aimed? (4) What should be the content of atheist messages? We will deal with each question in turn.

1. Official policy, affirmed in countless directives and commentaries, demands a vigorous struggle against religion. Nonetheless, the view that religion need not be, or ought not to be, combated is apparently widespread. Some atheists point to the Constitutional guarantee of "freedom of conscience" and argue that any interference with people's personal beliefs is unwarranted and illegal.[84] Others feel that a policy of "militant atheism" is no longer appropriate, although it was necessary during the early years of the Revolution, "when a cruel and desperate armed struggle with the old was in progress . . . , when the church put at the service of the Counterrevolution the entire power of its organization, the entire influence of its ideology over the untutored masses."[85] Today, they argue, religion does not represent a social danger, and legal restraints placed on the church are sufficient to prevent the reemergence of a problem. Moreover, they say, continued social and economic progress guarantees that religious beliefs and practices will disappear eventually.[86]

2. While policy toward the church has always involved a mixture of

persuasion, coercion, and the threat of coercion, the period since Stalin's death has been marked by increased reliance on propaganda and education measures. As Nancy Heer has pointed out, "the rejection of terror as the central instrument of control requires a much heavier reliance upon internalized or subjective norms."[87] At the same time, however, the laws regulating religious practices continue to be harsh, and there have been authoritative demands that they be enforced even more strictly in the future.[88] Extralegal and illegal measures have been used to close churches and intimidate believers. During the Khrushchev period, for example, the Russian Orthodox, Baptists, Lutherans, and Catholics lost approximately half of their churches. The Jewish faith was treated even more harshly: synagogues were reduced in number from some four hundred to less than one hundred.[89]

Although the massive campaign of closing churches ceased with the fall of Khrushchev, extremist behavior and demands can still be encountered. "Why are there churches in every city?", one atheist has asked. "Close them, all of them!"[90] While such demands are publicly rejected, churches are still closed forcibly. Instances of official interference with religious ceremonies and pilgrimages as well as the expulsion of believers from universities or from their jobs are also reported in the Soviet press. Still other incidents have been revealed by underground sources.[91]

3. Propaganda specialists disagree about how and where to concentrate their efforts. Their disagreements center around three related issues: (a) whether to try to convert believers to atheism, or to reinforce the convictions of atheists, (b) whether to direct antireligious efforts toward youngsters or toward older people, and (c) whether to work with ordinary believers or with clergymen and other church officials.

a. Some argue that atheist efforts ought to be directed exclusively to undermining the religious views of believers, while others contend that nourishing the doubts of agnostics is likelier to bring success. Still others, aware of the substantial difficulties involved in both of these approaches, suggest that atheist work focus on reinforcing the convictions of atheists. They point out that believers and agnostics are highly resistant to atheist propaganda, while people who claim to be atheists are not always worthy of this designation. Indeed, they say, a person who does not have sufficiently strong atheist convictions "can prove to be defenseless in his first serious clash with religion . . . when faced with the craftily woven conclusions of experienced missionaries and 'fishers of souls.' "[92]

b. Those who advocate that atheist efforts be directed primarily at children argue that it is easier to socialize young people than to resocialize adults. Moreover, they say, older people who believe in God are not going to change their views and should therefore be left alone. (See Chapter 2.) According to the opposing view, it is precisely the older believers who keep religion alive: they take their grandchildren to church, insist that they be baptized, and teach them the Gospels.[93]

c. Propaganda specialists who try to persuade clergymen to give up their religious views do so for two reasons. First, they argue that without constant inspiration and reinforcement from church leaders, the typical congregation will dissolve. Second, they feel that clerical apostasy will be a direct and powerful inducement to other believers to question their religious beliefs. Other propagandists argue that, despite the obvious and continuing threat that clergymen represent, they are hardly likely to succumb to the blandishments of professional atheists. They therefore recommend working with ordinary believers, whom they regard as less sophisticated and more susceptible of conversion.[94]

4. Questions of propaganda content and style are also debated vigorously. Some propagandists choose only to criticize religious views and practices, while others seek to emphasize the alleged virtues of "scientific atheism" or "communist morality." Similarly, some consider the dissemination of scientific information sufficient to undermine religion, while others think that questions of morality or aesthetics deserve greater attention. Finally, some think that criticism of religion should be phrased in intellectual, if direct, language, while others believe that blunt, even crude, denunciations will prove more effective.·

Any method of dealing with any of these questions has certain advantages and disadvantages. But because there have been virtually no serious studies of the strengths and weaknesses of the various approaches, it has been impossible to choose rationally from among them. The result has been to dissipate much official energy in futile or even counterproductive activities.

The presence of problems, even problems as basic and far-reaching as those we have noted, has not deterred the Soviet authorities from attacking religion. Official uncertainty has not meant official timidity.

Concluding Note
Soviet ideologists have traditionally distinguished between propaganda and agitation. In theory, propaganda involves the dissemination of complex ideas to a small audience, while agitation entails the communication of a

small number of relatively simple notions to the masses. In Plekhanov's words: "A propagandist presents many ideas to one or a few persons; an agitator presents only one or a few ideas, but he presents them to a mass of people." [95] In recent years, however, these terms have lost much of their original distinctiveness, and they often are used interchangeably. Moreover, a new term, "political information *(politinformatsiya)*," has come into use. The political information specialist *(politinformator)* is essentially an agitator who performs his task in a more sophisticated manner, taking into consideration the fact that people are now more educated.[96]

For the purpose of this study, differences among these forms of political communication are not important. All involve efforts to win acceptance for official policies and the official ideology. They use the same instruments—the mass media, lectures, discussions, consultations, etc.—and all are aimed at stimulating the masses to implement the Party's program. The Party, as William Johnson has observed, "utilizes every possible means to create and nurture the political attitudes it deems desirable." [97] Our interest is in the communication of political messages. Whether this communication is called propaganda, agitation, political information, indoctrination, or education is, for our purposes, of no consequence.

2 The First Half Century

. . . we have separated the church from the state, but we have not yet separated the people from religion.

V. I. Lenin

Two opposed ideologies, two opposed views of life, two opposed moralities; they are as incompatible as freedom and slavery, as light and darkness. One of them brings man happiness, the other puts fetters on his heart and mind, trying to persuade him that he is only "God's slave."

Kommunist Tadzhikistana, March 23, 1972

Marxists, Leninists, and their followers in Russia have always been hostile to religion. Before 1917, they vilified organized religion as one of the principal props of the tsarist autocracy and denounced religious sentiment as a major barrier to the modernization of Russia. Since coming to power, the Communists have continued to be antagonistic toward the church. While their methods of dealing with religion have shifted over time, from an initial wariness, to persecution, to accommodation, and now to a relatively muted form of repression, they have not deviated from their ultimate objective. They seek a society completely free of religion. As a leading Western authority has put it, Marxism-Leninism is "incompatible with any faith but a faith in its own infallibility." [1]

Although at first they disclaimed any interest in attacking religion—partly out of fear of antagonizing the faithful, partly out of disingenuousness—they soon made clear their determination to undermine the churches. Their aim was radical: they wanted not merely to limit the influence of the Orthodox Church but to subordinate all churches to Soviet power and, eventually, to eliminate religion altogether.

It is impossible to "blame" one side or the other for the clash between church and state. Each saw the other as "servants of darkness" and a menace to decent society; neither was willing to make concessions or to compromise. Religious leaders regarded the Bolsheviks as enemies of social stability (which they were), while the Party denounced the churches as enemies of social progress (which they were). Both Party and church authorities considered it their duty to "liberate" or "enlighten" the masses, especially the younger generation—the former with the message of atheism, the latter with diametrically opposed religious teachings. As the years have gone by, however, both church and state have revised their initial attitudes.

Virtually all religious groups in the USSR have abandoned their earlier policy of uncompromising hostility and have adapted themselves to the new order. Motivated by what some see as absolute necessity, but what others denounce as lack of principle or even abject servility, organized religion has been able to survive. While church officials can hardly be content with the restrictions placed on them, they have learned to support the regime and its policies.

Similarly, the Party has changed its approach to religion. The Bolsheviks expected religion to wither away after they seized power, or at least to disappear after being subjected to official terror. When the Party's expectations failed to materialize, it resolved instead to conduct "a protracted engagement with the forces of religion to make its prophecy of their extinction come true." [2] Official policy has shifted often, sometimes dramatically, as the regime has pursued its "cyclical but inexorable drive toward atheism." [3] At times, the Party has dealt with religion so vigorously that it has "seemed purposely to confuse the withering of religion with liquidation of the religious, . . . with shuttered churches, jailed priests and persecuted believers." [4] At other times, the secular authorities have tolerated or even encouraged religion. In fact, during the Second World War, the Party actively supported the Russian Orthodox Church, treating it, in the words of one Western specialist, as a "junior partner of the state." [5] Today, while the regime continues to affirm its intention to eliminate all vestiges of "religious superstition," it no longer resorts to outright terror and emphasizes instead the power of atheist propaganda.

The Party has invested a great deal of energy and manpower in trying to achieve its atheist objectives. It has relied sometimes on coercion, at other times on persuasion, and most often on a combination of the two. But, for a number of reasons, it has sometimes proved difficult to distinguish among these approaches. The coercive and persuasive aspects of official policy can be so intimately intertwined that they simply cannot be separated; some policies can only be understood as "coercive persuasion." [6] Moreover, coercive measures applied to curb the actions of some have a persuasive effect on others. The threat of coercion (itself a form of coercion) can also have a persuasive impact, serving to deter or promote certain kinds of behavior. (Law, for example, is an instrument of coercion, but it is also a means of persuasion.) Finally, the line separating proper from improper application of laws and administrative regulations is sometimes elusive.

Despite these caveats, it is both desirable and possible, if only in rough terms, to deal separately with coercive and persuasive efforts. Certain measures are purely coercive, while others are clearly persuasive. We will examine the major steps taken by the Party, focusing first on coercive measures, then on attempts to persuade the citizenry to abandon religion.

Coercive Measures

Efforts to restrict organized religion in Russia began before the Bolshevik Revolution. In July 1917, the Provisional Government moved to end the Russian Orthodox Church's official status. It promulgated a law guaranteeing freedom of religious profession, freedom to change religion, and freedom to profess no religion at all. In addition, it placed the nation's parochial schools under the jurisdiction of the Minister of Education and made religious education in the public schools optional rather than compulsory.[7] But the Kerensky government was not interested in doing battle with the Orthodox Church, or with any other church. The Bolsheviks were. They were ready to use the law, as well as extralegal and illegal measures, to gain control over the churches.

A number of the Soviet government's first legislative acts severely restricted church power. Immediately after the October Revolution, landed estates (which included monasterial and church lands) were placed under government control. State subsidies for churches, clergy, and religious ceremonies were halted, and the government's control over education was expanded to include the ecclesiastical seminaries. Divorce laws were relaxed, civil marriage was decreed, and responsibility for the registration of births and deaths was placed in the hands of civil authorities.[8]

At the same time, there were numerous instances of violence, aimed primarily at the Orthodox Church. Churches and monasteries were desecrated and looted, and individual clergymen were physically assaulted and sometimes murdered. Whether these acts were part of a plan devised by top Party officials, or were instead simply scattered, uncoordinated local excesses, is unclear. In any event, they outraged the leaders of the various churches. Angered by the government's ruthlessness and anticipating even more severe measures, Patriarch Tikhon of the Russian Orthodox Church issued his famous pastoral letter on February 1, 1918. In this document, the Patriarch anathematized the Bolsheviks and called upon "faithful children of the Orthodox Church . . . to have nothing in common with these outcasts of the human race."[9] Officials of other churches reacted similarly.[10]

The government's response was direct and sweeping. On February 5, the Council of People's Commissars issued a lengthy decree outlining its attitude toward the church. This document is probably the single most important statement of government policy toward religious groups. Church and state were separated, and religious instruction (except that undertaken privately) was outlawed. Religious organizations were prohibited from owning property and buildings and articles used for worship could thenceforth be rented to such groups only with the consent of the secular authorities. (As Western commentators have pointed out, making religious groups dependent on the state for their legal existence and for the right to use church buildings made a mockery of the decree separating church from state.)[11] Moreover, religious organizations were not permitted exclusive use of "their" buildings; churches could be used for lectures, concerts, films, dances, political meetings, and other secular (and even antireligious) purposes as well. Even the right to perform religious rites was restricted; they were to be permitted only if they did not "disturb public order or interfere with the rights" of other citizens. To guarantee adherence to this stipulation, local government officials were authorized "to adopt all necessary measures to maintain public order and safety." [12]

The new regime, which at first was hesitant to move vigorously against organized religion, soon became vindictive in persecuting the church. Economic pressure and physical terror were quickly brought to bear. Asserting that a considerable segment of the clergy had come out openly against Soviet power, which it had, the Party initiated a "sharp class struggle" to inhibit and punish its enemies. The government's position was expressed succinctly by Mikhail Kalinin, Chairman of the Central Executive Committee of the Soviets: ". . . the heads of the Church have declared civil war against the government . . . there cannot and will not be mercy for those princes of the Church." [13]

Thus, religious and secular authorities refused to recognize each other's legitimacy, and a period of intense conflict began. It was particularly savage in the case of the Orthodox Church, although other denominations suffered as well. Both Tikhon and his successor, Sergii, were arrested. Vast sums of church properties were seized, and thousands of "counterrevolutionary" church figures were imprisoned or executed. Thousands of churches were closed illegally, and individual believers and clerics were harassed. Much of the story is too familiar to bear repeating here; we need only mention the principal measures that were adopted.

The clergy were for a time disenfranchised, deprived of the right to hold public office, compelled to pay higher taxes, and subjected to discrimination in the allocation of housing and rations. Clergymen were ridiculed and humiliated. Some were searched or arrested while performing religious rites, while others were compelled to clean streets or perform other demeaning services. Churches, mosques, and synagogues were stripped of their religious ornaments; these in turn were made into revolutionary banners and decorations. The teaching of religious doctrine to anyone under the age of eighteen was sharply restricted. (Somewhat later, in 1923, religious instruction to groups of more than three children was banned.)[14]

Policy toward the non-Orthodox faiths differed somewhat, although the differences usually involved little more than matters of timing. The government's hostility toward all churches was never in doubt. Conflict with the Jewish and Catholic communities was particularly intense, in great part because their response to the new regime was uncompromising. As Zvi Gitelman has noted, very few Jewish religious leaders were willing to reconcile themselves to the new order, and the Party "made no attempt to win over the Jewish religious establishment." [15] The Catholic hierarchy, too, condemned the Bolsheviks and refused to accept the February 5 decree. The government's response was to arrest leading church officials, imprisoning, executing, or expelling them from the country.[16]

Efforts to undermine the influence of Islam proceeded more slowly.[17] Although the Bolsheviks had no less contempt for Islam than they had for other faiths, four considerations led them to deal cautiously with the Moslems. First, other problems were more urgent: the Soviet regime was not yet secure, and it would have been premature to tackle the question of Islam at this time. Second, the Moslem faith exerted such a powerful and pervasive influence on the peoples of Central Asia that an attack on the Moslem clergy would have been less effective than attacks on Orthodox or Jewish clergymen. Islam is not only a religion but also "a legal framework, a way of life and . . . a whole network of institutions." [18] (Even a Soviet historian of this period has acknowledged that "Moslem traditions . . . continued to be a strong force, and the Moslem priesthood still enjoyed great authority and influence.")[19] Third, the Party was an alien force in the Moslem areas: in the first years of Soviet power, there were very few Moslem communists, and only a handful of these were prepared to undertake an assault against Islam. Finally, the Bolshevik leadership may have feared that anti-Moslem excesses would impede the prospects for world revolution. At the very least, attacks against Islam would have alienated the "exploited toilers" of the Middle East and presumably would have diminished their revolutionary ardor.

To be sure, the new government was far from passive in its dealings with Islam. Mosque lands were confiscated, *Shari'ah* courts were forbidden, and religious schools—termed by one observer "workshops for dulling children's abilities" [20]—were abolished. There were also scattered instances of violence, particularly as the Civil War drew to an end.[21] But Lenin and Stalin personally discouraged direct attacks on Moslem institutions and officials,[22] and other Bolsheviks were equally cautious. As a result, policy "on the religious front" was basically different in Central Asia from policy elsewhere. While the authorities waged an "all-out merciless struggle against religious institutions"[23] in the Christian areas of Russia, they preferred to postpone the inevitable conflict with Islam until a more opportune moment.

In attempting to weaken the major churches, especially Russian Orthodoxy, the Party at first actively supported some of the smaller denominations. The decree of February 5, which was aimed primarily at the Orthodox Church, encouraged many Old Believers and members of the smaller sects to come out into the open. The government also encouraged the growth of "sectarianism" more directly. It authorized the publication of a number of Protestant religious books and pamphlets, and it permitted religious conscientious objectors (most of whom were members of one of the sects) to serve in hospitals instead of in the Red Army. But the policy of special treatment proved so successful—membership in the various sects grew rapidly—that the Party had to abandon this policy. In 1923, it decided to include all the sects in its antireligious efforts.[24]

With the introduction of the New Economic Policy (NEP) in 1921, church-state relations grew more tense. Despite official promises to ease pressure against religion, efforts to undermine church influence were intensified. In March, 1921, the 10th Party Congress urged that atheist efforts not be "overemphasized." Continued struggle against religion, it was said, would only undermine what remained of the "worker-peasant alliance."[25] Directives issued by the Central Committee a year later further emphasized the need for moderation. They pointed out that "the present period is not at all opportune for pressing the antireligious struggle."[26] In point of fact, however, these directives were ignored, and relations between the Party and the churches deteriorated.

The devastating famine of 1921–1922 helped to precipitate a major church-state crisis. In early 1922, the government demanded that the Orthodox Church donate its precious stones and other valuables for famine relief. When Tikhon refused to give up consecrated articles, the government seized large quantities of church treasures. (Their value has been estimated at several billion rubles.)[27] The confiscation order led to widespread violence, and in the ensuing trials, many leading church figures were imprisoned. Some, including Metropolitan Veniamin, were executed. The confrontation, over an issue of the Party's choosing, produced "a massive strategic victory" for the regime.[28] As Walter Kolarz has observed, the Orthodox hierarchy "was made to defend not religion as such but material interests against a government which championed the cause of a starving people."[29]

What is more, new laws were adopted, and existing legislation was applied more rigorously. In December, 1922, sermons were subjected to censorship. Churches were soon required to adopt a new calendar whereby religious holidays became working days, and religious instruction in churches was banned shortly thereafter. Taxes on church lands were raised, and a system of compulsory insurance of church property (with the state as beneficiary) was introduced.[30] Religious organizations were restricted to the performing of religious services. They were prohibited from organizing mutual aid funds, cooperatives, youth and women's groups, or providing religious instruction.[31] As Grigori Zinoviev put it, NEP concessions granted in the economic field had to be offset by extreme vigilance on the ideological front.[32] But while congregations were harassed, and some churches, synagogues, and mosques were closed forcibly, large-scale repressions against organized religion were deferred until the end of the decade.

In 1922, the Bolsheviks sought to split the ranks of the clergy by supporting a schismatic movement, the so-called "Living Church," within Russian Orthodoxy. The Living Church was the organizational expression of a desire among parish priests to reduce the authority of higher church officials and bring about a liberalization of church regulations and practices. But many of its leaders were unscrupulous men who were ready to utilize the government's police powers in order to engineer a *coup d'église*. In turn, the government was anxious to exploit the ambitions of the schismatics, and it intervened openly in support of them.[33] (Indeed, the Bolsheviks may well have been responsible for the schism itself.)[34] Clergymen and high Church officials loyal to the Patriarch were arrested and deported, while the government helped place Living Church candidates in clerical offices throughout the country.[35] Until 1927, the Living Church enjoyed a privileged position as the only officially recognized Orthodox Church body.[36]

The purpose of government aid, of course, was further to undermine the unity of the Church and thereby diminish its ability to influence the masses. As one Soviet official admitted, the regime hoped to "profit by the discord existing among the clergy with the sole purpose of drawing the people away from . . . religion."[37] The freeing of Patriarch Tikhon at this time (in mid-1923) was probably motivated, at least in part, by a desire to set the two Church factions against one another. (A Soviet newspaper cartoon at the time depicted Tikhon and a leader of the Living Church engaged in hand-to-hand combat, while a smiling worker stood nearby observing the contest. The caption reads: "While the two are engaged in a struggle, the hands of the third are free.")[38]

But the Living Church never gained much of a following; it "was stronger in its apparatus than in its popular support." [39] Its enthusiasm for the new order produced suspicion and hostility among Orthodox laymen, rather than enthusiasm and respect. What is more, the modernist movement lost its usefulness to the regime within a few years, as the previously recalcitrant Old Church leaders began to adopt an attitude of loyalty toward Soviet rule.[40] Once they professed loyalty, the Bolsheviks withdrew their support from the Living Church, and without official support the Renovationist effort quickly died out. As William Fletcher has noted, "A movement which had been successful largely because of state repression of those who disagreed could scarcely hope for continued growth once the State ceased taking sides in the dispute." [41] Similar efforts to nourish dissident movements in Judaism and Islam were, if anything, even less successful.[42]

When the Patriarch was released from prison, he had promised that the Church would remain aloof from politics. But this position was acceptable to the regime only while Tikhon was still alive; after his death in 1925, the Party undertook a major offensive against the Orthodox hierarchy. The three men Tikhon had appointed to succeed him were arrested, as was Metropolitan Sergii, who ultimately was permitted to become the new Patriarch. But in order to win the regime's acceptance, Sergii had to abandon Tikhon's policy of political neutrality, in favor of a policy "which offered active cooperation with the State in matters political." [43] Under Tikhon, then, the Church learned that "it could not survive if it remained neutral toward the State." [44] Only by adopting this new political course was Sergii able to obtain from the government enough concessions to survive.[45]

Toward the end of the decade, the regime undertook a major offensive against all faiths. At the time of agricultural collectivization, thousands of Orthodox priests were executed or exiled. (Many had been seized in retaliation for the murder of local officials by peasants resisting the government's demands.) Places of worship were closed by decree; churches and seminaries were requisitioned for use as schools, sanatoriums, and asylums, and church bells were seized (under the pretext of requiring the metal for industrial purposes).[46]

The offensive against the Moslem faith was equally severe. Islam had been treated more leniently than other religions during the first decade of Soviet power, and it was probably inevitable that this anomaly would be eliminated. In 1927, the regime began an intensive anti-Moslem campaign.

It began with the so-called "Hudjum" or "attack"—the struggle for the emancipation of women. The authorities chose to focus their immediate attention on persuading women to discard their veils. As had happened five years earlier in the confrontation over Orthodox Church valuables, the government was able to put its enemy in an unenviable position. The Party "maneuvered its Moslem opponents into a position where they defended not religion but an out-of-date reactionary point of view about women." [47]

A year later, the Party began a campaign of terror against Islamic institutions. The Moslem clergy "was drastically reduced in numbers," and large numbers of mosques were closed, destroyed, or secularized. Some mosques were converted into schools, clubs, movie theaters, and reading rooms, while others became museums, hotels or prisons. All were seized over the protests of the Moslem faithful.[48]

A 1929 amendment to the Constitution deprived religious institutions and individuals of the right to proselytize. Until 1929, Article 4 of the Constitution stated that "freedom of religious and antireligious propaganda is recognized for all citizens." The amendment revoked the right to engage in religious propaganda and provided only "freedom of religious worship and freedom of antireligious propaganda." [49] In addition, "the commission of acts of deceit, with the purpose of encouraging superstition among the masses of the population and with a view to deriving profit of any kind therefrom" was made punishable by law.[50]

That same year, the government issued two major decrees further clarifying the duties and circumscribing the rights of citizens in religious matters. The two documents, "On Religious Associations" (April 8, 1929) and "Instructions to the People's Commissariat of the Interior" (October 1, 1929), established strict guidelines for religious groups, calling for official supervision over their registration, organization, and operation. The sweeping language used in these documents, which remain in force today, further facilitated state control. As a leading Western scholar has noted, the language is so ambiguous that it enables the authorities "to curtail or halt the normally permitted activities of a religious association whenever they deem it expedient." [51]

To disguise its violations of existing laws and procedures, the Party resorted to various forms of chicanery. At political meetings or antireligious lectures, for example, the local authorities "proposed resolutions to close certain churches and . . . [took] a mere majority vote at such unrepresentative gatherings as a mandate to close them." [52] Similarly, meetings of local Communists and Komsomols often voted over the heads of the congregations to seize religious properties.[53]

Official enthusiasm for such measures soon subsided, for it became apparent that the Party had gone too far. As late as March, 1930, the 16th Party Congress adopted a resolution urging that "the considerable successes attained in the work of liberating the masses from the reactionary influence of religion" be "strengthened and developed." [54] Before the month was over, however, the line had changed dramatically.

Stalin had observed in January, 1930, that "great confusion reigns" in the atheist movement. "Extraordinarily stupid acts are sometimes committed," he said, "which play into the hands of our enemies." [55] Six weeks later, he charged that those responsible for agricultural collectivization had become "dizzy with success," and his remarks were echoed by antireligious leaders. "Leftist deviationism," especially the seizure of icons and the forced closing of churches, was condemned. These "inadmissible distortions in the Party line" were severely criticized at a meeting of the Party Central Committee in March. Local Party organizations were instructed

Positively *to put an end to* the practice of closing churches forcibly, fictitiously disguising it as the public and voluntary wish of the population. To permit the closing of churches only when this is the genuine desire of an overwhelming majority of the peasants. . . . To bring to the strictest accountability those guilty of mocking the religious feelings of peasant men and women.[56]

Over the course of the following decade, the Party continued to attack religion, while taking pains to offer a number of minor concessions. These few hints of a conciliatory attitude, which were probably linked with the ever-present danger of war, foreshadowed the concordat of the World War II period. Thus, the 1936 Constitution ignored the distinction between "working" and "nonworking" citizens, restoring to clergymen the right to vote. At the same time, the clergy were accorded better treatment in the payment of taxes, and the government removed the ban on the admission of children of "nonworking" persons to institutions of higher learning.[57]

But these concessions did not indicate any fundamental change in the Party's outlook. Hostility toward religion remained the official policy, and the regime "gave no ground for hope that doles parceled out to believers betokened anything more than the largesse of a Party that felt so secure against Church resurgence that it could afford to be generous to a condemned victim." [58] During the purges that shook Soviet society during the latter half of the decade, organized religion suffered substantial losses. Leading figures in the Orthodox, Moslem, and other churches were imprisoned, exiled, or executed during the Great Purge, while churches and mosques were accused of hiding "nests of spies," "diversionists," and other "anti-Soviet elements" and were closed.[59]

It was not until the eve of World War II that a genuine accommodation was reached. After the Hitler-Stalin Pact was signed in 1939, church-state relations changed radically. Once Stalin had decided to annex certain neighboring territories in Eastern Europe, he turned to the Russian Orthodox Church "to smooth the process of their absorption" into the USSR.[60] The churches in the newly acquired territories had to be reorganized on a pro-Soviet basis, and in order to avoid a repetition of the ten-year struggle with Orthodoxy after 1917, Stalin decided to use Sergii's services "to bring the situation under control." Indeed, territorial annexation in 1939 and thereafter may well have saved the Church from extinction.[61]

After the Soviet Union was attacked in 1941, leaders of the Orthodox, Moslem, and other churches responded by supporting the Soviet government and mobilizing the faithful for a patriotic war. Orthodox leaders denounced the German invaders as "Fascist bandits" and urged every citizen to defend "the sacred frontiers of our fatherland." They collected money to purchase arms, to care for the wounded, and to aid widows and orphans.[62] Officials of other churches were equally outspoken, although their contribution to the war effort was more modest.

This support was a major factor in bringing about the change in Soviet policy, but it was reinforced by other considerations as well. The Orthodox Church was no longer a threat to the regime, as it had been in the first years after the Revolution. In addition, Stalin was anxious to make a favorable impression on Western public opinion, which had often been critical of Soviet policies toward religion. Most important, Stalin realized that a more liberal policy toward the church would help mobilize popular support within the Soviet Union, both in German-occupied and Soviet-held areas. Indeed, in those areas occupied by the Germans, there was a spontaneous religious revival. The occupation authorities permitted and even encouraged the mass reopening of churches, which in turn stimulated a revitalization of religious life.[63] Because upward of half the population retained its allegiance to religion,[64] continued antireligious efforts might have had a serious effect on morale.

Stalin's concessions, especially those made to the Orthodox Church, met many of the needs of clergymen and ordinary believers. A number of churches were reopened (in addition to those reopened by the Germans), and Radio Moscow began to broadcast a religious hour. Parents were again permitted to obtain private religious instruction for their children, and the government again began to supply oil for icon lamps. Sunday was reinstituted as a day of rest, and public celebration of Easter was again permitted. *The Journal of the Moscow Patriarchate* renewed publication after a lapse of nearly a decade, and the regime authorized the printing of a limited number of religious books. Leading clergymen were included among those receiving medals "For the Defense of Leningrad" and "For the Defense of Moscow," and arrangements were made to resume the training of additional clergy. In September, 1943, Acting Patriarch Sergii, together with other Orthodox Church leaders, was granted an unprecedented meeting with Stalin, where the terms of the new modus vivendi between church and state were worked out. When Sergii died in 1944, the regime in no way impeded the installation of Metropolitan Alexei of Leningrad as his successor.[65]

The church-state détente reached in 1943 continued into the postwar period; in fact, it left its imprint on Soviet policy until Stalin's death. Except in his dealings with the Jews and with religious groups in the newly acquired Western territories, Stalin continued to treat the churches indulgently. In 1945, religious groups were granted the right to construct or rent buildings, and they were promised the active support of local officials. In 1946, the remaining Orthodox monasteries were freed from the heavy taxes that had been placed on them. Additional churches, seminaries, and theological academies were opened, and new bishops were consecrated. Patriarch Alexei and other high officials of the Orthodox Church were awarded orders and medals for their patriotic services.[66]

Members of most other faiths also profited from the continued détente. For example, Islamic religious academies were opened in Bukhara and Tashkent, and permission was given to publish an edition of the Koran. Several groups of Moslems were permitted to make a pilgrimage to Mecca, and the Soviet government even provided them with aircraft for this purpose.[67]

In the Baltic States and the Western Ukraine, however, many clergymen were arrested and accused of war crimes. They were said to have collaborated with German occupation forces, aiding in the pacification of the population and even helping to send Soviet citizens to forced labor in Germany. Catholic and Uniat churches were closed, and the Uniat Church itself was forced to break with Rome and join the Russian Orthodox Church.[68]

In the last years of Stalin's reign, the Jewish religion, too, was subjected to a campaign of terror and intimidation. While this campaign was directed primarily at Jewish Communists and atheists suspected of nationalist or pro-Western leanings, it seriously affected all Jews. Jews were attacked as "bourgeois nationalists" and "rootless cosmopolitans" who were enemies of

Soviet power. At the end of 1948, all Jewish organizations and Yiddish publications were shut down, and leading Jewish intellectuals and cultural figures were imprisoned or executed. Two months before the dictator's death, a group of "saboteur doctors," most of whom were Jewish, were charged with plotting to poison Soviet leaders at the instigation of Jewish organizations abroad.[69] They were exonerated only after Stalin died, when the "Doctors' Plot" was revealed to be a fabrication.

Propaganda Measures
The Soviet leaders recognized shortly after the Revolution that religion could not be abolished by administrative fiat. They therefore initiated a long-term atheist propaganda effort, whose purpose was to persuade people of the falsity of religious belief. Although the RSFSR Constitution of 1918 allowed both church and state the right to disseminate propaganda, the two parties were unevenly matched from the beginning. As Robert Conquest has noted, "antireligious propaganda was to be pursued with all the forces of the State and the Communist Party, while religious propaganda was to be undertaken by Churches weakened, if not crippled, by discriminatory legislation." [70]

The Program adopted by the Party at its 8th Congress (1919) promised to organize "the broadest scientific-educational and antireligious propaganda." [71] A year later, the Party's Central Committee issued a directive calling upon atheists to intensify their efforts.[72] Party and government officials soon began to visit houses of worship to explain the new regime's policy toward religion, and agitators and propagandists traveled around the country on "agitation trains" to bring the same message to the peasants.[73]

In 1921, the Central Committee called for the publication of atheist pamphlets, books, and newspaper articles,[74] and the 10th Party Congress in 1921 pointed to the battle against religion as one of the principal tasks of Party propaganda. The Congress adopted a resolution calling for "wide-scale organization, leadership, and cooperation in the task of antireligious agitation and propaganda among the broad masses of the workers," using the mass media, films, books, lectures, and other devices.[75]

Among the earliest propaganda measures was the "unmasking of clerical frauds," i.e., showing that the bodies of saints, purportedly preserved through miracles, had turned to dust or were only wax images. To aid in the campaign against holy relics, mummified rats were placed in shrines next to the bodies of saints. If nothing else, this presumably inhibited religious pilgrims from kissing the relics.[76]

As the Civil War drew to an end, the Party began to experiment with a number of new approaches to atheist propaganda. Among the most imaginative was the system of secular holidays (designed as a substitute for traditional religious holy days and festivals) and secular rituals (to replace religious ceremonies). Debates between atheists and clergymen were also arranged, and the Komsomol organized antireligious carnivals and processions on the eve of religious holy days. Young people in various localities would march to the city center, carrying torches, caricatures, and posters, singing parodies of religious chants, and burning images of the gods to symbolize the dying out of religion. Demonstrators often clashed violently with angry citizens, and the Party Central Committee soon introduced restraints on future demonstrations.[77]

In 1924, the State Publishing House for Antireligious Literature was founded; it translated foreign works and published the writings of Soviet atheists as well. By the end of the year, nine other publishing houses throughout the country were printing atheist materials.[78] A weekly newspaper, *Bezbozhnik (The Godless)*, was established to coordinate and systematize antireligious propaganda, and an organization was soon created around the newspaper, calling itself "The Friends of the Newspaper *Godless*." In 1925, the organization changed its name to the "League of the Godless" and then to the "League of the Militant Godless." This association expanded its activities to include the publication of other atheist materials and was soon made responsible for formulating and conducting virtually all antireligious propaganda.[79]

League members were instructed to be models for other citizens and to conduct atheist work with them. In fact, the League's rules stipulated that "the best agitation for the League's ideas is the personal example and personal life of the atheist propagandist." [80] A children's godless movement —"The Young Godless"—was also set up to aid in the socialization of youngsters.[81]

Guided by the motto, "The struggle against religion is the struggle for socialism," [82] the League became a mass organization, reaching a membership of five and a half million persons in 1932. Its publishing activities expanded rapidly.[83] Besides *Bezbozhnik,* the League published many other newspapers and journals in Russian, Ukrainian, and other languages.[84] Circulation of these newspapers increased rapidly; the monthly circulation of *Bezbozhnik* alone reached almost half a million by 1931.

In addition to publishing atheist literature, the League arranged lectures, question-and-answer evenings, plays, concerts, films, and discussions with individual believers. It organized displays, parades, and mass demonstrations, and set up antireligious museums as well. The League emphasized organized group activities. Competitions between christened and unchristened infants were arranged, to see if there would be any difference in their health or growth. Contests were arranged between a "godless field" (an agricultural plot using new methods of soil and plant science) and the field of a religious peasant who used old techniques and relied on a priest's blessing. "Godless meteorology" was introduced to undercut the belief that prayer could influence weather, and "godless miracles" (elementary physics and chemistry experiments) were performed in clubs and auditoriums.[85]

Antireligious museums were opened in former monasteries and cathedrals in Moscow, Leningrad, and provincial centers. The first of these was opened in 1924; two years later, a large museum was opened in Moscow, and in 1932 the most famous one of all (now known as the Museum of the History of Religion and Atheism) was opened in the Kazan Cathedral in Leningrad.[86] These museums contained exhibits exposing the "falsity" or "crimes" of various religions, showing the "irreconcilability of science and religion," and mocking various religious beliefs and practices. For example, the exhibits on display at the Central Antireligious Museum in Moscow included the relics of several Russian saints, whose remains were placed alongside those of a mummified cat, a dog, and a rabbit.[87] By 1930, forty-four antireligious museums were open, and they were visited by millions of persons each year.[88]

Movies were also employed to propagandize atheism. The films *The Miracle-Maker* (1922) and *Brigade Commander Ivanov* (1923) mark the beginning of antireligious propaganda in the Soviet cinema. After 1924, when the 13th Party Congress urged that steps be taken to develop motion pictures as "a powerful method of Communist education and agitation," the number of films on atheist themes increased. Typically, they depicted Orthodox Church officials conducting counterrevolution under the guise of religion, portrayed nuns as depraved and attacked religion as a capitalist trick to disarm the workers. Clergymen invariably duped rank-and-file believers for personal gains or conspired with capitalists to sow counterrevolution and undermine Soviet power. These films were so crude, however, that they were of little propaganda value.[89]

The entire genre was subjected to harsh criticism in 1928 at a Party conference on the cinema. This gathering denounced the film industry's clumsiness and recommended a more subtle approach to the problem of religion. The conference appears to have been effective, for script writers and directors thereafter "tried to convey a deeper conception of religion as a social phenomenon and to disabuse believers [of their religious notions] by presenting characters that were artistically convincing."[90]

Antireligious posters also tended to be crude. They linked religion to capitalism and war, referred to clergymen as "black crows" and "filth," and generally dealt with religion in a coarse manner.[91] One poster showed the pregnant Virgin Mary looking at a billboard advertising a film on abortion. In the caption, she exclaims: "Oh, why didn't I know that before!"[92]

Toward the end of the twenties, as the government intensified its pressure on the churches, educational institutions were called upon to combat religion. Whereas the educational authorities had decided in 1925 that "special implanting of antireligious views into each child is not needed," by the end of the decade this policy was reversed. The term "nonreligious education" was abandoned, and antireligious instruction was begun.[93] Special "antireligious universities" were also set up to indoctrinate groups of workers, peasants, and Red Army soldiers. By 1931, there were eighty-four of these "universities" in various regions of the country. Students were given one year of classroom instruction and were then assigned to conduct atheist propaganda.[94]

In 1929, "Godless shock brigades," "Godless factories," and "Godless collective farms" made their appearance. These detachments of industrial or agricultural workers vowed to fulfill high production quotas, while simultaneously carrying on antireligious propaganda.[95] Although they were constantly urged to be uncompromising toward religious belief, their members rarely demonstrated the requisite militancy. In fact, the atheist press frequently published complaints that these units were being infiltrated by believers who used them as a protective cover.[96]

The League, like other Soviet institutions, sought unsuccessfully to find a path between Leftist and Rightist deviations. In 1930, when the antireligious effort was relaxed, the League's work was criticized as excessively harsh. (Its activities during the first years of its existence were later characterized by a Soviet commentator as "bluster," the work of an "atheist sect." The League was said to have "completely adopted all of its adversary's worst features of intolerance and fanaticism."[97] The description, it would appear, is entirely apt.) But in predictable Stalinist fashion, the victorious battle against Leftist Deviationism gave rise to a flourishing Rightist Deviation. By 1932, more than half of the members of the League of the Militant Godless were in arrears in the payment of dues. Without encouragement from above, local activists and rank-and-file members lost interest in the fight against religion. The press carried accounts of inactivity in Godless cells, and some of the "successes" of the atheist movement were revealed to be fabrications. Membership figures for branches of the League had been inflated, and fraudulent reports of antireligious activities had been recorded. Yemelian Yaroslavskii, head of the organization, observed in 1930 that whole towns and villages had declared themselves "Godless." Even if there were some basis in fact for these claims, he said, "when entire districts are declared Godless, in a county where there is nothing, no culture, no [antireligious] work—this is a joke. . . ." [98]

During the next few years, the Party sought to consolidate its gains on the "atheist front." A Central Committee Plenum in the spring of 1936 called for more subtle and sophisticated efforts to undermine religion. The Party and Komsomol programs soon were revised to include a statement underscoring the need for "patience" in antireligious propaganda. Chastened by revelations of shortcomings and outright falsification during the first half of the decade, Yaroslavskii acknowledged that it was necessary to exercise caution to create an "atheist mentality" among the populace. "Open assaults" were specifically rejected, and a policy of "deep, insistent, and patient" persuasion was stressed. [99] Atheist propaganda was continued, but its tone was far less strident than it had been earlier.

Two decades of experience had produced a chastening effect on the *antireligiozniki*. As one authority admitted in 1939, "it is much more difficult to uproot religion from the minds of the workers than to liberate them from the exploitation of capitalism." [100]

Once the war began, antireligious propaganda became still less virulent and soon ceased altogether. The League of the Militant Godless issued no publications after the autumn of 1941 and was disbanded not long afterward. During the war, the production of atheist films was suspended. In fact, in some films of this period, heroes refer to God, turn toward icons (often conspicuously displayed), and cross themselves. In one film, *The Rainbow*, a partisan actually replies to a traitor who begs for mercy in the name of God: "He's our God, not yours!" [101]

As World War II drew to an end, however, the Party began once again to move against the church. In September, 1944, the Central Committee adopted a decree calling for renewed antireligious efforts through "scientific-educational propaganda." Party members were reminded of the need to combat "survivals of ignorance, superstition, and prejudice" among the people." [102] Less than a year later, the Central Committee repeated its call for intensified atheist propaganda, and the mass media also called for more aggressive efforts in this area. [103]

These exhortations appear to have been routine and almost perfunctory. They certainly did not lead to a substantial increase in the level of atheist propaganda. Moreover, most of the propaganda that did follow was confined to criticisms of the Catholic Church, which was said to have been allied with the Axis powers during the War. In antireligious films of the postwar period, for example, Catholicism was singled out for particular abuse. In *Conspiracy of the Doomed* (1950), a Catholic Cardinal directs a gang of murderers, spies, and saboteurs. In *Dawn Over the Neman* (1952), Catholic clergymen spread poisoned seeds, set fires, conceal murders in their churches, and help those resisting Soviet "liberation" of Lithuania.[104] (Soviet hostility toward Roman Catholicism did not die with Stalin. Even after 1953, scurrilous propaganda continued to be published. The Vatican was termed "the Catholic branch of the [U.S.] State Department," while Pope John XXIII was accused of trying to establish "a kind of spiritual NATO.")[105] Despite the production of such works, the volume and intensity of atheist propaganda did not return to the levels of the earlier Stalin years until the dictator died.

The Post-Stalin Era

Official policy toward religion has gone through a number of phases since Stalin's death. Only a year after he died, another major antireligious campaign was begun. On July 7, 1954, the Party Central Committee issued a resolution calling for more vigorous measures against the church. According to the resolution, religious groups had "intensified their activities and skillfully adjusted to contemporary conditions." There had been, the decree continued, "a rise in the number of citizens observing religious holy days . . . as well as an increase in pilgrimages to holy places." It concluded with a demand for a "broadening, strengthening, and deepening" of atheist efforts." [106]

The *antireligiozniki,* once again "unleashed" after a lengthy period of quiescence, responded so harshly that the Party was compelled to call a halt to the campaign only four months later. On November 10, the Central Committee issued another decree, signed by Nikita Khrushchev, that criticized "insulting attacks upon the clergy and believers who perform religious rites." It cited "cases of administrative interference . . . in the activities of religious associations and groups," and condemned the "rude attitude" manifested toward the clergy by some local Party organizations.[107]

The four-month episode remains to this day rather puzzling; it began suddenly, quickly assumed savage proportions, and ended just as suddenly as it had begun. Some have attributed the campaign to Georgi Malenkov and other high-ranking opponents of Khrushchev. According to this point of view, only after Khrushchev had ousted Malenkov could the First Secretary put an end to a program he did not favor.[108] But this argument does not account satisfactorily for Khrushchev's later attacks on religion.

Thus, others have been led to argue that the 1954 campaign was initiated by Khrushchev. One Western scholar has suggested that the episode was "the first portent of the open and intense campaign which marked the years of Khrushchev's unchallenged rule." [109] While the evidence for this hypothesis is largely circumstantial and certainly not unambiguous, it is consistent with Khrushchev's general attitude toward the church. Indeed, during the fifties, official attacks on religion "followed the wavering course of Khrushchev's rise to power," reaching their greatest intensity only after the defeat of the so-called Anti-Party Group in 1957.[110]

Whatever the explanation, the campaign had a considerable impact on antireligious efforts for the next few years. Until the end of the 1950s, the regime made only sporadic and superficial attempts to combat the church. Toward the end of the decade, however, a new offensive was begun, this time with the enthusiastic public support of the top Party leadership. In fact, Khrushchev himself gave the signal for the new campaign: in his speeches, the First Secretary underscored his concern about the problem of religion, and he demanded that the Party act vigorously to combat it.[111]

The new antireligious drive, which began in 1959, has involved a sharp increase in the use of both coercion and propaganda. While the clergy and laymen have been spared the excesses of the Stalin era—there have been no executions for "counterrevolutionary" or "anti-State" activity—there has been widespread use of crude and/or illegal measures. For example, the secular authorities have forbidden priests to administer more than one parish; many of the churches thus deprived of their ministers have been declared unusable and have been closed.[112] Indeed, thousands of churches and more than half of the remaining seminaries were closed forcibly within the span of a few years. Between 1959 and 1966, the number of Orthodox churches fell from some 17,500 to only 7,500,[113] while the eight Orthodox seminaries that were functioning as late as 1958 were reduced to three by 1965.[114] (See Table 2.1.)

What is more, the authorities have arbitrarily refused large numbers of congregations permission to register, offering them the equally unappealing alternatives of disbanding or assuming an illegal status. This policy has brought forth numerous protests, some of which have reached the West through underground channels. Thus a Baptist congregation in Vladivostok wrote to Khrushchev in 1961:

Here the principle of freedom of conscience has been severely violated. There is not a single registered [religious] community in the region. We are all forced to assemble without registration, although we have asked for it continuously and insistently. There is not a single community where

Table 2.1   Churches and Synagogues in the USSR

Year	Number of Orthodox Churches	Number of Synagogues
1914	54,000	
1917		1,034
1928	39,000	
1929–30		934
1941	4,200	
1945	16,000	
1948	15,000	
1956		450
1958	17,500	
1963		96
1966	7,500	60–62

Sources: Robert Conquest, *Religion in the USSR* (New York: Frederick A. Praeger, 1968), pp. 11, 20, 29, 37; A. Veshchikov, *Nauka i religiya*, No. 11 (1962), p. 59; Zvi Gitelman, "TheJews," *Problems of Communism*, Vol. XVI, No. 5 (September–October, 1967), p. 92; Walter Kolarz, *Religion in the Soviet Union* (New York: St. Martin's Press, 1961), p. 386; *Spravochnik propagandista i agitatora* (Moscow, 1966), pp. 149–150; Joshua Rothenberg, *Synagogues in the Soviet Union* (Waltham, Mass.: Institute of East European Jewish Studies, Brandeis University, 1966), pp. 6–8; Bohdan R. Bociurkiw, "Religion in the USSR After Khrushchev," in John W. Strong (ed.), *The Soviet Union Under Brezhnev and Kosygin* (New York: Van Nostrand Reinhold Co., 1971), pp. 135, 151.

workers of the police have not appeared with threats to prohibit church services.[115]

The organizational structure of the Russian Orthodox Church has also been changed by the Party. In 1961, control of local church affairs was taken out of the hands of the parish priest and given to a council of twenty parishioners, the so-called *"dvadtsatka."* Since 1961, priests have been subordinated to the *dvadtsatka*, i.e., they no longer have legal control over the administration of their own parishes.[116] The government, operating through its Council for Religious Affairs,[117] has used these new regulations to intimidate believers and clergymen, to close churches, and to prevent others from being opened. According to official documents (obtained through underground channels but apparently authentic), the government has sought to infiltrate and, if possible, gain control over the parish councils. In the early 1960s, the Council for Religious Affairs instructed its local representatives to arrange for new elections to each *dvadtsatka.* Arguing that many of the existing councils of twenty were "untrustworthy," consisting chiefly of "illiterate or fanatical people," officials in Moscow demanded the selection of people "who would honestly carry out the Soviet laws and [government] suggestions and requests." Representatives of the Council for Religious Affairs were urged to take part "in the selection of members of such an executive body," in order to guarantee subservience to the government's will. "Only when such a 'council of twenty' is formed and . . . it satisfies you," the instructions concluded, "should you sign an agreement with it." [118] This procedure, which involves direct interference in religious affairs and is a clear violation of the laws separating church from state, was widely used during the Khrushchev era. It continues to be applied under Brezhnev and Kosygin.

While the harshness of the Khrushchev period has been muted somewhat since the First Secretary was deposed, the struggle against religion continues to be pursued energetically. The most visible form of illegality— the forcible closing of churches (see Table 2.1)—has been all but abandoned, but the houses of worship, monasteries, theological academies, and other religious institutions that were shut down earlier remain closed. Moreover, most of the legislation passed during the Lenin, Stalin, and Khrushchev eras is still in force;[119] congregations and individual believers continue to be harassed and are sometimes terrorized by measures of questionable legality.

The laws regulating religious activity, which were drafted in very broad terms and contain a good deal of ambiguous language, continue to be interpreted strictly. Loosely drawn codes provide the authorities with considerable latitude and facilitate arbitrary application of the law. Indeed, it is "all but impossible for believers to satisfy their religious needs without compromising their positions as . . . law-abiding citizens." [120]

Since the Bolshevik Revolution, thousands of churches, mosques, and synagogues have been closed "legally" because the law has been drafted so broadly. Houses of worship, according to Soviet law, can be closed under any of the following circumstances: (1) if the congregation violates a law; (2) if the congregation violates the agreement governing use of a building; (3) if the lawful instructions of a state organ are not obeyed; (4) if the buildings are to be demolished as part of a program for rebuilding an area; (5) if their age represents a danger to occupants; or (6) if "the need arises to transform a house of prayer because of state or public needs." [121] Each of these reasons, particularly the last, admits of broad and varied interpretations.

In point of fact, churches often are closed under the pretext of widening a street, laying out a park or square, or because of some other urban renewal project. The government has sometimes taxed churches at such a high rate that they have been forced to close, or else classified them as "historical monuments" and transformed them into museums. The secular authorities may also interfere with the selection of a church council; while the church is "abandoned," pending selection of an official governing body, it is closed for want of use.[122] The latitude given to local authorities, it would seem, is almost limitless.

Similarly, the criminal codes of the various republics use vague and sweeping language, covering virtually any form of religious activity. Article 227 of the RSFSR Criminal Code, for example, makes it illegal to organize or direct a group

. . . whose activity, carried on under the guise of preaching religious beliefs and performing religious ceremonies, is connected with causing harm to citizens' health, or with any other infringement of the person or right of citizens, or with inducing citizens to refuse social activity or the perform-ance of civic duties, or with drawing minors into such a group. . . .[123]

Under this statute, circumcision, baptism by immersion, fasting, refusal to let a child wear the Pioneer neckerchief, and a host of other acts are criminal offenses. "Under the guise of religious dogma," a leading official has argued, certain religious groups "circulate anonymous anti-Soviet letters, spread rumors which cause panic, and make criminal attacks on the rights of Soviet citizens guaranteed by the Constitution, on their health and even on their lives." [124]

Article 142 of the Criminal Code makes it illegal to advocate the acts prescribed in Article 227. It prohibits "the commission of fraudulent acts for the purpose of arousing superstitions among the masses," as well as "compelling others to perform religious rites." [125] This article is directed primarily against clergymen, although it can also be applied to religious parents.

The mere act of bringing up children "in a religious spirit" may warrant depriving parents of their parental rights.[126] According to one émigré scholar, the withdrawal of children from their religious parents was elevated to a "national virtue" during the Khrushchev years.[127] While this view is highly exaggerated, it is nonetheless clear that the regime will not tolerate religious instruction within the family. In the words of a leading ideologist of the Khrushchev era,

We cannot and we must not remain indifferent to the fate of the children on whom parents, fanatical believers, are in reality inflicting an act of spiritual violence. We cannot allow blind and ignorant parents to bring up their children like themselves and so deform them.[128]

If the authorities consider criminal sanctions too severe to deter or punish a particular form of religious activity, they may apply the anti-parasite statutes, cancel or refuse to grant residency permits, call up seminary students for military service, or confine dissident clergymen and believers to mental hospitals.[129] The available evidence suggests that the authorities make substantial use of the wide variety of weapons at their disposal.[130]

The Constitutional guarantee of religious freedom, then, remains less important than the right and obligation to combat religion. Indeed, the state's "protection" of its citizens from "encroachments on their conscience and on their freedom by fanatical obscurantists" has been cited as evidence of the "lofty humanism" of the Soviet system.[131] Soviet law, it is said, "does not recognize 'freedom' for religious fanaticism or other antisocial acts." [132]

The official Soviet position is that citizens are not punished simply for their religious convictions. "[Only] for breaking the law is punishment meted out by the Soviet State," it is argued.[133] But the law is vague, and those who apply it tend to be extremely zealous. Even a cursory examination of the Soviet press reveals that believers may be refused employment, lose their jobs, be dismissed from a university, be denied an apartment or a pass to a sanatorium, or suffer other privations solely because of their religious convictions.[134] These acts are a product of the sweeping and ambiguous language of Soviet law, constant demands in the media and at Party and Komsomol meetings that atheists adopt an "aggressive" stance toward religion, and the cavalier attitude of Soviet authorities toward believers. A half century of official hostility toward the church continues to stimulate official acts that are clearly outside the law.

There are serious reasons for questioning the value of these coercive measures, however. Closing churches, arresting clergymen, or harassing religious citizens seldom deters people from believing in God. Thus, as soon as Stalin gave his approval to a church-state détente during World War II, Soviet citizens (many of whom had claimed to be atheists) filled the churches. As a Soviet observer has remarked, "It was enough to open the temples of God during the war, and many of the atheists of yesterday found themselves in church. Thus, we see how shallow are the roots planted by crash methods and lack of genuine knowledge." [135]

Countless numbers of people who had denied or disguised their religiousness felt free to admit it during the war. Two decades of coercion and clumsy propaganda had only inhibited their public expression of religious belief. It had not eliminated their faith. Today, too,

. . . over a large part of the territory of the Soviet Union there are no churches . . . or clergymen. But there are believers. If not Orthodox, then sectarians of all possible shades. . . . They are former members of the church. . . . [Cutting] off access does not turn believers into atheists. On the contrary, it strengthens people's leanings toward religion. . . .[136]

Antireligious measures, then, have affected people's behavior far more than their beliefs. While official persecution may reduce the number of churches, it also increases the number of illegal parishes and parishioners. To quote a Soviet commentator, "Withdrawal of registered status frequently results in a mere increase in the number of unregistered but functioning religious societies and groups." [137]

Concluding Remarks

Official policy toward religion has shifted somewhat as the attitudes of religious leaders have changed. By the time of the German invasion in 1941, Stalin could rightly say that the "reactionary clergy" had been all but completely eliminated,[138] and today organized religion in the USSR is even less hostile toward the regime. In fact, almost all denominations actively support Soviet domestic and foreign policy. (Some groups, it is true, resist particular measures, while others encourage their members to withdraw from society and avoid politics.) Leading church figures are lavish in their praise of the political system and support the government's position on all international issues. They have echoed the Party line on questions of arms control, peaceful coexistence, and the elimination of colonialism, and have supported the government whenever a major international crisis has erupted.[139]

Because of these developments, the church's loyalty to the Soviet state is no longer questioned. While religious leaders who were active half a century ago are still described as "clerical counterrevolutionaries" and "the fiercest enemies of Soviet power," clergymen today are regarded as politically loyal.[140] Therefore, the Party has tolerated, approved, and sometimes even encouraged a measure of religious freedom. Religious delegations visit foreign countries with the government's enthusiastic approval, and leading clerics receive official recognition for their services to the regime. Patriarch Alexei, for example, was awarded the Red Banner of Labor in 1962 and again in 1968 for his "great patriotic activity in defense of peace." [141] These measures do not represent a change of heart on the part of the authorities, nor do they indicate an intention to fulfill the Constitution's guarantee of religious freedom. Instead, it appears that the Party, while anxious to combat religion, is at the same time willing to exploit it.[142]

Religious groups consider it expedient to support the political system as the price for their continued existence. But their political loyalty has been exchanged for an uneasy and uncertain toleration of religious practices.[143] The church-state détente is highly fragile; government tolerance may be eroded gradually or abandoned suddenly. In fact, in the period since

Stalin's death, the unofficial concordat with the church has grown increasingly unstable. The Party has again resolved to create an atheist society and has invested considerable energy and resources in an effort to achieve this objective.

The secular authorities have unilaterally abrogated the concordat reached in 1943, demonstrating, of course, just how unequal the two parties were and are. The two officials who had symbolized the détente between church and state, Metropolitan Nikolai and Georgi Karpov (head of the government agency responsible for church affairs), were replaced in early 1960.[144] The Communist Party once again called for a war against religion, although it promised to make that war a limited affair. The objective is still to vanquish the enemy, but limited means are now brought to bear in pursuing this goal. Outright terror has been abandoned as an instrument of policy, and the campaign to close churches seems to have ended with the fall of Khrushchev. Atheist propaganda has come to play the dominant role in the struggle against religion.

In 1959, the antireligious journal *Nauka i religiya (Science and Religion)* was established, and two years later a similar journal in Ukrainian appeared. A new course, "Fundamentals of Scientific Atheism," was introduced in institutions of higher learning. Special chairs in the history and theory of atheism were established in some of the major universities at this time, and a research institute dealing with religion was set up shortly afterward under the Academy of Social Sciences. As the years have gone by, atheist propaganda has become an increasingly visible and audible feature of Soviet life.

The emphasis in combating religion today is no longer on terror, administrative measures, or ridicule. It is on the propaganda of science, atheism, and "communist morality." Since the late 1950s, the Party has sustained an antireligious propaganda effort of massive proportions. The features of this program, and an assessment of its efficacy, are the subject of this book.

3 The Institutional Framework

Although they guarantee complete freedom of religion, Soviet laws reject the clerical demand for freedom of religion, i.e., the demand for unlimited freedom of activity for religious organizations and for the arbitrary rule of priests, for in fact that would lead to the abridgment of the freedom of conscience of nonbelievers.

Sovetskaya Litva, March 30, 1969

Because there is at present no body that enjoys the prestige and authority that the League of the Militant Godless did in Stalin's time, the Party has granted operational control over the atheist movement to a number of organizations. All of the major instruments of political socialization and communication—the mass media, schools and universities, the Pioneers and Komsomol, the Knowledge Society, the trade unions, the cultural-enlightenment institutions (libraries, clubs, and museums), the political enlightenment network, the system of people's universities of culture, and the vast array of propagandists, agitators, and political information workers *(politinformatory)*—are involved in this effort. Not all of these organizations and institutions contribute equally, of course; we will concentrate on those that make the greatest contribution. This chapter will focus on the institutions responsible for directing and controlling the flow of propaganda, while the chapters that follow will describe and analyze their activities.

Ultimate responsibility for organizing and supervising antireligious propaganda is vested in the Propaganda Department of the CPSU Central Committee and analogous bodies at each level of the Party hierarchy. These bodies set the goals of the atheist movement, devise, approve and/or reject specific propaganda techniques, and supervise the implementation of the Party's atheist programs. At every administrative level, a Party secretary controls this work. By and large, he will be assisted by a staff of experts organized as a "council of scientific atheism." Such councils exist in most cities and districts, and in some farms and factories as well. They are arranged in a hierarchy, with higher-level councils providing instructions and recommendations to those below.[1] They are a major force stimulating atheist propaganda: without their prodding, Party organizations would devote considerably less attention to the struggle against religion.

On the lowest level, the Party requires each of its members "to aid in forming and educating the man of communist society; to struggle decisively against all manifestations of bourgeois ideology . . . [including] religious prejudices. . . ." [2] This does not mean that the Party requires its rank and file to become specialists in atheist work. It means only that Party members must, or should, exploit every opportunity to criticize religion. While some respond enthusiastically to the call, most are too busy with other problems, are indifferent, or lack the training necessary to devote much attention to atheist propaganda. They feel that the struggle against religion is a task for "professional" atheists.[3] Given this lack of enthusiasm, the Party has had to organize segments of the population to do the job.

Both specialists and ordinary citizens are drawn into this work. At the highest levels, the Party has sought to recruit, train, and retrain personnel from the scholarly and ideological communities. To supplement their efforts, the authorities seek to enlist a broad *aktiv* of scientists, schoolteachers, former believers, and pensioners. At lower levels, officials seek to organize as atheist propagandists those whose views are most respected by their friends and fellow workers. They, in turn, must create and organize an "atheist public opinion," mobilizing the atheists and indoctrinating the believers and agnostics. As a Soviet philosopher has observed, if the official doctrine of scientific atheism "is not organized, not consolidated, and has not penetrated to the depths of the collective," it is unlikely to be accepted by the masses.[4]

The Knowledge Society

The Knowledge Society (known until 1963 as the All-Union Society for the Dissemination of Political and Scientific Knowledge) is the most important institution operating in the field of atheist propaganda. When it was founded in 1947, it inherited the functions of the League of the Militant Godless (along with certain other functions), and many of the League's personnel as well. It has carried out its tasks far more responsibly than its predecessor did.

It is organized in much the same way as the Communist Party. Each of the union republics has its own Society, and there are branches in every region, territory, city, and district. Most of the large villages have set up their own branches, and some have even been created in individual factories and plants. In most branches of the Society, there is a special section that deals with scientific atheism; its members are responsible for delivering antireligious lectures and arranging other atheist activities. The administration of each republic's Knowledge Society aids provincial and district branches by arranging conferences and seminars and by setting up permanent "scientific methodology councils" to deal with the various spheres of propaganda work.[5] A higher branch of the Society may prepare lectures for local propagandists to deliver, and sometimes local branches request speakers from regional or district centers.[6]

The Party exercises, or is supposed to exercise, direct control over each branch of the Society. Local Party officials appoint the head of the local branch and sometimes even the chiefs of the various sections. This practice, it is said, "naturally makes Party leadership . . . more effective, allows the spiritual needs of the workers to be satisfied more fully, and attracts leading workers to speak before them." [7] But Party control is often imperfect and sometimes nonexistent. Many Party organizations do not pay sufficient attention to the activities of the Knowledge Society. They do not recruit adequate numbers of "volunteers" to handle propaganda work and fail to exercise direction over the Society's efforts. Moreover, the organizational links between the central administrative board of the All-Union Knowledge Society and local branches often exist only on paper.[8] As we shall see, the Party's response to such problems of coordination and control has been to establish additional organizations, in the hope that some measure of unity can be achieved.

Like its predecessor, the Society uses a variety of propaganda devices, e.g., books, pamphlets, periodicals, lectures, question-and-answer evenings, and discussions with believers. Unlike the League, however, the Society eschews such boisterous measures as antireligious carnivals, parades, and demonstrations. It has kept the struggle against religion on a relatively intellectual plane, contrasting the unscientific religious weltanschauung with the "scientific materialist world-view" of Marxism-Leninism and scientific atheism. Since 1959, the Society has published a monthly journal, *Nauka i religiya (Science and Religion),* which is devoted entirely to the struggle against religion. In 1961, a Ukrainian-language monthly, *Voivnichii ateist (The Militant Atheist),* began publication; since 1964, it has appeared under the title *Lyudina i svit (Man and the World).* It is principally through these periodicals and through public lectures that the Society presents its message to the masses.

The Knowledge Society is said to be a "public scientific and educational organization of the Soviet intelligentsia." [9] Membership is voluntary, but to be a member one must be sufficiently informed to contribute to the Society's work. At first it was a limited association of scientists, intellectuals and *agitprop* functionaries, but membership has grown steadily over the years. Its size hardly rivals that of the League of the Militant Godless, which in 1932 numbered five and a half million members. But, as we have seen, the League enrolled entire factories and villages in spurious membership drives, while the Knowledge Society continues to rely on an

Table 3.1   Growth in Membership of the Knowledge Society (Society for the Dissemination of Political and Scientific Knowledge), 1947–1972

Year	Number of Members
1947	1,414
1950	130,000
1958	800,000
1959	850,000
1960	900,000
1963	1,200,000
1964	1,300,000
1967	1,800,000
1972	2,500,000

Sources: Partiinaya zhizn, No. 18 (1959), p. 37; Partiinaya zhizn, No. 4 (1960), p. 36; Izvestia, January 26, 1960, p. 2; Pravda, September 11, 1963, p. 3; Pravda, June 21, 1972, p. 1; G. Merkurov, Mass Organizations in the USSR (Moscow, n.d.), p. 36; Walter Kolarz, Religion in the Soviet Union (New York: St. Martin's Press, 1961), p. 16.

intellectual and political elite. The ranks of the Society now include approximately two and a half million persons, and each year another 100,000 new members are added. Table 3.1 shows the growth of the Society's membership.

While no figures have been published that give a nationwide breakdown of Knowledge Society personnel, selected data indicate that approximately 40 percent are Party members, 10 percent are Komsomols, and 50 percent are non-Party people.[10] New members are recruited primarily from two groups: the younger intelligentsia and the ideological specialists, i.e., journalists, the heads of clubs, agitators, and propagandists. The Party has tried repeatedly to persuade the more prominent members of the Soviet intellectual community to participate in the Society's antireligious activities, but their response has invariably been unenthusiastic. The CPSU Central Committee noted some years ago that "significant groups among the intelligentsia still have not been drawn into the Society's work," while many of those who *had* joined did not participate in its activities.[11] The complaint is no less appropriate today, despite continuing criticism of intellectuals' lack of involvement in antireligious efforts. At present, only the lesser-known scientists, novelists, and playwrights are actively involved in atheist propaganda.

The problem of intellectual apathy or hostility is particularly significant among scientists; as *Sovetskaya Rossiya* put it, "the voices of scientists are not to be heard."[12] Most members of the scientific community simply refuse to associate themselves with the atheist campaign. Some consider any criticism of religious views inappropriate in a serious scientific work; they say that antireligious propaganda is the task of popularized works. Others argue that science is itself atheism; they see no need to draw explicit atheist conclusions from scientific data. In their view, the facts speak for themselves, demonstrating the validity of atheism and "refuting" religion.[13] Whatever the reason, it means that atheist work is often conducted by people with inadequate scientific backgrounds. The consequences of this for the struggle against religion are obvious. As one commentator has observed, atheist propaganda "not infrequently is reduced to the repetition of prepared conclusions and the unsubstantiated denial of religious ideology, instead of the unmasking of its scientific bankruptcy." [14]

The regime continues to try to persuade the intellectual community to participate in the fight against religion. Some Party organizations rely on appeals and exhortations; others provide financial inducements to draw the intelligentsia into the Society's work; still others simply assign certain of their members to combat religion. The available evidence suggests that compulsion and persuasion are not always necessary. Some persons, particularly those who are on pension, apparently volunteer for altruistic reasons. While many are simply bored and hope to find an outlet for their restlessness, others evidently see religion as such a dangerous social and moral force that they voluntarily contribute their energies to combating it. Thus, one atheist lecturer, when asked why he had chosen involvement in this work rather than retirement, replied:

To be frank, life forced me to. I saw that clergymen and sectarians were intensifying their activities, seeking new ways and means to influence people, while the struggle against their influence is waged in a weak manner. For a man who has not grown accustomed to a quiet life, the struggle against religion is a most appropriate job. You feel yourself on the main line of the ideological front. . . . And what a joy to realize that your work helps people to break away from the path of religious ideology and renounce their faith in god! [15]

Few persons are so enthusiastic, however, and the Party has had to recruit propagandists and utilize other institutions to bring the message of atheism to the Soviet people.

The School System

The school system is potentially the Party's most powerful weapon in the struggle against religion. By inculcating the appropriate views into the minds of impressionable young children, the regime can, at least in theory, utterly eradicate religion within the space of a few generations. In fact, however, while the schools have made some effort in this direction, their influence has not been nearly so pervasive and profound as might have been expected. The major impediments to their success have been (1) prior socializing experiences in the family and (2) the lack of interest and skill of most teachers in dealing with religion.

As Nigel Grant has observed, the relationship between school and family is a partnership, with each side making a contribution to the child's upbringing. According to Soviet theory, "the teachers are . . . the senior partners, the experts," and the school is "firmly in control." [16] But reality is sometimes very different. Even little children attending school for the first time have had socializing experiences, and some of these seriously impede the Party's antireligious efforts. Relatively few children are sent to nurseries or kindergartens,[17] and a great many grow up in homes where at least one member of the family is a believer. These youngsters, who are exposed to religious views by their parents or grandparents, are said to lack "atheistic immunity" [18] and may have difficulty in assimilating the regime's antireligious messages. Suggestions that preschool and school activities be oriented chiefly toward atheism[19] are, by and large, ignored. Educational authorities have their own set of priorities and tend to be unresponsive to the demands of the atheist movement. To be sure, Soviet youngsters receive some antireligious training in school or through organized extracurricular activities. But atheist messages are presented very infrequently, and when they are, they are likely to be too indirect and mild, or else too heavy-handed, seriously to influence the children.

Resourceful teachers can, and do, weave attacks on religious beliefs and persons into virtually any kind of lesson. Physics, biology, chemistry, astronomy, mathematics, history, geography, and literature can all serve as jumping-off points to instruct pupils on the evils or falsity of religion. For example, the laws of motion and the laws of the conservation of matter and energy are used to refute religious miracles and the notion that God created the world out of nothing. Science and history lessons can discredit Biblical descriptions of the origin of man and criticize the persecution by church authorities of such figures as Galileo or Giordano Bruno. Elementary school reading or writing lessons sometimes are transformed into attacks on religion. Students are asked to write compositions on such themes as "Whose enemy is religion?" or "Why is it necessary to combat religion?" After spring (Easter) vacation, some teachers arrange discussions on the subject "How I Spent the Holiday." They are urged to acquaint themselves with the children's attitudes toward religion and are even asked to observe the pupils' eating habits in order to determine who observes Lent.[20] Students in non-Russian schools often receive antireligious propaganda in their Russian language classes. In pursuing the apparently innocuous task of learning Russian grammar, pupils in Central Asian schools are taught such antireligious proverbs as "There will be no friendship between the Caucasian bard and the mullah." The children are instructed in the following catechism:

Q. Who is the Caucasian bard?
A. He is a troubadour—a singer of folk songs.
Q. And what does the mullah do?
A. Mullah reads the Koran and when someone dies, he reads prayers. . . .
Q. Why is there no friendship between the mullah and the Caucasian bard?
A. Because the troubadour loves people, life, weddings, merriment, songs and holidays, but the mullah loves prayers, fasting and funerals. There is no place for the mullah where the Caucasian bard is.
Q. Who has the greater esteem for the people?
A. The troubadour, because his songs make people happy and glorify life, noble feats, and his native land.[21]

Pupils in the upper grades receive atheist training in social studies or social science courses. A few schools, generally in areas where religion is widespread, have even introduced a course on the principles of scientific atheism. But the course is usually offered only as an elective and is taught in very few schools.[22]

Extracurricular activities, sometimes involving parents as well as pupils, are also directed toward antireligious objectives. Atheism clubs and circles, lectures, and field trips are organized, and even physical education and sports can be utilized to combat religion by attracting to school those who usually stay home on religious holidays. On hikes and excursions the instructor can point out monasteries, churches, or holy places; these provide a starting point for atheist discussions.[23]

The most elaborate extracurricular activity involves "young atheists' clubs." These clubs operate during and after school, and they are designed to harness peer group pressure to achieve atheist objectives. Their activities are a smaller-scale version of adult atheist propaganda; they include surveys of religious belief, as well as antireligious plays, puppet shows, films, lectures, excursions, newspapers, photographs, and posters. Some clubs assign the children to individual believers (adult or child) in an effort to persuade them of the falsity of religious belief.[24] The Club for Young Atheists in one primary school in the city of Gorky has even put together its own antireligious museum, which takes up an entire floor of the school building. Pupils conduct guided tours for visiting schoolchildren, parents, and other adults, and the museum's holdings are loaned out to various factories in the city. In addition, members of the Club stage antireligious plays and deliver lectures in both Gorky and neighboring cities.[25]

Despite the elaborateness of some of these programs and activities, their contribution to the atheist effort is limited. Only a small number of pupils are actively involved in atheist circles and clubs. While the program provides them with training and experience in antireligious propaganda, it hardly touches the other boys and girls in school.[26] Moreover, antireligious propaganda tends to be conducted episodically, primarily when major religious holy days occur. More important, religious students often work diligently at mastering their school lessons—even in the natural, physical, and social sciences—and still retain their religious beliefs. They have already been subjected, it is said, to parental censorship and therefore cannot assimilate their school lessons.[27] One report in *Nauka i religiya* tells of a schoolteacher who explained to her classes that Soviet cosmonauts had reached an altitude of 300 kilometers in their flights and had never encountered God. Therefore, she concluded, God does not exist. She then asked one of her second graders (whom she knew to be religious) whether she found this logic convincing. The child responded: "I do not know if 300 kilometers is very much, but I know very well that only those who are pure of heart will behold God." [28] It is an argument that is difficult to rebut.

To compound the problem, few teachers share the enthusiasm of professional atheists. "Why are the school and teachers so timid, at times even clumsy," one atheist has asked, "in gaining access to . . . families in which children are stupefied and maimed?" Alluding to the fact that most teachers are reluctant to mix atheism and formal school lessons, she went on, "Are we not committing an unpardonable error by sometimes keeping the sword of atheism in its scabbard during school lessons in physics, botany, zoology, history, and literature?" [29] Some teachers conduct antireligious discussions only during the period before Christmas and Easter, while others make no effort whatsoever to undermine religion or inculcate an attitude of militant atheism. Teachers and school officials generally refuse to act against pupils' religious beliefs as long as the children perform adequately in class.[30]

There appear to be many teachers who choose not to spend class time discussing religion. Some consider the subject irrelevant; others lack the requisite knowledge or simply prefer not to explore such an awkward and personal matter; still others themselves harbor religious beliefs and thus refuse to attack religion. Moreover, few teachers have the necessary training for atheist work. Until recently, the subject of scientific atheism was not even taught in universities and pedagogical institutes, and, as of early 1972, only a third of all schoolteachers had taken the course.[31] Not all of these had a "correct understanding" of the relevant problems, and seminars, refresher courses, and other official training programs for teachers have had only limited impact on the others.[32] Because few teachers share the zeal or skill of antireligious specialists and ideological functionaries, only a handful of teachers and administrators actively attack religion. Some of these are overly zealous, resorting to intimidation, threats, and other forms of pressure. They insult the feelings and dignity of religious youngsters.[33] Most teachers, however, avoid the issue entirely; they spend their time in more familiar academic pursuits.

The widespread neutrality or tolerance has been criticized by educational authorities and antireligious specialists alike. In the words of two commentators,

Today we can still meet teachers who harbor a certain misconception about atheist education in the school. In most instances, this view is formulated as follows: The great majority of schoolchildren today are free of religious prejudices, so that there is no longer any need for open antireligious propaganda. If, however, the need should arise to expose religious prejudices, the teacher must present atheist material indirectly and surreptitiously, rather than in a direct fashion, in order not to attract the attention toward religion of children who know nothing about it.[34]

Antireligious indoctrination, according to this view, is undesirable. It is pointless—and perhaps dangerous—to arouse "an unwholesome interest" in religion. But in point of fact, schoolchildren and graduates are said to find themselves "in a blind alley at their first encounter with religious manifestations in life." Their "spontaneous, superficial and uncomprehended atheism" usually is no match for the religious person who is able to explain and defend his faith.[35]

The available textbooks provide only marginal assistance to the schoolteacher who would like to combat religion in his or her classroom. Until the mid-1960s, ministries of education devoted little or no attention to the atheist training of schoolchildren or preschoolers. Neither the *Program of Instruction* nor the *Teacher's Commentary*, both of which are used in all Soviet nurseries and kindergartens, makes any reference whatsoever to religion or atheism.[36] As late as 1963, the list of works recommended for class use in the lower grades included none devoted entirely to religion and atheism.[37] The study program for outside reading for pupils in the lower grades showed a similar lack of concern with these problems, listing few books on antireligious themes. The various teachers' manuals and workbooks either made no mention of religion or gave teachers vague and insubstantial cues on how to introduce atheist materials.[38] The situation since that time has changed only slightly.

Conditions in institutions of higher learning are not appreciably better, although there has been some intensification of antireligious propaganda in the past decade. Until 1959, Soviet higher academic institutions provided small doses of antireligious material, primarily in history and social science courses. The required course "Dialectical and Historical Materialism," the subject most concerned with questions of religion and atheism, devoted only six hours of lectures and seminars (out of 140) to these problems.[39] In 1959, a new course, entitled "Fundamentals of Scientific Atheism," was introduced in higher academic institutions.[40] The course was offered as an elective, and few students registered for it; of those who did, most did not attend lectures. Indeed, in some institutions the course was not given at all because no students enrolled in it.[41] This situation led to a number of major changes. At present, the course calls for twenty-four hours of instruction (twelve lectures in a single semester), and the new syllabus devotes particular attention to the organization, forms, and methods of antireligious propaganda.[42] In 1964 the Central Committee made it a requirement for all university students and for those enrolled in medical, agricultural, and pedagogical institutes.[43]

The purpose of the course is not simply to provide students with knowledge of antireligious theory. Classroom instruction is accompanied by "practical work." Students take part in various antireligious activities under the guidance of the Komsomol or the scientific atheism faculty. They deliver antireligious lectures to the general public and sometimes conduct "agitation tours" of nearby collective farms.[44] In addition, the Komsomol organizations in some institutions of higher learning have set up atheism clubs or "schools for atheist propagandists." Young scientists and students in the upper levels of technical schools and institutes are given intensive training by experienced antireligious specialists. Each student is responsible for delivering lectures and arranging discussions on atheist themes on Sundays or during vacation periods.[45] Thus, while the basic purpose of atheist training in institutions of higher learning is to ensure that Soviet youngsters reject religious notions, the training serves a second purpose as well. Many young people serve as antireligious propagandists while still in school, and some go on to become atheist specialists in later life. Even while being socialized, they are called upon to socialize others.

Antireligious work in Soviet universities suffers from many of the same problems visible in primary and secondary schools. Separate departments of scientific atheism have been set up in very few universities and institutes, and antireligious training in other universities is extremely superficial. Textbooks and other sources are often unavailable, particularly in the non-Russian republics. Those that are available are dated and/or tendentious.[46] Some faculty members choose not to interfere with the personal religious beliefs of students, while others are insufficiently well trained in scientific atheism. The faculty at most schools is more interested in the conventional academic disciplines than in conducting a propaganda war against religion.[47] The lack of interest of teacher and student alike is expressed in another way as well. Very few persons register for graduate work in scientific atheism in the Institutes of the USSR Academy of Sciences or in the faculties of higher educational institutions. In the period 1957–1963, only three doctoral dissertations and some sixty candidates' theses dealing with scientific atheism were defended.[48] There has been some increase in academic attention to atheism in recent years, but not much. For example, at present, only slightly more than 10 percent of all dissertations in philosophy deal with some aspect of religion and atheism, and the number of students in history, pedagogy, jurisprudence, literature, and aesthetics interested in atheist matters is even smaller.[49] The lack of scholarly research and interest, combined with faculty and student indifference to atheist themes in their regular classwork, suggests that the effectiveness of university-based antireligious programs is likely to be quite limited.

Atheism Clubs

At the end of the 1950s, when the Party became more concerned about the atheist upbringing of the Soviet people, it created two new kinds of organizations to coordinate antireligious propaganda in individual cities or districts. Called either "atheism clubs" or "houses of atheism," these bodies rely on a broad *aktiv* of scientists and ideological specialists. Like the Knowledge Society, they are "voluntary, public organizations." Their members are doctors, teachers, scientists, and representatives of the creative intelligentsia, as well as Party, Komsomol, and trade union officials and workers in cultural-enlightenment institutions. Both sets of organizations perform their work under the guidance of the city or district Party committee and, at least in theory, coordinate their activities with the local branch of the Knowledge Society. In larger communities or enterprises, there may be a central club, as well as branches in the various brigades or shops. They are set up in libraries, red corners, propaganda reading rooms, or in the factory or farm club.[50]

In addition to coordinating the work of atheists in a particular community, atheism clubs engage in antireligious propaganda. They arrange meetings, hold lectures, and show films and plays. They also set up training programs for atheist activists and provide methodological aid through their libraries and special consultation programs.[51] Generally, any citizen who is eighteen years of age or older can join an atheism club. He must promise to combat all manifestations of "religious prejudice," acquaint himself with the political and scholarly literature on religion and atheism, and "serve as a personal example at production and in daily life." [52]

The work of an atheism club or house of atheism is organized in any of three ways. Sometimes groups of members are assigned responsibility for dealing with different religions. Thus one section may be responsible for combating the Orthodox Church, another for Judaism, and a third for the various sects. A second approach involves setting up sections to handle specific propaganda techniques, e.g., sections for atheist discussions, lecture propaganda, literary and artistic measures, civil ceremonies (designed to supplant religious ceremonies), and natural science experiments (which expose miracles as "clerical fabrications"). A third organizational pattern takes into consideration the features of target groups *and* individual propaganda techniques. Typical sectors include those dealing with the training of antireligious propagandists, mass-cultural measures, the press, agitation by visual means, work among youth, and work among women.[53] (See Appendix 2.)

Atheism clubs and houses have proliferated in the past decade and are now one of the major institutional supports for the Party's antireligious effort. They may, in the not too distant future, become the principal vehicle for arranging, coordinating, and controlling atheist propaganda.

Museums

Among the most distinctive of Soviet institutions engaged in atheist propaganda are the nation's museums. While only a few of the approximately one thousand museums in the USSR are aimed exclusively at combating religion, most of the others make some contribution to the atheist effort.[54]

Museums of science, for example, set up exhibits dealing with artificial earth satellites and other scientific discoveries and achievements. These are designed to show that man, not God, is the master of nature. Some displays focus on the persecution of "progressive scientists" by various churches, while others are arranged to refute the Biblical description of the creation of the world and the origin of man. All are designed to contribute to the scientific atheist upbringing of the Soviet people.[55]

Similarly, art museums can display paintings depicting the church's support of reaction or the alleged debauchery of priests. Thus, an architectural museum in Pskov, situated alongside a monastery, has set up a display detailing the drunken orgies, which the monastery was said to have arranged for the German occupying forces during World War II.[56] Museums of regional lore *(kraevedcheskie muzei)* can also help to discredit local religious groups or leaders. Some of these museums exhibit materials from court proceedings in cases involving "religious fanaticism," while others display published statements of people who have renounced religion.[57]

Historical museums, too, can bring their influence to bear by attacking church movements, individual religious leaders, or the pernicious influence of religion. For example, the Museum of the History of Bukhara (in the Uzbek SSR) has a major display dealing with Islam. It consists primarily of amulets and emblems from the tombs of Moslem officials. In addition, there is an *ukaz* signed by a Bukharian emir, calling for the execution of a driver who refused to carry several religious leaders to mosque free of charge. (The driver was declared an apostate and was beheaded.) The same display contains a photograph showing the punishment of a peasant who was whipped for failing to perform certain Moslem prayers.[58] The purpose of the display, of course, is to demonstrate the cruelty that religious narrow-mindedness and fanaticism can bring.

While such exhibits have been set up in many localities since the late 1950s, museum officials in general have not been very responsive to pleas for intensified antireligious propaganda. Thus it has fallen to special museums, set up explicitly to combat religion, to wage the battle for scientific atheism. These have been established in a few of the major cities, and in certain provincial centers and villages as well. Virtually all are situated in buildings that formerly served as churches. The most famous, Leningrad's Museum of the History of Religion and Atheism, is located in what was formerly the Kazan Cathedral. Other major antireligious museums in Vilnius and Lvov used to be Catholic churches, while the Bukhara museum formerly was a mosque and Moslem shrine. According to present plans, as other houses of worship are closed, "at the wish of the working people," many will be transformed into atheist museums.[59]

The Leningrad Museum is by far the largest and most important antireligious museum. Its holdings include paintings, photographs, sculptures, models, and various religious artifacts (medallions, fetishes, etc.), all directed at showing the origins and development of various religions, the history of atheism, and "the struggle between materialism and idealism." [60] Displays are organized according to eight major themes: (1) Science and

Religion, (2) The Origin of Religion, (3) Religion and Atheism in the Ancient World, (4) Religions of the East, (5) The Origin of Christianity, (6) Religion and Atheism in the West, (7) History of Russian Orthodoxy and Russian Atheism, and (8) The Overcoming of Religious Survivals in the Period of the Expanded Construction of Communism in the USSR.[61] Exhibits in the Vilnius museum focus on "the crimes of the [Catholic] church," the Inquisition in Lithuania, the clergy and capitalism, and "the church's support for imperialist wars." [62]

To ensure that these exhibits will be seen by the public, worker and student groups are brought from local plants, schools, institutes, and universities; they are taken around by museum staff members or specially trained guides. Several thousand such excursions to Leningrad's museum are arranged annually, and it is primarily through these tours that the museum has been able to attract hundreds of thousands of visitors each year.[63] (See Table 3.2.)

Most organized efforts involve young schoolchildren who are more likely to find a field trip exciting and educational. To reach the older students, as well as workers and farmers, museum exhibits are lent out to other institutions. Many museums set up displays in schools, public squares, red corners, parks, factories, or collective farms and are thus able to reach far more citizens than Table 3.2 indicates.[64]

Other Institutions
The political enlightenment network, the Komsomol, the armed forces, the trade unions, and other institutions also contribute to the antireligious program, but their efforts are not very substantial. They conduct atheist

Table 3.2   Number of Visitors to the Museum of the History of Religion and Atheism, 1956–1966

Year	Visitors
1956	257,000
1957	317,000
1958	375,000
1959	465,000
1960	501,000
1963	700,000
1966	700,000

Sources: *Kratkii nauchno-ateisticheskii slovar* (Moscow, 1964), p. 383; A. A. Vershinskaya et al., "Massovaya rabota muzeya po preodoleniyu religioznykh perezhitkov," *Yezhegodnik muzeya istorii religii i ateizma*, Vol. V (1961) (Moscow-Leningrad, 1962), p. 349; G. V. Voronstsov, *O propagande ateizma* (Leningrad, 1959), p. 53; I. Zhernevskaya and L. Laskina, "Kazanskaya ploshchad, dom 2 . . . ", *Nauka i religiya*, No. 11 (1967), p. 27.

work in a desultory fashion, often, in fact, ignoring it entirely.

At the highest level, an Institute of Scientific Atheism was established in 1964 in the Academy of Social Sciences of the Party Central Committee. This body coordinates all scientific research efforts in the field of atheism, operates a training program, and provides methodological aid to local atheist groups.[65]

Its publications, especially the semiannual collection *Voprosy nauchnogo ateizma (Problems of Scientific Atheism)*, compare favorably with two earlier series, *Voprosy istorii religii i ateizma (Problems of the History of Religion and Atheism)*, issued by the Institute of History's Sector on the History of Religion and Atheism, and the *Yezhegodniki (Yearbooks)* of the Museum of the History of Religion and Atheism. What is more, *Voprosy nauchnogo ateizma (VNA)* appears to be of considerably greater value to atheist activists than the other two series were. Although all three sets of studies usually include first-rate scholarly works, authoritative in their field, the earlier publications focused chiefly on historical and/or philosophical questions. In contrast, *VNA* is oriented primarily toward "concrete sociological research," which provides propagandists with useful information.

Besides issuing a modest number of studies, the Institute of Scientific Atheism does not itself engage directly in antireligious propaganda. It confines its efforts to providing assistance and training to atheist propagandists, who seem to be greatly in need of the Institute's sophisticated insights and recommendations.

The political-enlightenment network, especially in the post-Khrushchev period, has had the important responsibility of training and retraining antireligious propagandists. Although it is aided in this task by other agencies, it carries the major burden. "People's universities" and departments of scientific atheism have been established within many branches of the political enlightenment network, and the regular and evening universities of Marxism-Leninism have also been active in this effort.[66] However, not all of those who undergo special training put their knowledge and skills to use. For example, only half of those who completed the program in the city of Saratov subsequently assumed responsibility for conducting antireligious propaganda.[67] Even fewer, 22 percent, of those in the first four graduating classes of the Department of Scientific Atheism at the Voronezh Evening University of Marxism-Leninism subsequently conducted atheist propaganda.[68] (When this became known, a program of obligatory "practical work" was introduced. Judging from experience elsewhere, we can say that these graduates, too, will soon be inactive.)

Members of the Komsomol (approximately 27 million young people) are required to be "irreconcilable opponents of vestiges of the past," who must "passionately and convincingly propagandize the communist world-view." [69] To this end, the organization has set up various councils, commissions, and "problem groups" to guide the atheist upbringing of Soviet youth under the direct supervision of local Party authorities. Within the Komsomol's own system of political education, "militant atheist" groups have been organized. Komsomol atheism clubs, like their counter-parts for adults, arrange lectures, show films, distribute antireligious literature, visit nearby plants and farms, and try in other ways to combat religious tendencies among youngsters.[70] Despite the presence of these institutions and activities, the Komsomol's contribution to the fight against religion is not very great. It consistently underestimates the "pernicious influence" of religious views on Soviet youth. Because of its pervasive lack of concern with atheist indoctrination, the Komsomol's antireligious efforts have been termed "unsatisfactory." [71]

The failings of both the Komsomol and the regular school system have been satirized by the editors of *Krokodil*, the Soviet humor magazine. The two cartoons reproduced as Figures 3.1 and 3.2 mock the unsuccessful effort to transform Soviet youth into militant atheists.

Other institutions are even less concerned with combating religion. The trade unions are far more concerned with increasing labor productivity and fulfilling the economic plan, while the armed forces are preoccupied with technical training and instilling feelings of patriotism into their personnel. Both organizations arrange antireligious measures only on rare occasions, and even then do so in a perfunctory manner. They do not systematically engage in atheist propaganda. The little they do is artless and, as one might expect, of negligible value.[72]

Conclusion
The struggle on the religious front is more decentralized than it was several decades ago. Consequently, certain institutions have been established to provide a measure of central coordination. Party committees, the Knowl-edge Society, and atheism clubs or houses are the most significant of these. On the local level, atheism clubs are the principal centers of antireligious propaganda. Working with local branches of the Knowledge Society and with local atheist activists, these bodies carry the major burden in dealing

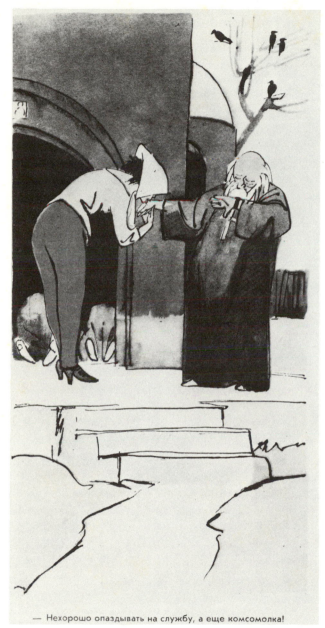

Figure 3.1   You shouldn't be late for services—you're a Komsomol!
Source: Krokodil, No. 18 (1963).

Figure 3.2   Vera Petrovna, don't you recognize me? I studied in your class. . . .
Source: Krokodil, No. 17 (1963).

with believers. It is their responsibility to coordinate antireligious activities in each community, train local activists, and serve as a clearinghouse for literature and advice on religious matters. The evidence suggests that they have carried out their responsibilities with less than total success.

4 Secular Holidays and Ceremonies

... is there any sense in keeping in the center of a village or a town an absurd church built out of the charity ... of a rich merchant ... ?

Pravda Ukrainy, August 31, 1971

... man's consciousness not only reflects the objective world, but also molds it.

V. I. Lenin (1895)

Certain aspects of religion have proved to be particularly resistant to the Party's propaganda. In particular, the regime has experienced great difficulty in its effort to do away with religious holy days and ceremonies. These are said to have become "ingrained traditions," accepted more as folk customs than as formal components of a religious belief system. In the official view, church leaders many centuries ago appropriated a number of pagan rituals, gradually linking them with church dogma. Now, many of these practices have developed a life of their own; they are popular customs that even nonreligious persons honor.[1]

The Party is seeking to eliminate these rites and replace them with a set of new practices, devoid of religious content and infused with positive secular symbols. A network of secular holidays and ceremonies, which affirm "socialist" or "communist" traits, has been created. It is the role of these new rituals in the overall Soviet program of antireligious propaganda that will concern us in this chapter.

The new holidays and ceremonies clearly are counterposed to religious rituals; indeed, their central purpose is to supplant the familiar religious holy days and ceremonies. But the new secular rituals, though an instrument of antireligious propaganda, are intended to perform other functions as well.

On the one hand, they play an economic role. Religious holy days and ceremonies are said to lead to excessive drinking, debauchery, hooliganism, crime, and economic waste. (According to a report from one *kolkhoz,* the local collective farmers did no work on the thirty-nine different saints' days they celebrated each year.)[2] Fasting, too, causes physical and economic harm. The new rites, it is hoped, will eliminate these costly excesses. Indeed, they are supposed to be celebrated by "a new upsurge of competition to implement the program of communist construction" and "great successes in labor." The essential features of the new holidays are connected with the "cult of labor," in contrast to the emphasis in holy days on the worship of God.[3]

On the other hand, they are expected to contribute to a more far-reaching goal: "the ideological, ethical, and aesthetic upbringing of the builders of communism," and the "rearing of . . . citizens . . . devoted to the ideas of the Party." [4] Thus, the new rites are not merely an "atheist" measure; they are supposed to satisfy basic human needs for beauty, ritual, and entertainment. "There will come a time," it is said, "when religion will have died out, but people's need for ceremonies will remain." [5] As we shall see, the new secular ceremonies do more than merely fulfill this need. They serve the political and ideological purposes of the Party by undermining religion and contributing to the political socialization of the Soviet people. Although their purpose is "not simply to spite the clergy," [6] their antireligious implications are enthusiastically endorsed by the Party.

The new celebrations are of two types: (1) public holidays and festivals, which the entire nation or entire population of some locality celebrates annually, and (2) rites that mark significant events in the lives of individual persons. We will deal with each of these in turn.

New Secular Holidays

The official Soviet view, to which most Western scholars would subscribe, is that Christian holy days are not truly the anniversaries of the events they purport to mark. The Soviets claim that Christ never existed and characterize historical references to him as folk legends or myths. Moreover, they say, over the course of many centuries, the dates of Christian holy days were deliberately fixed to coincide with ancient pagan festivals. Thus, the church is said to celebrate spring with Easter, and to celebrate the new year with Christmas. The new Soviet system of holidays and festivals, then, only appears to be an artificial substitute for long-accepted religious celebrations. By and large, the regime is reviving ancient folk festivals and holidays that the church earlier had appropriated for its own purposes. The Party can reasonably argue that *it*, not the church, is the true heir and bearer of the culture of the past. The secular authorities have advanced this view vigorously. To quote one official, "We must take back from religion that which it stole from the people." [7] Another commentator has echoed these remarks in even cruder terms, demanding that ancient customs be "cleansed of the scum of religion." [8]

The authorities were not always so ready to assault church holy days. After seizing power in 1917, the Bolsheviks moved rather haltingly against the religious holidays officially recognized by the tsarist regime. When the Council of People's Commissars in the spring of 1918 decided to commemorate revolutionary, rather than religious, events as the first Soviet state holidays, it also authorized local government officials to set aside another ten "rest days" to celebrate religious holy days. Concessions to holy days soon were curtailed, however, and after the Five-Year Plans were introduced, the Party's line hardened considerably.[9]

At present there are six state holidays: (1) New Year's Day (January 1), (2) International Women's Day (March 8), (3) International Labor Day (May 1 and 2), (4) Victory Day (May 9), (5) the Anniversary of the October Revolution (November 7 and 8), and (6) Constitution Day (December 5). Other days have been set aside from time to time as "revolutionary holidays," only to be abandoned eventually. Thus, January 22 (commemorating the 1905 Revolution), March 12 (celebrating the overthrow of the tsarist regime), and March 18 (in honor of the Paris Commune), which were among the first Soviet holidays, are no longer celebrated.[10]

Each holiday provides an occasion for celebrating the regime's achievements; all are marked by a profusion of propaganda, public speeches, demonstrations, and ceremonial meetings. Nonetheless, the number of holidays is still deemed insufficient to meet the needs of the Party and the people, or to provide an adequate challenge to religious holy days. Special "labor holidays" and festivals, connected with the beginning or end of some phase of the production cycle, have been devised to meet these needs. Celebrated primarily (but by no means exclusively) in the countryside, these events are aimed at drawing people's attention away from religious holy days and to the successes of the Soviet regime. The principal Christian holy days (Christmas, Easter, and various patron saints' days) are the primary focus of these efforts.

An elaborate spring holiday, known by various names in different regions of the Soviet Union, is now celebrated at Eastertime. It is held in late March, at the conclusion of the spring field work, or, in the Christian calendar, at Eastertime. Individual days usually are set aside during the festival period, coinciding with the various holy days of the Easter period. In the Baltic States, for example, Spring Holiday is held for the entire week before Easter Sunday; a "week of purity" is proclaimed, a direct parallel to the familiar Week of Passion. The climax of the holiday is a series of processions, concerts, dances, and games, and a rather pagan ceremony honoring spring. A pretty girl, adorned with flowers and ribbons, is chosen to represent "Spring." "Spring" will then greet "Winter" (usually an exemplary female worker, perhaps a member of a local Brigade of Communist Labor), offering thanks for the abundant snowfalls and promising to provide a rich harvest.[11]

A winter holiday, similar to the spring festival in both form and function, is designed to help undermine the celebration of Christmas. Again, the Party claims to be reviving ancient pagan practices, which antedate Christian religious ceremonies. The winter festival celebrates either the advent of the new year or the winter solstice. But the New Year Holiday seems to be linked more closely with Christmas than with pre-Christian festivals. The quasi-religious nature of Christmastime apparently has influenced those who developed the winter festival. Thus, the New Year Holiday has retained many of the elements of the Christmas celebration, which never had, or which have lost, religious significance. A jolly character named "Grandfather Frost," who closely resembles our Santa Claus, is a central figure in the holiday. Christmas trees, known now as New Year's trees *(novogodniaia yolka),* are decorated, and a red star is placed atop each tree. New Year's trees can be seen throughout the country, even in the Georgian Republic, where snow almost never falls. Trees are decorated and displayed in homes, clubs, and schools, at enterprises, on public squares, and even in the Great Kremlin Palace.[12]

Other pre-Christian holidays have been revived and are celebrated in various regions of the USSR. "The meeting of spring and summer," for example, is the occasion for celebration in a number of communities. In Latvia, an ancient pagan agrarian holiday known as Ligo, which marks the summer solstice and was originally designed "to worship the spontaneous forces of nature," is again being celebrated, although in a new guise. In the fall, a Harvest Holiday, also called "Day of the Harvest" and "Holiday of the Hammer and Sickle," is celebrated throughout the USSR. (Since 1966, October 9 has been set aside as the All-Union Day of Agricultural Workers, and it is on this day that the Harvest Holiday usually takes place.)

Each of these holidays is designed not simply to replace a religious holy day but also to emphasize the values and strengths of the communist system and to stimulate future economic successes. "The social and educational significance of these holidays and new ceremonies is great," a high Ukrainian official has remarked; "they inspire, they call people to labor feats." [13] The Ukrainian Holiday of the Hammer and Sickle, for example, which extols "the social, political, and ideological unity of society under socialism" by underscoring "the indestructible union of workers and peasants," is supposed to generate dramatic economic achievements.[14] The new holidays honor labor, collectivism, and the Soviet system in general. At the same time, they honor those workers who distinguish themselves by their high productivity.

For example, the Latvian holiday of Ligo, which is celebrated in the countryside at the conclusion of spring field work and in industrial areas at the end of the second economic quarter, is "a holiday of summing up the results of socialist competition." It is said "to propagandize the best labor traditions, achievements in the socialist economy, to honor the best people in the city and the countryside. . . ." The best workers and peasants are given bonuses and other prizes, are awarded ribbons and banners, and are chosen to represent their work groups in various ceremonies that take place during a holiday.[15]

Those whose work is disappointing, who have not met their socialist obligations, are exposed to criticism during the festival proceedings. The Holiday of Russian Winter celebrated in the city of Petrozavodsk even includes a procession comprised entirely of negative types, e.g., drunkards, rowdies, hooligans, parasites, and bureaucrats.[16]

Thus, by rewarding some and criticizing others, and by underscoring those traits which characterize the New Soviet Man, the system of secular holidays not only fulfills an antireligious function but performs a crucial socializing role as well.

New Secular Ceremonies

In addition to these public holidays and festivals, various ceremonies and rites marking significant events in people's personal lives have been introduced. These celebrations are designed to serve as a substitute for the traditional religious consecration given to such events and simultaneously to help mold the New Soviet Man. While most of the effort has been directed at devising adequate substitutes for religious ceremonies, a good deal of attention has been focused on the creation of completely new "daily-life ceremonies" that have no religious counterpart, or that are not performed in the Russian Orthodox Church. The major purpose of the new Soviet ceremonies, however, has been to provide secular rivals to the principal religious sacraments, those which mark birth, coming of age, marriage, and death.

The Soviet conception of what constitutes personal or family joy or grief is substantially different from the Western notion. In the USSR, a celebration ought not to be merely personal or spontaneous; it must be organized by and for the entire community. "In our country," one Soviet writer has pointed out, "people's personal lives are not only their private affairs, but also a profoundly public matter. The collective must be far from indifferent as to what sorts of morals one or another comrade adheres to." [17] This notion of collectivism, repeatedly underscored by Soviet authorities, is a central feature of all new Soviet ceremonies. In the USSR, it is said, "a

man's happiness is possible only in the collective, and not outside of it."
Therefore, celebrations are arranged by factories and farms, by and for "the
entire production collective." [18]

In the first decade after the Revolution, special Bolshevik ceremonies
were created to compete with the religious sacraments, i.e., the "Oktyabrin"
or "Octobrist" ceremony for newborns, "red weddings," and "red funerals."
They met with only limited success and gradually were abandoned. They
are now regarded as a crude device for disseminating anticlerical propaganda, completely devoid of the beauty and ritual that religious ceremonies
provide. The *Oktyabrin* ceremony suggests why this is so. The parents of
several newborn children would promise to bring up their children "not as
slaves for the bourgeoisie, but as fighters against it." Individual mothers
would declare: "The child belongs to me only physically. For his spiritual
upbringing, I entrust him to society." [19] Such ceremonies could hardly have
been expected to satisfy the needs of people other than Party or Komsomol
activists, and it is clear that they did not.

The regime encountered similar problems in its attempt to popularize
"revolutionary names" for newborns. Conscious of the religious origin and
significance of most people's names, the Party encouraged citizens to give
their children names more in keeping with the new order. Among the more
unconventional names given were Molot (Hammer), Serp (Sickle), Krasarm
(Red Army), Svoboda (Freedom), Komintern, Ninel (Lenin spelled backward), Lentrozina (an acronym derived from the names Lenin, Trotsky,
and Zinoviev), Rem (an acronym derived from Revolution, Electrification,
and Moscow), and Kim (the Russian abbreviation of the Communist Youth
International). By and large, use of these names was confined to political
activists.[20]

Within a decade, the Party completely abandoned its initial enthusiasm
for "revolutionary" ceremonies and names. Births, marriages, and deaths
were viewed thereafter simply as vital statistics, not as the occasion for a
festive, solemn, or even propagandistic celebration. Responsibility for
recording such events had been taken from the church in December, 1917,
and placed in the hands of civil authorities. The institution that performed
this function, the *zags* (the Russian acronym for Bureau of the Registry of
Marriages, Births, and Deaths), interpreted its duties rather narrowly. The
zags simply recorded births and deaths, while the wedding "ceremony" it
provided was perfunctory at best. (According to one description of *zags*
weddings during the 1920s, the civil registrar would demand rudely: "Your
passports!" After having married the couple, he would declare: "Congratu-
lations on your lawful marriage: that will be 3 rubles.")[21]

The ceremonies that have been developed over the past decade are better suited to achieving the Party's objectives. The authorities have tried to avoid the formal, bureaucratic, and often disagreeable atmosphere of the *zags*. Moreover, there are now more rituals: people can celebrate most of the key events in their lives, from birth to death. In fact, Party activists in some areas begin to conduct atheist propaganda before a child is born. Agitators and medical personnel are instructed to tell women in maternity hospitals, or, preferably, at an earlier stage of pregnancy, of the evils of baptism and circumcision.[22]

The new ceremony celebrating the birth of a child has two objectives: to provide politically relevant messages to parents, and at the same time, to introduce the child to the official belief system. It has proved difficult to achieve both aims. "Children are not born atheists or believers," a Soviet scholar has observed; "they become one or the other under the influence of their environment or upbringing."[23] A child who is kept from religious influences and is instead confronted with those symbols of which the regime approves is unlikely to become a believer and, it is hoped, will become an enthusiastic supporter of the political system.

Several variants of the new ceremony have been worked out. Some are relatively simple, involving nothing more than a visit to the family's home by local dignitaries to present a birth certificate to the child and flowers to the parents.[24] More elaborate ceremonies, either for a single child or for a group of newborns, are staged as a "Day of Family Happiness." The infants usually are given memorial medals, medallions, certificates, or gift packages that emphasize political themes and symbols. These vary from Oktobrist pins, Pioneer neckerchiefs, and Komsomol badges to ornate medals heavily laden with political symbols. Medals given to children in Leningrad and Kiev, for example, are adorned with pictures of a Russian birch tree, a tractor, a freshly plowed field, a high-voltage line, an electric power station, and a picture of Lenin. It is said that these medals "help engender feelings of love toward the Soviet Fatherland and the Soviet people," that they "fill a person's heart with patriotism."[25] At the very least, they acquaint children at an early age with those values and symbols that the Party supports.

At the same time, the ceremony accompanying the registration of a newborn links parents, relatives, and close friends to the official value system. The official presiding at such a ceremony instructs them in their responsibilities to the child and to the country. In Moscow, for example, he declares to the parents: "Raise your children to be honest, courageous, joyous, true patriots who love the Fatherland and labor. . . ."[26] Relatives or close friends may be asked to serve as "social godparents," "favored ones," or as "honorary mothers and fathers," the Soviet equivalent of godparents. They promise to help raise the child to be "an honest and fair citizen . . . a devoted patriot who loves labor and is a cheerful builder of Communism." [27] Other elements in the ceremony underscore the state's solicitude for its citizens. Posters and slogans present in the ceremonial hall bear such inscriptions as "Children are our joy, our happiness, our future!" and "To ensure a happy childhood for every child is one of the most important tasks in building a communist society." [28] The presiding official often reinforces this message by declaring to the parents: "This is a joy not only for you, but for the entire Soviet people as well, for what is most valuable in the Soviet Union is man. . . ." [29] Thus, the ritual connects the personal joy parents feel in celebrating the birth of a child with appreciation for the Party's magnanimity and concern, and with the officially approved values of collectivism and patriotism.

The ceremony seems to provide an experience in political socialization for the parents and friends, while providing for the *future* socialization of the child. Because the children are infants and are too young to participate, the ceremony itself cannot be instructive for them. A number of districts, therefore, now defer celebrating the birth of a child until he or she is several years old. In Latvia, for example, a "Holiday of Childhood" is arranged for children from two to four years of age. (It usually is held on June 1, International Day for the Defense of Children.) This ceremony is not an adequate substitute for baptism, because parents who wish to baptize their children usually do so when the children are still infants.[30] To devise a ritual that is politically instructive both to children and to adults, and that at the same time can help to counteract the religious rite of baptism, has thus far proved impossible.

The second special event in an individual's life that has become the occasion for nonreligous, ceremonial celebration is the attainment of maturity. New rites, designed in part to supplant the Christian practice of confirmation (especially prevalent in the Baltic States) and the Jewish bar mitzvah ceremony, have been devised. There are two basic patterns, one focusing on the receipt of a passport, the other organized around graduation from secondary school.

The issuance of passports, formerly a rather pedestrian event in the life of Soviet citizens who reached the age of sixteen, is now the occasion for a special coming-of-age ceremony. While different communities arrange rites with varying degrees of pomp and imagination, all provide a socializing experience. The passport is used as a symbol of adulthood, and its acceptance is made to imply the simultaneous acceptance of the obligations and duties of an adult. The ceremony itself is designed to stimulate patriotism and love of labor. The national anthem is played, and a Komsomol official urges the young people to emulate advanced workers, to "do nothing which might disgrace the revolutionary and labor traditions" of the Soviet people. "You must value your Soviet passport," he says. "This passport was earned by our fathers with their toil and blood. . . . Love your Fatherland and be its heroes!" [31]

In some areas of the country, particularly in the Baltic States, the Urals and the Altai region, officials arrange a coming-of-age ceremony for eighteen-year-olds. They have been influenced, of course, by the Lutheran practice of confirming youngsters at this age. (The Lutheran Church still has a large following in the Baltic region.) Because most young people finish their schooling and become workers sometime near their eighteenth birthday, graduation from secondary school is a convenient symbol of transition to adulthood.

In Latvia, a day-long Coming-of-Age Holiday *(Prazdnik Sovershennoletiya)* is held for groups of young people shortly after their graduation from secondary school. The boys and girls are assembled in a local club or ceremonial hall, where they symbolically take on adult responsibilities. They "solemnly promise to devote themselves to the Fatherland, to labor, and to the construction of communism." [32] Representatives of the previous year's celebrants, who have since distinguished themselves at work, entrust "the most deserving" eighteen-year-olds with a special banner symbolizing the link between school and productive labor. In Estonia, a more elaborate holiday, called Summer Days of Youth, is held at the time of secondary school graduation. The boys and girls are sent to nearby youth camps for up to two weeks, to participate in athletic, cultural, and political activities. Lectures and discussions on political and social questions are arranged with officials, writers, leading workers, and World War II veterans. The actual coming-of-age ceremony, reserved for the final day of the holiday, closely resembles its counterpart in Latvia.[33]

A third major event that is now celebrated with an elaborate secular ceremony is marriage. This is an event that people, including many whose religious convictions are by no means firm, have long celebrated in solemn surroundings in a place of worship. The occasion is generally regarded as demanding dignified and elaborate celebration, and the church traditionally has been the only institution that provided an appropriate setting and ritual. It is not surprising, therefore, that a good deal of energy has been channeled into an effort to attract young couples in the USSR to special buildings and halls in which an elaborate, but nonreligious, wedding ceremony is performed.

In recent years, there has been much criticism of the inadequacy and ugliness of the civil registrar's office, where all Soviet weddings formerly took place. As an *Izvestiya* reporter remarked in 1959,

We cannot list all the letters [to the editor of *Izvestiya*] on the shortcomings of our *Zags*. The very word *Zags*, official and sterile, is irritating to everyone. . . . People are furious also at the official and soulless atmosphere in these institutions. Indeed, for some reason or other it has become the custom to employ sullen uncles and aunts there; they force the beaming newlyweds to mix with people who have come to register a relative's death, abruptly snarl their demands for 15 rubles [old money] for the registration and forget even to congratulate the newlyweds. . . .[34]

Indeed, the editors of *Krokodil* were moved to print a cartoon upbraiding local officials for providing surroundings so obviously inferior to those available in church. (See Figure 4.1.)

The official response to such criticism has proceeded in two directions. On the one hand, special courses have been set up for the directors of local registry bureaus. Their purpose is to teach officials the proper ceremonial atmosphere for weddings, avoiding the stiffness and formality that had prevailed for so many years.[35] On the other hand, the Party has established a nationwide network of "wedding palaces." These are special buildings that have been set aside in all large cities, and in some provincial centers as well, to provide attractive surroundings for the new secular marriage ceremony. The first such palace was opened in Leningrad in 1959, and today others can be found even in the most remote regions of the country.[36]

The ceremony itself is similar in form to Western weddings, although some of its features are quite distinctive (particularly in Moslem sections of the country).[37] The bride is dressed in white, Mendelssohn's Wedding March is played (music had been prohibited in *zags* marriages), and there are flowers, gifts, champagne, and an elaborate dinner. Certain elements, however, are uniquely Soviet. In a typical ceremony in the Krasnodar Territory, for example, young couples are urged "to work faithfully for the sake of our beloved Fatherland." They are told to rear children who will be "ardent patriots of the Soviet Fatherland, diligent builders of Communism." [38] The conspicuous use of political slogans and inevitable references to the state (a kind of "brooding omnipresence" at all Soviet ceremonies) help to emphasize the profoundly public nature of the personal events they celebrate.

Soviet authorities have experienced a good deal of difficulty in devising a

Figure 4.1   It's not like in a church here—one, two, and that's that!
Source: Krokodil, No. 31 (1963).

satisfactory funeral rite, primarily because of the delicate nature of the task. Difficulties in introducing "reforms" in this area are not new. The "red funerals" held during the early years of Communist rule were incongruous and ineffective. When the first crematorium in Russia was opened in 1920, it was viewed as a powerful instrument to undermine religion; it was expected to end the church's control over the last rites for the dead.[39] However, the practice of cremation never became very widespread, and the authorities have renewed their quest for a "revolutionary," but dignified, funeral ritual.

The new funeral ceremony, like the other ceremonies we have described, is similar to religious services. Before being interred, the body is placed in a special room in a House of Culture and surrounded by an honor guard, who also serve as pallbearers. On the day of the funeral a procession is arranged for the mourners; funeral music is played, and farewell speeches by close friends and local dignitaries are offered. The service itself takes place either at the gravesite or in specially equipped rooms somewhere on the premises of the cemetery. Until recently, there was no alternative to using the cemetery's chapel, i.e., a religious edifice. Some new buildings have been constructed to replace them, and many chapels have been remodeled. Religious symbols have been removed, and new Soviet symbols have been installed.[40]

As might be expected, the speakers at funeral rites focus on the contributions that their late comrade made to his factory or farm and to the national economic effort. The medals, orders, and other awards that he may have received often are displayed and carried on red pillows as part of the funeral procession. As the deceased is honored and memorialized, so too is the idea of productive labor; the life and death of the deceased are given meaning in the context of official values and symbols.[41] Thus, while it obviously is too late to socialize the deceased, a considerable effort is made to socialize the survivors.

Annual memorial ceremonies for the dead, which were introduced a decade ago, are perceptibly different from traditional church services. According to the official view, family and friends used to visit cemeteries merely to listen to "priestly ravings." [42] "The people used to gather, were swindled out of money, a prayer was read, and that was it. Then a drinking bout began." [43] The new memorial ceremony seems more festive than mournful. Flags and banners are raised, and "popular and revolutionary songs" are sung. Old communists, production leaders, and schoolchildren deliver speeches. Professional lecturers may even be invited to cemeteries, to talk about the dead who, "by their labor and revolutionary struggle," should serve as an example for future generations.[44] Memorial Days ("Civic Days of Remembrance" in the Baltic States) are specifically designed to honor "the fighters who have perished and the toilers who have died," those who have "fallen in the revolution," the martyrs of the Komsomol and the Party who died protecting the Revolution.[45] But the ceremony and speeches are not really addressed to those who have died or to their families; their essential purpose is to inspire the living and to glorify and magnify the purposes of the Party.

Other Holidays and Ceremonies

Other festivals, holidays, and ceremonies, in addition to those described above, are arranged in the USSR, and suggestions have been made to introduce still more. The events now celebrated publicly include departure for military service, taking a job, and retirement from work.[46] Although few communities or enterprises arrange such ceremonies at present, their number is growing rapidly. A solemn ritual, usually centered around some sort of oath, has been devised to mark each of these events. In the city of Tashkent, for example, factories greet their new workers with a special "Initiation of Workers" ceremony. Each of the new employees takes the following oath:

I, a son of the toiling people, entering the ranks of the great working class, in the presence of my comrades, swear: to toil honorably and increase the wealth of my fatherland, to live and work like a Communist. I will never in any way sully the lofty title of worker . . . I will preserve sacredly the revolutionary labor traditions of the working class.[47]

The symbols emphasized here—hard work, patriotism, and proletarian internationalism—are familiar.

Many other proposals for new celebrations have been advanced. Thus, a newspaper specializing in rural affairs has suggested that youngsters living on farms be formally inducted into their *kolkhoz* when they reach the age of sixteen. (Unlike young people in the cities, they do not at present receive internal passports and labor books.) At the induction ceremony, boys and girls would take the following oath:

Entering upon the honorable ranks of the tillers of the soil of the USSR, I solemnly promise to love labor, which is the source of abundance and happiness; to cherish and honor my collective farm, to live and work like a Communist; to remember always that land is the greatest natural resource.[48]

The proposal would seem to merit careful consideration, in view of the greater incidence of religious belief among rural dwellers. Other suggestions for new rituals, however, have substantially less merit. They have been rejected as too elaborate, expensive, or inappropriate. Among the more striking of these are that the daily number of births in each city be announced on special "pyramids" during the day and on electric signs at night, and that shotguns be fired in the streets (using blank shots) during wedding processions.[49] Soviet authorities thus far have recognized the need to retain a sense of proportion in devising new rites. To arrange elaborate ceremonies involves the expenditure of considerable sums of money and man-hours, and there always are competing demands on the limited resources available to any enterprise or community.

Effectiveness

It is difficult to assess how much holidays and ceremonies contribute to the political socialization of the Soviet citizenry or help combat religion. Clearly, the new rituals suffer from shortcomings in planning, design, and execution. They have been described variously as "banal," "prosaic," "stereotyped," "dull," "artificial," "primitive," and "pompous."[50] Composers, writers, and artists have not cooperated in working out attractive and inspiring new rituals. As a result, the choral and orchestral works that are performed are "insipid and empty."[51]

It has proved particularly difficult to strike the appropriate balance between the political and artistic sides of the new ceremonies. "A genuine rite," a leading Soviet analyst has suggested, ". . . while entertaining, is at the same time instructive, gradually and unobtrusively inspiring certain kinds of thoughts, views and moral norms."[52] In practice, however, one or the other element has taken precedence. Some rituals are simply theatrical spectacles incapable of performing the political function assigned to them, while others are so filled with propaganda messages that they become didactic and wearisome. Indeed, sometimes the program of a particular celebration is so filled with political lessons that it becomes "a sort of seminar or short course."[53]

The very impersonal character of the new rituals is another impediment to their success. Large numbers of persons are invited to take part in or view a given ceremony. Dozens of newborn infants may be registered at one time, and the practice of marrying fifteen or twenty couples simultaneously, while not the norm, is by no means uncommon.[54] If an essentially intimate and personal experience is celebrated with and for strangers in a large public place, its impact is not likely to be great. Indeed, it may even be transformed into an offensive charade.

Experience with the secular funeral rite provides some insight into the problem. Soviet authorities have expressed dismay at the practice of hiring paid, professional lecturers from the Knowledge Society to speak at funerals. In condemning these "Cemetery Ciceros," one journalist observed several years ago:

> . . . we are firmly convinced that when a funeral speech is delivered by a person who is a complete stranger, be he an orator to end them all, if he speaks only by virtue of having a glib tongue and the membership card of a respectable enlightenment society, this becomes insulting and resembles a carnival hoax.[55]

These remarks can be applied to the entire effort to inroduce new ceremonies and holidays. Party secretaries, chairmen of Soviet executive committees, Wedding Palace directors, and other officials who are the principal figures in these affairs are little more than complete strangers to most participants. They may be unavailable, uninterested, hostile, intoxicated, or indicate in some other way that they feel no sense of personal involvement. Whether or not the ceremonies are therefore "insulting" or "resemble a carnival hoax," their overorganization, impersonality, and highly propagandistic nature clearly have limited their appeal. They will require substantial modification if they are to gain popular approval.

While Soviet citizens have made greater and greater use of the new ceremonies, particularly the new marriage ritual, they have done so reluctantly and only with a good deal of "guidance" from the authorities. Soviet writers acknowledge that the process of introducing new rites is directed "from above," for people do not willingly renounce centuries-old traditions spontaneously. In the words of one specialist: "Of course nothing can happen by itself . . . a serious battle [is to be expected]." [56] This need not involve pressure or outright compulsion, although it is clear that some officials do resort to such tactics. Komsomol or Party activists may be asked to take the initiative, in the hope that their personal example will win additional converts to the new rites.[57] At other times, Party agitators and propagandists are mobilized to perform "explanatory and organizational work," describing the merits of the new rites and the harmfulness of religious celebrations.[58] All of these factors—the intrinsic merits of the new rituals, the efforts of Party and Komsomol activists, propaganda meetings, and various kinds of pressures—help to explain the successes achieved thus far. Tables 4.1, 4.2, and 4.3 provide some indication of the magnitude of this success.

To be sure, the program has not been uniformly successful. In certain areas, especially in the Moslem republics of Central Asia, few citizens have accepted the new rites.[59] Many people still seek religious sanctification for

Table 4.1   Births, Weddings, and Funerals Marked by Religious Ceremonies (in percentages)

	Births	Weddings	Funerals
Ryazan (1960)	60	15	30
Penza (1962)	48.5	6.4	20.9
Tallin (1963)	14.3	3.2	28.4
Tartu (1963)	—	4	51
Odessa (1964)	55.2	14.5	35.7
Komi ASSR (1964)	22	0.2	—
Yekabpilskii District (Latvia) (1964)	25.7	7	19.4
Lithuanian SSR (1966)	50	33	50

Sources: Voprosy istorii religii i ateizma, Vol. XI (Moscow, 1963), pp. 67, 73, 80–82, as cited in Bohdan R. Bociurkiw, "Religion and Soviet Society," Survey, No. 60 (July, 1966), p. 70; M. D. Shevchenko, "Rol semeinykh traditsii v nasledovanii religioznykh perezhitkov detmi i podrostkami," Vestnik Moskovskogo universiteta, Seriya VIII (Filosofiya), No. 2 (1966), p. 33; V. Pomerantsev, "Eksperiment," Nauka i religiya, No. 1 (1965), p. 4; Ts. A. Stepanian et al. (ed.), Stroitelstvo kommunizma i dukhovnyi mir cheloveka (Moscow, 1966), pp. 225–226; L. N. Terentieva, "Rasprostraneniye ateisticheskogo mirovozzreniya i bezreligioznykh form byta sredi kolkhoznikov Latyshei," in N. P. Krasnikov (ed.), Voprosy preodoleniya religioznykh perezhitkov v SSSR (Moscow, 1966), p. 65; P. P. Mishutis, "Opyt sozdaniya sistemy ateisticheskogo vospitaniya v Litovskoi SSR," in A. F. Okulov et al. (eds.), Voprosy nauchnogo ateizma, Vol. 1 (Moscow, 1966), p. 207.

Table. 4.2   Births, Marriages, and Funerals Marked by Religious Ceremonies: Estonia, 1957–1970 (in percentages)

	Baptisms	Church Weddings	Religious Funerals
1957	55.8	29.8	64.5
1958	49.3	28.0	65.9
1959	42.5	25.6	65.1
1960	34.5	18.0	62.8
1961	28.7	13.6	60.9
1962	22.3	9.1	55.4
1963	20.0	6.7	52.6
1965	15.1	3.4	—
1970	12.7	2.7	44.0

Sources: V. Pomerantsev, "Eksperiment," Nauka i religiya, No. 1 (1965), p. 4; P. P. Kampars and N. M. Zakovich, Sovetskaya grazhdanskaya obryadnost (Moscow, 1967), p. 220; V.Ranne, "Ateisticheskoye vospitaniye: problemy i zadachy," Sovetskaya Estonia, October 9, 1971, p. 2.

Table 4.3   Secular and Religious Coming-of-Age Ceremonies: Estonia, 1957–1970

	Number of Summer Days of Youth Celebrants	Number of Church Confirmations
1957	36	10,000
1958	2,200	8,100
1959	6,300	6,400
1960	6,950	3,950
1961	7,000	2,730
1965	—	550
1968	6,000	—
1970	—	488

Sources: L. Alekseyeva, Sovremennyye prazdniki i obryady v derevne (Moscow, 1968), p. 20; G. Gerodnik, "Grazhdanskiye i bytovyye obryady," Nauka i religiya, No. 7 (1962), p. 49; I. G. Kebin, Sovetskaya Estonia, April 11, 1969, p. 2; V. Ranne, "Ateisticheskoye vospitaniye: problemy i zadachi," Sovetskaya Estonia, October 9, 1971, p. 2; I. A. Galitskaya, "Izucheniye kanalov vospriozvodstva religioznosti v novykh pokoleniyakh—odno iz trebovanii sistemy ateisticheskogo vospitaniya," in A. F. Okulov et al. (eds.), Voprosy nauchnogo ateizma, Vol. 9 (Moscow, 1970), p. 76.

significant personal events, and it is not unusual for a family to utilize both the old and the new rituals when marking special occasions.[60] But it should be emphasized that these persons represent a minority. The number of those using the new ceremonies continues to increase, while the proportion relying on religious rites is declining. As the Party devotes additional attention and resources to developing its new network of ceremonies and holidays, this decline should continue.

The authorities have already begun to rationalize and improve matters. First, the organizational machinery responsible for introducing new ceremonies has been centralized. Day-to-day responsibility continues to lie in the hands of the cultural departments or "commissions for daily life ceremonies and holidays" set up under raion ispolkomy (the executive committees of district soviets). These commissions are comprised of deputies to local soviets, representatives of the Party, Komsomol, and trade union organizations, as well as persons active in the arts. Since 1964, special councils have been set up at various levels to provide assistance to local soviets and to coordinate the work of the numerous organizations active in this effort.[61]

Second, the republics have begun to give greater support to local groups. Republic ministries of culture are increasingly active in providing advice and leadership, and full-time, paid personnel have replaced some of the volunteer "cultural-enlightenment workers" who had hitherto exercised responsibility in each locality.[62] "Departments of Soviet traditions" have been set up within the system of "people's universities," and government funds have been made available to supplement the limited resources of individual farms and factories.[63] Competitions for the best songs, rituals, posters, and decorations for each of the celebrations have been organized, and prizes have been awarded.[64] Some ceremonies are broadcast live over radio or television, and literature, films, and phonograph records describing prize-winning efforts have been distributed to local officials and activists.[65] Finally, new buildings have been erected specifically for the new ceremonies. Indeed, the RSFSR Council of Ministers has instructed the RSFSR Gosstroi (the Committee on State Construction) to include in its blueprints for new construction projects plans for special ceremonial halls.[66] These measures indicate that Party and state authorities intend to develop and improve the existing system.

Concluding Remarks

It is clear that the network of new Soviet holidays and ceremonies is designed to play a major role in combating religion and promoting the political socialization of the Soviet people. The Party hopes to reach every citizen, to celebrate every major event with him, constantly emphasizing and reiterating a basic set of propaganda themes. All of the rituals are directed toward developing the qualities of the New Soviet Man—collectivism, patriotism, proletarian internationalism, and love of labor. The new rites emphasize the partnership between the individual and the state; it is hoped that citizens will identify their personal joys and sorrows with the Party's purposes. At the same time, they provide numerous opportunities to propagandize the achievements of the regime, thereby stimulating and reinforcing the political values, symbols, and notions that the Party advocates.

If it is clear that the network of new celebrations has been assigned a central role in Soviet political socialization efforts, it is also clear that the program has failed to live up to expectations. It has proved difficult to devise rituals that provide both political propaganda and an aesthetically pleasing experience. Moreover, efforts to nurture collectivism have clashed with the objective of satisfying people's needs for personal or family celebrations. And the task of uprooting traditions that have endured for centuries has sometimes generated frustration and impatience among officials. This has led to excesses and errors that have harmed the entire program. Perhaps most important, religious families have resisted the intrusion of these secular affairs into their private lives.[67] Their recalcitrance, nourished by tradition and supported by the activities of church organizations, has impeded the success of the Party's efforts. While we cannot gauge precisely the extent of the Party's success in the face of these difficulties, we should underscore that it recognizes many of the problems and continues to mobilize additional resources in an effort to overcome them.

Finally, it should be emphasized that the introduction of new holidays and ceremonies is only one part of the overall Soviet antireligious effort. The new rituals serve an essentially negative function by distracting believers and potential believers from religious activities. To be sure, the new rituals may serve a positive function by inspiring Soviet citizens and giving them pleasure, thereby stimulating support for the regime. But the new ceremonies are directed essentially at drawing people away from the ritual beauty and fascination of religion. They compete with religion by appealing to many of the same motives and predispositions that cause people to find religious rites satisfying and inspiring.[68] Their acceptance by the citizenry requires positive steps that can transform believers and nonreligious persons into atheists. As the author of a major Soviet antireligious textbook has argued,

. . . nonreligious holidays and ceremonies, although an important aspect of atheist propaganda, only distract believers from performing religious ceremonies, but by no means destroy religious notions. Therefore they must be supplemented with systematic propaganda of the scientific, materialist world-view and principles of communist morality.[69]

It is to the Party's criticisms of the antiscientific and immoral character of religion, then, that we now turn. We will examine the three basic channels of communication: the mass media, mass oral propaganda, and discussions with individual believers. We will deal first with the mass media.

5 The Mass Media

Just as an army cannot wage war without weapons, the Party cannot conduct its ideological work successfully without such a sharp and militant weapon as the press.

N. S. Khrushchev (1957)

Political socialization in all countries is carried out by means of communication. In the West, where the chief socializing agents are the family, schools, and peer groups, the mass media are usually relegated to a secondary role. While mass communications provide direct learning experiences for some citizens, this is not their major function. They serve more to reinforce socializing processes initiated by primary agents, and rarely help to develop political cognitions and values.[1]

In the USSR, where the communications process is subject to far-reaching controls and where virtually all official communications have a political character, we might expect the media to be more influential in socializing citizens. The Soviet regime has an explicit program of political socialization and allocates vast resources in order to achieve its goal of rearing the New Soviet Man. It sees the mass media as a major weapon to inculcate into each Soviet citizen values and views that it considers appropriate.

Each of the media contributes to the regime's antireligious program. Their relative importance has changed surprisingly little over the half century of Communist rule, in great part because of the conservatism and inertia of Party leaders and ideologists. At present, the press is far more active and aggressive than the other media in combating religious belief and behavior. But the radio, television, and film industries all play some part in the struggle for atheism, supplementing and reinforcing messages transmitted through other channels.

The Press

The press has always played a major role in the Soviet effort to eradicate survivals of the past. Long before the Bolshevik Revolution, Lenin demanded that the press perform certain basic political functions. "A newspaper," he said, "is not only a collective propagandist and a collective agitator, it is also a collective organizer." [2] Although Lenin's remarks were designed chiefly to help the Bolsheviks come to power, they have continued to guide Soviet press policies since the Revolution. Even today they help to orient the press in the struggle against religion.

Professional atheists view the press as the principal vehicle for indoctrinating the masses. In the words of a former editor of *Nauka i religiya*, "The press is the most basic, the most powerful instrument for the communist upbringing of the masses, for overcoming survivals of capitalism in their minds."[3] To be sure, there is considerable debate on how it can best perform this function, and even more disagreement on how well it has done the job. Nonetheless, it is clear that the press has been assigned a vital role in pursuing the regime's antireligious objectives.

The kinds of materials that receive newspaper coverage reflect the values of the Soviet leadership, primarily their desire to legitimize the regime and to socialize the citizenry. The official conception of the nature and function of the press centers on three qualities: *partiinost'* (party-mindedness), *ideinost'* (ideological content) and *narodnost'* (intelligibility to the masses). In practice, any question raised in the press must serve a social, political, or economic purpose and further "the struggle for communism." In a lecture to journalism students, a former director of TASS emphasized this instrumental view of news reporting.

News must be organized; otherwise it is mere events and happenstance. . . . News must not merely throw light on this or that fact or event—it must pursue a definite purpose. . . . News is agitation via facts; it must educate and instruct. . . . In selecting the news topic, the writer of the news story must proceed above all from the realization that not all facts and not just any event should be reported in the press. The aim of news must be to present selected facts and events. . . .[4]

Articles on antireligous subjects, like articles on any other subject in the Soviet press, are selective and highly political. They emphasize the wisdom and success of the Party's policies. They attack religious ideology and religious leaders, while affirming the virtues of atheism and communist morality. Although their stereotyped form, moralistic content, and heavy-handed character disturb some newspapermen and officials, Soviet journalism continues to be extraordinarily didactic.

Until the end of the fifties, antireligious articles seldom appeared in the Soviet press, and very few journalists concerned themselves with atheist themes. On the rare occasions when articles on religion or morality were printed, they were played down. They were, to quote the editor of *Izvestia*, merely the "subordinate clauses . . . of an essay on a production theme."[5] Newspaper efforts to combat religion usually took on the character of a campaign. Prolonged lulls were interrupted only in connection with some religious holiday, and these brief propaganda revivals were immediately followed by official silence.[6] While the press today still is concerned far more with economic and foreign policy issues than with the struggle against religion, and while press attacks still take the form of campaigns, the past decade has witnessed a perceptible resurgence of atheist propaganda. This resurgence began in the second half of 1958 and reached a peak in the middle of 1959. A second peak occurred in 1964, after the Party Central Committee called for an intensification of atheist propaganda. Figure 5.1 lists the number of articles on atheist themes published in the principal Soviet newspapers since 1957. A similar pattern can be seen in the figures on book publishing and magazine articles (Figures 5.2 and 5.3).

Although each newspaper is supposed to have a plan governing the content and frequency of antireligious articles, few papers go about the task so systematically. Many of the atheist articles printed in the Soviet press are sent out by the press bureau of *Pravda* or are prepared by TASS or some other news agency. These items deal with topics that the leadership considers especially important, and they are put together by the best-informed and most-experienced authors. Newspaper editors are instructed to use such materials "creatively," adapting them to the specific problems and conditions of their area and supplementing them with appropriate materials of local origin. A number of papers feature regular columns devoted to religion and atheism; they are given such names as "The Atheist's Corner" or "The Militant Atheist." Most editors, however, confine their antireligious efforts to publishing articles prepared by TASS or to reprinting items from other newspapers.[7]

Soviet newspapers, books, and magazines speak to both the atheist and the believer, providing facts and opinion that can be used to gain a better understanding of the evils of religion. But these materials are directed primarily toward the politically active and nonreligious members of the population, because most citizens, particularly religious believers, avoid items on atheist themes. Propagandists and agitators are urged to familiarize themselves with the day's newspaper and then discuss its contents with friends, relatives, and fellow workers. Activists carry out this task by reading aloud to groups of workers, conducting discussions with them, or arranging displays of newspaper or journal articles.[8]

Most of these articles are written by professional journalists, few of whom are specialists in religious matters. Lacking both scholarly and religious training, they sometimes commit blatant errors that only amuse or irritate their audience. Editors therefore try to recruit outside experts— teachers, scientists, and others who possess the requisite knowledge and skills—to provide consultations for newspaper staffs and write guest articles.[9] In addition, letters to the editor account for a substantial portion

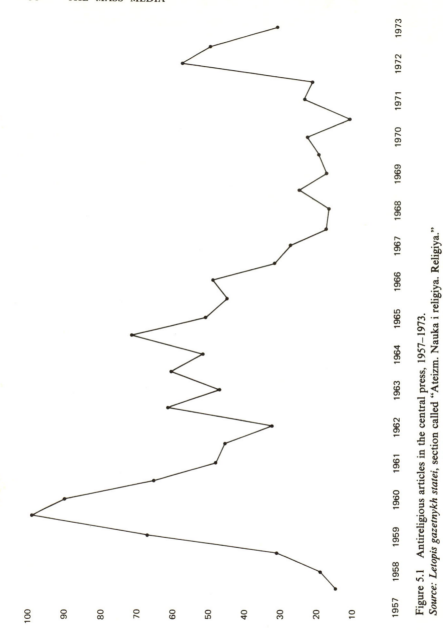

Figure 5.1   Antireligious articles in the central press, 1957–1973.
Source: Letopis gazetnykh statei, section called "Ateizm. Nauka i religiya. Religiya."

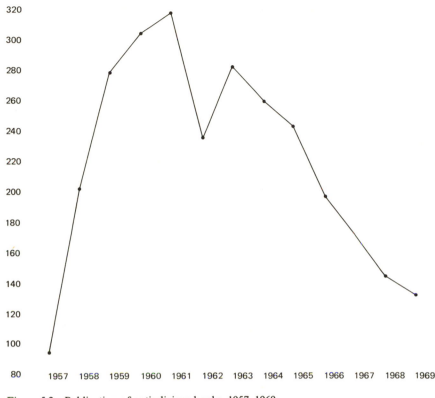

Figure 5.2   Publication of antireligious books, 1957–1969.
Source: Yezhegodnik knigi SSSR, section called "Ateizm. Nauka i Religiya. Religiya."

of atheist items in the press. Friends and relatives of believers sometimes write to newspaper editors (often acting on the suggestion of an atheist agitator), seeking assistance in freeing the "afflicted" individual from the pernicious influence of religion.

Articles and letters by persons who have renounced their religious views also appear in the press; the authors usually explain how they were first attracted to religion and what persuaded them to change their minds. A particularly dramatic example of public apostasy occurred in late 1959, when A. Osipov, a professor at the Leningrad Ecclesiastical Academy and Seminary, announced in a latter to *Pravda* his conversion to atheism. It is worth quoting at some length.

. . . I have abandoned that world, which I now believe to be one of illusions, of retreat from reality, sometimes even of conscious deceit for the sake of financial gain. . . .

. . . how did I come to this? Briefly: as the result of an honest historical

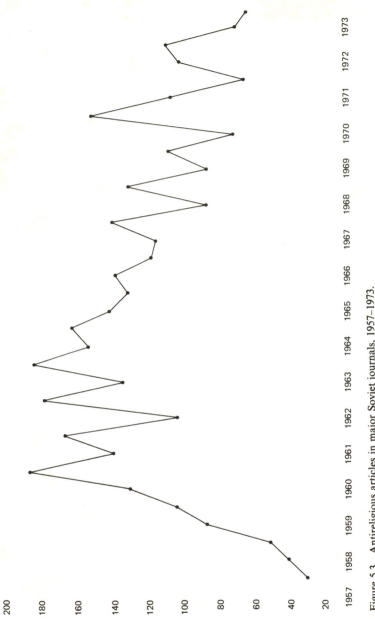

Figure 5.3   Antireligious articles in major Soviet journals, 1957–1973.
Source: Letopis zhurnalnykh statei, section called "Ateizm. Nauka i Religiya. Religiya."

and critical study of the Bible, of careful study of the history of religion, of following the development of the natural sciences, of a practical acquaintance with all the repulsiveness of the capitalist world and the pitiful, despicable role which religion plays there; as a result of studying Marxism-Leninism and its philosophy; and finally as a result of seeing our own Soviet reality which powerfully invites us to follow its unique path of truth.[10]

Osipov eventually came to play a major role in the antireligious effort; his writings were widely publicized, and he was a frequent guest on atheist radio and television programs. (After his death in 1969, however, it was rumored that he had repudiated his earlier apostasy and on his deathbed reconverted to Christianity.)

Propagandists urge those who have renounced religion to write about their experiences and sometimes even help draft articles or letters to the editor. While many of the published articles seem to be legitimate, some people who claim to be apostates apparently are Party or police workers who were asked to masquerade as clergymen or believers.[11]

Letters to newspapers from religious people requesting spiritual guidance or aid in settling church problems also seem less than credible. To write such letters is hardly in keeping with the acknowledged reticence of believers; indeed, it violates every canon of good sense. Nevertheless, newspapers publish what they claim are such letters. To quote from one,

Dear Editor: I am a believer. . . . I am worried about the behavior of our pastor. . . . He loves to drink and consorts with several women. He threw his former housekeeper . . . out of the house; she could no longer work because of her age.

Our pastor drinks not only with his own funds, but with church funds, too. Could not a surprise audit of the church's funds be carried out, as is done in stores? Help us please.[12]

It is not possible to verify the authenticity of such letters. Very likely the authors of some turn to the press out of genuine concern, but others simply seek to redress personal grievances. Whether spurious or not, these letters serve a definite purpose. They illustrate the alleged depravity, wickedness, and callousness of religious authorities and, at the same time, suggest that the Party is the only true source of wisdom and virtue. According to the editor of *Sovetskaya Latvia*, such letters show that "people see who personifies true morality and who must be turned to for truth and assistance." [13]

Antireligious propaganda is supposed to focus on religious ideology, criticizing it and contrasting it with Marxism-Leninism or scientific atheism. Journalists and newspaper editors are instructed to exercise moderation and tact in exposing the wrongdoings of the clergy; they are told to refute the dogmas of religion without offending believers. However, the official policy—to avoid giving offense and to stay within the bounds of good taste and truth—often is violated in practice, so often, in fact, as to cast doubt on the authenticity of the policy. Many items are printed that cannot help but alienate believers, and even Soviet commentators have spoken out against what they term the "primitiveness" or "one-sidedness" of atheist propaganda.[14]

The headlines and language used in atheist materials frequently are lurid or insulting. It is not unusual to come across such offensive headlines as "The Howls of the Obscurantists," "The Vultures," "The Wolfish Fangs of 'God's Harmless Creatures,'" and "Swindlers in the Guise of Holy Fathers." Believers are called "toadstools," "rotten elements," or other ugly names.[15] While there seems to be increasing recognition that tasteless and crude language offends believers and impedes the struggle against religion, materials of this sort still are printed regularly.

Examples of offensive stories are not difficult to find. They focus on allegations of excessive drinking, licentiousness, corruption, misappropriation of funds, and the like. "The newspapers eagerly print material about clergymen who are drunkards and embezzlers," a Soviet journal acknowledged several years ago.[16] They also devote an inordinate amount of attention to highly sectarian groups, e.g., the Jehovah's Witnesses or the Skoptsy, focusing on bizarre or dangerous practices. Articles usually imply (and sometimes state explicitly) that these groups are representative of all that is undesirable about religion. Many articles depict sect membership as a threat to the well-being of the believers themselves, as well as a danger to the common good. In such articles, one commentator has remarked, every sectarian is presented "as a barbarous fanatic and a criminal." [17] Seldom is it mentioned that these sects have few members and exert little or no influence on the rest of the population.

Official policy emphasizes that materials that "unmask" the illicit and immoral behavior of clergymen play an important role in atheist propaganda; they are said to help undermine a believer's faith in his minister and, indirectly, in religion itself. Journalists and Party activists have praised such items for vigorously exposing the true face of religion. However, the publication of such articles sometimes becomes an end in itself. Although criticism of clerics is supposed to play only an accessory, subordinate role in atheist propaganda, it often becomes a primary goal. Efforts to "unmask" the antisocial or amoral acts of individual clergymen should show that such behavior stems directly from a religious value system that allegedly emphasizes self-interest, parasitism, bigotry, and hypocrisy.[18] But they seldom do, and scurrilous charges against certain clergymen are often substituted for a reasoned criticism of religion. In particular, distinctions between rank-and-file believers and religious leaders—the former are said to be merely "deluded," while the latter "maliciously profit from their credulity" and thus ought to be attacked—frequently are ignored by overzealous writers.[19]

It is evident that the level of printed propaganda is low; the tone of antireligious articles tends to be shrill. They are excessively concerned with deviant practices and minor groups, and they may even alienate believers and thus impede the attainment of the Party's atheist objectives. Like most Soviet materials dealing with contemporary affairs, they tend to be highly ritualistic and repetitious. "It is no wonder," a Soviet critic has remarked, "that people say you get used to these articles. Like the rumble of train wheels, you stop paying attention to them." [20] While there are no available figures on reader response to atheist materials per se, the available survey data support his view. Approximately 30 percent of *Izvestia*'s readers regularly read the newspaper's editorials (which, of course, include items on religion), and articles on "communist morality" are only slightly more popular. But these readers often are frustrated by the stereotyped and unpersuasive character of the materials presented to them. "They are not satisfied with the superficial treatment of moral conflicts as accidental clashes between 'good' and 'bad' individuals." [21] The implications of this for propaganda effectiveness are considerable.

Films

It is clear that the cinema can play a substantial role in combating religion and propagating the Party's atheist doctrines. As a special handbook for atheists points out,

The cinema is a formidable weapon in the struggle with religious superstitions. It possesses enormous capacity for exerting influence on people's minds, permits complex questions of science to be explained in depth and reveals in a striking and graphic manner the harmfulness of religious superstitions.[22]

There is a considerable difference, however, between the atheist potential of the film industry and its actual role in the communist upbringing of the masses. The authorities have not fully exploited the cinema in the struggle against religion.

During the 1950s, little attention was devoted to producing antireligious movies. One commentator acknowledged candidly in 1959 that "We simply

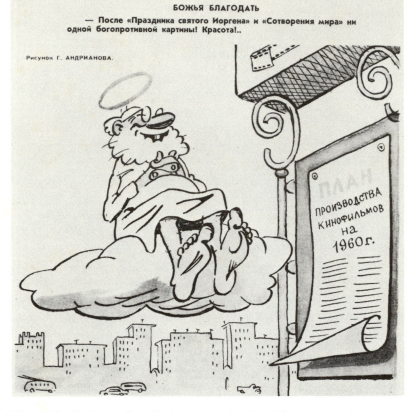

Figure 5.4   God's paradise. (Having examined a list of films to be produced in the coming year, "God" exclaims: "Other than *The Feast of St. Jorgen* and *The Creation of the World,* not one anti-God film! Beautiful! . . .)
Source: Krokodil, No. 11 (1960).

have no good antireligious films," [23] and a year later, the editors of *Krokodil* made the same point in a cartoon (Figure 5.4). Changes soon followed. In the past decade, several dozen atheist movies have been produced, and while there still are too few movies to satisfy ideologists, the situation is no longer regarded as critical. In the following pages we will describe some of these films and then consider the problems that have emerged in trying to fashion the cinema into an instrument of antireligious propaganda.

Most antireligious films deal with the machinations of sectarian groups and focus on what one Soviet specialist has termed "atheist detective story situations." The head of the sect is invariably either a criminal with several convictions against him or else a traitor who assisted the Nazis during the war and now is hiding from Soviet justice.[24] Just as there are standard villains, there are also standard heroes and scenarios. The heroes are pure in heart, and, if sometimes they fall prey to the wicked churchmen, they are always rescued. Their adversaries' plots are invariably foiled, and the culprits are always punished.[25] Typically, atheist films depict incidents of religious fanaticism; they feature such phenomena as crucifixions, murders, starvation, and cases of severe mental derangement. *The Truth About "Saint Misail,"* for example, exposes a self-assigned holy man who collaborates with the Germans during the Occupation, acquires enormous sums of money, drives two women mad, and is finally brought to trial.[26] *The End of the World* also makes use of numerous negative symbols in "unmasking" the exploitative, immoral, deceitful, criminal, and dangerous character of religious leaders. It is instructive to look more closely at this movie, for it is representative of an entire genre.

Philip, once a rich farmer and parasite, returns to his village after serving a term in prison. He is an accomplished liar, and so he decides to present himself as a "saint." He is assisted by several old women dissatisfied with the conduct of the local priest, who is partial to worldly pleasures such as drinking, women and modern dances. . . .

The activity of the sectarians in the village arouses the priest. At first he tries to "reason" with Philip and to come to some understanding with him. However, Philip declines categorically, and a "cold war" for the souls of the believers breaks out. Philip decides to use his maximum weapon and announces the hour of "doomsday," when all those who are not true believers must die. The sectarians are panic-stricken, torture themselves by fasting, and pray incessantly. However, the "end of the world" does not come to pass, and Philip has to run away, faced with the irate members of the sect from whom he has collected voluntary donations for his "holy" work. The sect falls to pieces in shame.[27]

Even Soviet critics wonder whether or not such movies come to grips with the challenge of religion. Indeed, there is a sharp division in their thinking on questions of plot, characterization, and even the very purpose of atheist motion pictures. Two approaches are evident. One sees the purpose of atheist films as "unmasking" religion's most evil or harmful qualities. Its adherents are interested in exposing as many people as possible to shocking scenes, in the hope that this will thoroughly discredit religion and persuade people to renounce their beliefs. They consider questions of style, character development, and plausibility of plot to be of secondary importance.[28] In contrast, other ideology specialists see a need for greater sophistication and subtlety. They are no less firm in their atheist convictions, but think that a frontal attack, using aggressive techniques, is likely to be counterproductive. They argue that standardized plots, stereotyped characters, and a preoccupation with unrealistic or grotesque situations will not help to overcome religion. At best these features are irrelevant to the demands of effective propaganda, and at worst they offend believers and intensify their religious beliefs.[29]

In fact, of course, "shock" techniques are fully exploited, and the most ghastly kinds of incidents are paraded before the viewer. To the traditionalists, this approach is a virtue, for it continually reaffirms the officially sanctioned conclusions about religion. It evokes revulsion for, and hatred of, religion and thus is conducive to the spread of atheism. To more sophisticated critics, the use of stock symbols and plots deprives a film of any force: it alienates the believer, bores the atheist, and impedes the spread of atheism. Thus what some see as a basic strength in antireligious films, others view as evidence of their weakness.

Those who approve of the repetitiveness of atheist movies are lavish in their praise. The films *Clouds over Borskoye, Ivanna, The Miracle-Working Icon*, and *I Love You, Life*, in the words of one reviewer, "tell the painful truth about different crevices in a common abyss—religion. . . . The atmosphere in the films is tense, the pitch of passions high, the polemic savage. There can be no reconciliation here."[30] Other reviewers are equally enthusiastic. According to one, *I Love You, Life* "tears away the mask from the Jehovah's Witnesses, a filthy sect that receives direct instructions from overseas," and *The Miracle-Working Icon* and *Clouds over Borskoye* "paint bitter pictures of the corrosive activities of Orthodox churchmen and Pentecostalists."[31] *The End of the World* is said to have been so effective in exposing the pernicious activities of religious groups in the town where it was filmed that the film's producer received several anonymous threats, and "the local sectarians did not know where to hide from the people's ridicule."[32]

Few atheist films are commended for handling antireligious themes in a subtle or sophisticated manner. This can be partially explained by the fact that those who make such films are lacking in knowledge and skill.[33] But a more basic factor is very likely at work—the propensity of propagandists to present problems in terms that are easy to understand. Antireligious films, one writer has remarked, "naturally tend toward a distinctive kind of polemic-dialogue form." [34] In practice, script writers have exaggerated this tendency, depicting a universe of absolute good and evil and heightening the tension between the two.

In the recent past, however, a growing number of critics have expressed reservations about such films. They are disturbed about the stereotyped characters, hackneyed plots, and bizarre situations that are explored so often. These elements, they argue, need not be abandoned, but they should be de-emphasized. If the basic task of the atheist film (and of atheist propaganda in general) is to expose religious ideology, today's movies are misdirected. They fail to show "the everyday work of destruction" that religious groups carry out, because they do not examine the most basic tenets of religion.[35] Religion, it is said, teaches passivity, helplessness, and love for one's enemy. It demands that potentially productive workers waste their time with prayer, thereby retarding the development of both the individual and the community. What should be emphasized, then, is what is truly typical, that which "inflicts the greatest harm on the practice of communist construction, which distracts believers from solving practical tasks." [36]

It is far more difficult, but also far more useful, to deal with everyday events and ordinary people. Only by making clear the ways in which religion influences people's behavior and thinking, only by examining true-to-life situations, can the "hypocrisy and falsity" of religion be demonstrated effectively. Adherents of this view claim that atheist films presently are confined to isolated, ugly, and sensational incidents that are seldom placed in a meaningful context. For example, one scene in the film *Clouds over Borskoye* shows the leaders of a group of Pentecostalists attempting to crucify a girl. An antireligious specialist has said of this scene:

. . . if we want to convince the viewers by artistic means of the harm done to Soviet citizens by religion, then such an incident cannot . . . be the basis for atheist conclusions. Why? Well, for the simple reason that this sort of thing is not typical of the activity of most churchmen and sectarian organizations and is indeed condemned by them.[37]

Such an occurrence is viewed by virtually everyone, including religious leaders and rank-and-file believers, as barbarous. To focus on bizarre characters and exceptional events, of which believers themselves do not approve, is to miss the mark.

The film propaganda program is also confronted with problems of resource allocation and utilization. Atheists complain that too few antireligious films are produced, and that too few copies of those that are produced are made. Three factors can be cited to account for this situation. In the first place, there are few novels, essays, or stories that can be made into scenarios for such pictures. The writers' organizations have simply not stimulated writers to explore the subject of religion.[38]

A second consideration involves rivalries and bickering among various cultural authorities. For example, the Moscow Popular Science Film Studio's picture *The Enlightenment* was for a time kept from circulation by Rosglavfilm, the Chief Film Distributing Office of the RSFSR Ministry of Culture, because officials of the latter agency thought the movie had "an insufficient atheist orientation." [39] At the same time, theater managers, apparently concerned about the limited box-office appeal of militantly antireligious films, try not to show them at all.[40] And on at least one occasion, local *political* authorities deliberately sabotaged the showing of atheist films. (The episode involved a conspiracy among high-ranking Tadzhik officials, who were faithful Moslems, and a group of "religious fanatics and charlatans.")[41]

A third element that impedes the flow of propaganda from the studio to the screen is the inefficiency of the distribution system. Listings of atheist movies available for rental are inadequate and frequently unavailable, and, because film rental agencies do not advertise the atheist pictures they have at their disposal, they usually send out only a small portion of their available stock. The head of the Department of Propaganda and Agitation of the Odessa Province Party Committee complained in 1963 that "hundreds of copies of natural science and scientific atheist films are lying on the shelves of film rental bases." Each copy, he added, was shown only two or three times a year.[42]

To compound the problem, film distributors often do their job mechanically, without taking into account which religious groups are active in a particular city or village. Antireligious film showings in Estonia, for example, seldom deal with the Lutheran Church, while anti-Catholic movies are shown in Moslem Central Asia.[43] The result, of course, is to leave religious citizens unmoved.

The authorities have made some effort to deal with such difficulties. In 1964, the Party Central Committee called for an increase in the number of prints of antireligious films, the production of new films (including cartoons on atheist themes), the showing of these films on television, and their duplication on special tapes. At the same time, steps were taken to improve the quality of scripts for atheist films. Cultural authorities, including officials of the Union of Writers and the State Committee on Cinematography were directed to arrange competitions (with incentive prizes) for the best artistic works on antireligious themes.[44] The Committee quickly formulated plans to increase the output of films on atheist themes: film studios were instructed to produce three or four antireligious films each year, including one or two for children. They were also told to put out four or five animated cartoons lampooning religion, plus another ten or fifteen popular science films and another dozen documentaries on atheist themes.[45] The Moscow "Filmstrip" studio alone has produced more than a dozen filmstrips on subjects ranging from *The Church and Religion in the Service of Imperialism* to *Religion and Medicine*.[46]

Despite the difficulties we have noted, a substantial portion of the population *is* exposed to antireligious motion pictures. An official of the Film Production Administration of the USSR Ministry of Culture reported in 1962 that 30 million people had seen *Ivanna*, while *The Gadfly*, *The Fire of Immortality*, and *Clouds over Borskoye* were each seen by 25 million persons.[47] In order to reach as many people as possible, antireligious movies are shown, often free of charge, not only in conventional theaters but also in schools, institutions of higher learning, atheism houses, museums, clubs, and other cultural-enlightenment institutions. Indeed, perhaps half the total audience attending atheist film showings is made up of organized groups of students and workers brought to such places.[48]

To attract more people to these pictures, some Party organizations have set up "film-lecture bureaus" under the local cultural-enlightenment institutions. On a given evening in a club or House of Culture, speakers deliver lectures on an antireligious theme, and then a film on a related subject is shown. Other Party organizations have created "atheism film clubs," which perform the same function and operate in much the same way. There are even antireligious film festivals, at which atheist or popular science films are shown. And, when conventional movie theaters are not available, propagandists make use of mobile projectors, traveling about the countryside on "agitation tours" in special "agit-vehicles." Through such means, cultural officials are able to bring atheist motion pictures to even the most remote localities.[49]

The assumption on which the authorities have been operating is that additional showings of such films will make for more effective propaganda. As we shall see, this assumption is faulty and has led to basic errors and shortcomings in the atheist effort.

Radio and Television

Radio and television are powerful instruments of propaganda and education. In the USSR especially, they are more than simple means of communication; they are also weapons for political agitation.[50] If used properly, they could be major assets in the Soviet effort to eradicate religious belief and behavior. Their principal advantage is that they allow the Party to present the same message to great numbers of citizens, both believers and propagandists. In addition, people are exposed to radio and television broadcasts when they are in familiar and comfortable surroundings, i.e., in an environment that facilitates effective communication. These would seem to offer compelling reasons for exploiting both media for atheist purposes.

Soviet ideological authorities, aware of the propaganda potential of radio and television, have urged that both media be given major responsibilities in the effort to mold the New Man. The Party Central Committee a decade ago demanded that radio "rear the Soviet people to be irreconcilable toward bourgeois ideology," and that television develop "a spirit of communist ideology and morality and of irreconcilability to bourgeois ideology and morality." [51] To achieve these objectives, production of radios and television sets has increased rapidly, while broadcasting and relay facilities have been expanded to reach the great mass of the population. By early 1972, there were more than 45 million television sets, 50 million radios, and 48 million wired speakers *(radiotochki)* in the USSR. (Another 6 million or so television sets are added to the total each year).[52] Soviet stations broadcast some 1,500 hours of television programs each day, along with 1,400 hours of radio programs. The entire population is exposed to radio, and television broadcasts can be received in an area inhabited by 170 million people. There are approximately 90 television sets for every 100 families living in the television reception zone, which means that there are almost 150 million viewers.[53] According to Soviet survey data, perhaps three-fourths of the population of the major urban centers watch television every day,[54] while a substantial (though doubtless smaller) percentage of the rural population is exposed to television propaganda.

What they see and hear, however, is decidedly nonideological. Neither radio nor television devotes much time to ideological activities in general or to antireligious propaganda in particular. Programs are devoted primarily to entertainment, and surprisingly little time is allocated to indoctrination. More than half (55 percent) of Radio Moscow's domestic programming is devoted to music, while only 10 percent is devoted to social or political broadcasts. Similarly, Central Television provides mainly entertainment and cultural enrichment; only about 8 percent of all broadcasts focus on social and political matters.[55] The establishment in 1961 of an editorial staff to aid Central Television with its atheist programs has not had much of an effect.[56]

It is particularly surprising that television's propaganda potential is exploited so inadequately. The "blue screen," as it is termed in the USSR, would seem to be particularly well suited to combating religion. Several Soviet specialists have spoken of its "tremendous potential" and suggested that it could be "extremely effective in the atheist upbringing of the masses." [57] There is some empirical evidence supporting this view. Soviet researchers have found that believers are more inclined to expose themselves to antireligious messages on radio and television than to similar messages transmitted through other media.[58] Nonetheless, the authorities seldom use either television or radio to combat religion.

The basic problem stems from a kind of cultural lag, although rivalries among the principal communications industries also play a role in keeping radio and television so inactive. Ideological specialists have been hesitant or unwilling to accept television's vast propaganda potential, feeling more at home with other media. One authority has spoken of the "traditional hierarchical order of propaganda media," in which the press, films, and radio are given priority. An "inertia of attitudes," he says, has created a "table of ranks," preventing a proper appreciation of the role television could play.[59] A decade ago, a television official complained:

It is sometimes considered more important to issue a small pamphlet in 10,000 to 15,000 copies than to televise a program on the same topic. There are those who feel that delivering a lecture on television is not particularly important, that it is a far more responsible task to speak in a hall that accommodates 300 to 500 persons. After all, you can count the number in attendance and the number of questions asked. It seems somehow not the thing to do, after a television lecture, to write that it was heard by six to eight million people and that hundreds of questions were asked in various places. . . .[60]

The problem persists to this day. The television medium still is relatively new and unfamiliar, and many propagandists apparently feel comfortable only with traditional approaches, e.g., the press and personal, face-to-face contacts.[61] There has been little effort to work out new forms of antireligious propaganda and exploit the distinctive features of these media, particularly television.

Moreover, the regime has also encountered difficulties in securing cooperation from the intellectual community. Attempts to find script writers for antireligious broadcasts have met with indifference, evasiveness, or hostility. Writers often refuse such work under one pretext or another. The better-known writers avoid antireligious themes entirely.[62] The philosophers are more interested, but their work usually lacks an emotional element—precisely that element which these writers possess.[63] This situation, of course, serves to reinforce the "inertia of attitudes" we have already described. The resources of radio and television thus remain underutilized.

Most of the programs directed at the problem of religion emanate from local or regional studios. The central authorities are, by and large, preoccupied with other matters. An official of All-Union Radio has argued that central broadcasting should present no more than two atheist programs per week, while the number of telecasts emanating from Moscow is even lower.[64]

Moscow's radio programs consist of lectures and discussions critical of religious doctrine or the behavior of religious officials. They are usually part of the regular series "Discussions on Atheist Themes." [65] Central Television broadcasts are quite similar, consisting primarily of panel discussions, lectures, plays, or films. Since 1962, the Moscow authorities have produced a "television magazine," at first called "The Truth About Religion" and after 1969 called "Man and Religion." The "magazine" consists of a series of programs on atheist themes and follows a plan drawn up by specialists on atheist indoctrination.[66] In addition, of course, a certain amount of antireligious propaganda can be found in programs that are ostensibly nonpolitical, e.g., news broadcasts, programs for young people, and literary and dramatic programs.

Few local stations compensate to any substantial degree for the lack of central programming. When they do, they try to enlist the services of local teachers, writers, scientists, doctors, and former believers, who serve as editorial consultants and sometimes even take part in programs. Broadcasts tend to be brief, usually lasting no more than fifteen or twenty minutes. They involve, in the main, atheist discussions, lectures, consultations, and plays arranged at local clubs or in the studio itself. Other popular formats include answering listeners' questions, reading selections from *Nauka i religiya*, arranging quizzes on religion and atheism, and reciting antireligious poetry.[67] A typical program, broadcast on Krasnodar Television, featured the play *Save Our Souls*, which explored the fate of a student in an ecclesiastical seminary. Under the influence of a girl in the Komsomol, he "breaks with the world of lies and deception and comes to a factory, to a workers' collective, in order to become a working man." [68]

More imaginative broadcasts include testimony from trials involving "religious fanaticism," as well as broadcasts of the protests of "outraged workers" from the area.[69] Atheist radio programs may even be confined to an individual factory or farm. Indeed, in at least one collective farm, activists set up *radiotochki* in the homes of several particularly unyielding believers, in an attempt to expose them to antireligious propaganda.[70]

Radio and television, like the press, do not confine their antireligious activities to propaganda. They may be called upon to serve an organizing function as well. For example, when one little girl wrote to the editors of the Voronezh "radio magazine," asking them to help free her mother from religion, they did more than broadcast an answer to her. They sent a copy of her letter to her school urging that her teacher assist the mother in renouncing religion.[71] Thus, radio and television perform the same three tasks Lenin fixed for the Communist press—to propagandize, agitate, and organize.

The value of antireligious broadcasts may be questioned on several grounds. We will have more to say on this subject in the final chapter, but here we can at least identify two basic problems. In the first place, the existence of several radio and television stations in a given locality means that listeners and viewers need not be a captive audience. As Anatoly Lunacharsky once said of the film viewer, the television or radio enthusiast "is not a patient who wishes a dose of medicine and not a schoolboy to be sat at a desk." [72] People cannot be compelled to watch or listen to propaganda broadcasts, particularly when they compete with cultural or sports programs. Soviet audiences apparently are strongly inclined to avoid broadcasts laden with propaganda, and atheist programs thus are not likely to have many followers.[73]

In the second place, propaganda broadcasts tend to be artless and dreary. The Party Central Committee observed in 1960 that radio broadcasts "arouse little interest or reaction among listeners," while television programs were characterized as "dull" and "unconvincing." [74] Similar assessments have been offered repeatedly since then. Thus, for example, Tashkent's television broadcasts have been criticized for their "serious ideological and artistic weaknesses and [their] drabness and stereotyped nature." [75]

Radio and television seem to add little to the struggle against religion. Atheist programs are produced infrequently, and when they are put on, they are not likely to hold the attention of the audience. Other instruments are called upon to wage the struggle.

6 Mass Oral Propaganda

It is necessary to present the masses with the most diverse materials on atheist propaganda, to acquaint them with facts from the most varied spheres of life, to approach them this way and that, in order to interest them, to rouse them from their religious dream, to shake them from the most varied sides, with the most varied means, etc.

V. I. Lenin (1922)

In its effort to mold the New Soviet Man, the antireligious movement has relied heavily on mass oral propaganda techniques. Soviet atheists have long argued that all forms of propaganda are suitable in combating religion, "except for those producing boredom or hurting believers' feelings." [1] On the basis of their experience with mass oral propaganda, however, it appears that one or the other of these reactions may be inevitable. An examination of the major techniques in use will indicate why this is so.

Lectures

The principal instrument of mass antireligious propaganda is the lecture. Despite the almost constant criticism to which atheist lectures and lecturers have been subjected over the years, lecturing remains a favored weapon in the struggle against religion. The years following Stalin's death witnessed a dramatic increase in the volume of lecture propaganda, followed by more modest increases in the post-Khrushchev period. (See Table 6.1.) In some regions of the country, where the antireligious effort is conducted with particular vigor, the lecture program continues to expand. In the Ryazan region, for example, the number of lectures on atheist topics almost doubled during the sixties. (See Table 6.2.) In the decade 1957–1966, the Knowledge Society in the Voronezh region expanded its atheist lecture program more than sixfold. (See Table 6.3.)

While such lectures represent only about 4 percent of the Knowledge Society's propaganda effort, they constitute a major part of the official antireligious drive.[2] Hundreds of thousands of lectures on atheist themes are delivered each year, and millions of people are exposed to the Party's views.

Lecture propaganda, like atheist propaganda in general, is heavily scientific in its orientation. It focuses on such questions as the formation of the universe, the origin of life on earth, and scientific discoveries "which confirm the correctness of materialist views on the development of nature and society." [3] While such information may help indirectly to undermine

Table 6.1   Number of Lectures on Atheist Themes Delivered Annually, 1954–1970

Year	Number of Lectures on Atheist Themes
1954	120,000
1958	303,000
1959	400,000
1963	660,000
1966	760,000
1970	679,000

Sources: D. Sidorov, "Za boyevuyu nauchno-ateisticheskuyu propagandu," *Politicheskoye samoobrazovaniye*, No. 2 (1960), p. 103; *Kalendar ateista* (Moscow, 1964), p. 153; I. Pantskhava, "Navstrechu chetvertomu sezdu obshchestva 'Znaniye,'" *Nauka i religiya*, No. 6 (1964), p. 3; "Ateisticheskoye vospitaniye segodnya," *Nauka i religiya*, No. 9 (1967), p. 4; "Za deistvennost ateisticheskoi propagandy," *Pravda*, July 27, 1968, p. 1; *Narodnoye obrazovaniye, nauka i kultura v SSSR* (Moscow, 1971), p. 310.

Table 6.2   Knowledge Society Lectures, Ryazan Region, 1960–1969

Year	Number of Lectures	Number of Lectures on Atheist Themes
1960	60,467	3,412
1961	63,530	3,209
1962	66,105	3,001
1963	66,898	3,221
1964	68,360	3,799
1965	73,087	4,160
1966	81,558	4,209
1967	92,256	4,990
1968	95,514	5,124
1969	101,708	5,936

Source: A. Kozhevnikov, "Ateisticheskoye vospitaniye selskogo naseleniya v sovremennykh usloviyakh," in I. Shatilov (ed.), *Zaboty i dela ateistov* (Moscow, 1970), p. 46.

Table 6.3   Knowledge Society Lectures on Atheist Themes, Voronezh Region, 1957–1966

Year	Number of Lectures on Atheist Themes
1957	1,532
1958	2,529
1959	4,584
1960	6,277
1961	6,324
1962	6,142
1963	7,396
1964	9,514
1965	9,525
1966	9,614

Source: A. V. Losev et al., *Sotsialno-ekonomicheskiye preobrazovaniya v voronezhskoi derevne* (Voronezh, 1967), p. 313.

people's religious convictions, it will not automatically persuade a believer to espouse atheism. Most believers are acquainted with the elements of physics, chemistry, and other sciences, but have not drawn the proper "atheist conclusions." The lecturer's responsibility, therefore, is not simply to present the relevant scientific data but also to explain the antireligious implications of these data.[4]

Lecturers who are not conscious of this dual responsibility may not only fail to shake anyone's faith but may even unintentionally reinforce the religious inclinations of their listeners. Nadezhda Krupskaya (Lenin's wife) used to tell about a worker who once visited the Moscow planetarium. After viewing the display, he is said to have remarked, "Well, well, who would have believed how wisely God has organized the world!"[5] More recently, a *Nauka i religiya* correspondent told of a lecturer who described recent discoveries in astronomy and physics, revealing "the secrets of the distant stars and the micro-world." The audience listened attentively, but afterward an elderly lady exclaimed in admiration: "See how cleverly everything in the world is arranged. And they say there is no God!"[6] Other such instances are reported from time to time; they illustrate clearly how difficult the professional atheist's task is.

To be sure, lecturers are encouraged to attack religion from other vantage points besides that of pure science. In the period since Stalin's death, the range of topics dealt with in public lectures has expanded appreciably. (See Appendix 3.) While there were only eight standard themes for atheist lectures in 1948, today there are more than a hundred.[7] Although some ideological specialists have expressed concern about the possibility of overspecialization,[8] the number of lecture topics continues to increase. Among the most popular subjects today are those dealing with religious morality, the alleged depravity of church leaders, and the dangers of fasting or engaging in frenzied prayer. A good deal of time is also devoted to analysis and criticism of religious doctrine, which, as might be expected, tends to be presented in a distorted manner.

It has proved difficult to deal effectively with these themes. Many lecturers confine themselves to anticlerical, rather than antireligious, propaganda. While criticism of "amoral conduct," "hypocrisy" or "money-grubbing" by church officials is encouraged, this effort sometimes becomes an end in itself. Lecturers often forget that the propagandist's primary responsibility is to combat religion as an "antiscientific world view," not simply to criticize individual religious leaders or believers.[9] As one Soviet commentator has observed, "it is easy to criticize priests; it is much more difficult to combat religious ideology."[10]

There are some speakers who deliberately insult the believers sitting in front of them. Instances of speakers calling members of the audience "obscurantists," "renegades," or other derogatory names have been reported. One Soviet authority suggested in 1963 that many lecturers engaged in this practice. They begin their talks, he said, with the "sacramental pronouncement, 'There is no God,' " and end by denouncing the "unseemly behavior of long-dead popes and the horrors of the Inquisition." These, he pointed out, are of no more concern to the audience than the ancient fire worshippers, "whom the orators also remember to 'condemn' in the course of the same lecture." [11]

Emotional appeals can of course play a useful role. Good propaganda should be directed not only toward people's minds but toward their emotions as well. While the more intellectual listeners may find the atheist's logical presentation satisfying, others in the audience require a somewhat livelier talk. Lecturers therefore are encouraged to "take pains to reach the hearts of their listeners." [12] Appeals to the emotions, it is said, will help the believer to see his own errors. They will make him aware of the "irreconcilable contradictions of religion, the discrepancy between a religious world-view and the life of Soviet socialist society." [13]

The ideal lecture thus mixes information, propaganda, agitation, and organizational efforts. The atheist lecturer is both scholar and advocate; he informs, persuades, denounces, and exhorts. He presents information and tries to stimulate his audience to join him in driving religion from the country. Appealing to his audience on both logical and emotional grounds, he will seem to be not an "official speaker" but rather "a comrade and conversationalist, a sincere story-teller." Those who attend his lectures will feel "like participants in a conversation," rather than like pupils. [14]

Until very recently, most antireligious lecturers were ill trained or totally without specialized training. According to A. F. Okulov, head of the Institute of Scientific Atheism, the entire "scientific baggage" of a large proportion of professional atheists consisted solely of the fact that they did not believe in God. [15] Not only did they lecture poorly, but their errors helped to discredit the atheist movement in general. Even now, after the introduction of atheist training and retraining programs, the standards of antireligious lectures have not improved appreciably. In fact, the presence of training programs has in some measure retarded the progress of lecture propaganda, allowing immature and uninformed speakers to present their views. Many of those who deliver lectures are inexperienced students trying to fulfill course requirements. Others have completed only one or two elementary courses; they cannot have acquired more than a superficial understanding of religion, atheism, or propaganda. A very high percentage, perhaps as many as half, of the people assigned to deliver antireligious lectures have had no training whatsoever in scientific atheism.[16] What is more, most of them are men, whereas most believers are women.[17] To make matters still worse, many lecturers are too young to be effective speakers. Their youth represents a major psychological barrier both to themselves and to believers, who, of course, tend to be older.[18] Thus the older, more experienced propagandists are not properly trained, while their younger, better-trained colleagues are too young and inexperienced to be taken seriously by believers.

Because so many lecturers are untrained and inexperienced, because they find themselves saddled with many other Party tasks, and because they are called upon to speak on a wide range of topics, they are not always able to write their own speeches. Some read from texts put together by local atheists, while others read drafts prepared by higher authorities.[19] If possible, a speaker will do some preliminary research, perhaps even studying local religious groups at first hand. Industrious propagandists visit local churches and listen to the sermons of the clergymen, in order "to expose their reactionary contents in a future lecture." [20] Other speakers read antireligious literature extensively, collecting reference materials for use in future lectures.[21] Party, Knowledge Society, and trade union organizations often assist propagandists by compiling dossiers on local religious groups or passing on materials prepared by higher authorities. There are even special handbooks listing answers to the most frequently asked questions on atheism and religion.[22]

In the final analysis, the lecturer himself is responsible for the success or failure of his speech. While a prudent propagandist will try to determine in advance what kind of audience he is to address and what their religious orientation is, some lecturers neglect to take even this basic precaution. One has written embarrassedly of an occasion when he was sent into a district to deliver an atheist lecture:

In one of the villages, 15–20 collective farmers had gathered for the lecture. Several of the men among them stood out because of their considerable age. At the beginning of the lecture, I managed to determine that these people were aggressively inclined and had come "to stand up for their faith in Christ." I anticipated a serious verbal battle, but to my surprise, the lecture went peacefully. One handsome old man even thanked me for the good lecture and asked whether I would not stay for another day, to repeat my performance on the morrow. He promised that there would be more listeners. I gladly assented.

Only when I arrived at the district center and spoke with workers from the district party committee did I understand the true reason for my "success." It seems that many Baptists lived in the village that I visited. In delivering my lecture, exposing "miracles" and the machinations of the Orthodox clergy, I was a "teacher" in the hands of the Baptists.[23]

Thus the lecturer, even when he delivers the "correct" message, must be certain to deliver it before the "correct" audience. That it may not be easy to determine what message is "correct" is revealed by the experience of another lecturer who neglected to prepare adequately for his presentation. In a speech in Central Asia on the evils of Islam, he criticized the Moslem clergy, focusing on those who "drink, lead a depraved life, and are engaged in illegal extortions." The audience, primarily faithful Moslems, was receptive to the lecturer's remarks: "indignant exclamations often rang out, directed against the unworthy behavior of the mullahs." The speaker naturally concluded that he was doing well. But when he had finished, he overheard several powerful members of the local Moslem community saying: "We must hold firmly to our mullah, for some sort of debauched person or someone interested only in himself could also come our way. . . ."[24] The speaker, of course, wanted to prove that the Moslem religion, like every other religion, is harmful. Instead of this, he "proved" that some ministers of this religion are wicked. In the terminology of Soviet propaganda, the speaker "substituted one thesis for another" and succeeded only in reinforcing the local population's high regard for its religious leader.

The typical audience is a heterogeneous group, and it is difficult for a speaker to find a common denominator. An audience is almost always comprised of people of different ages, educational levels, interests, and, most important, different attitudes toward religion and atheism. While nonbelievers are predisposed to accept the atheist's presentation, religious people in the audience are apt to respond "with well-known prejudices." Lectures directed at some sort of "average listener" are likely to miss the mark.[25]

Another problem confronting the lecturer is the fact that audiences do not always listen attentively. Religious believers sometimes try to distract the listeners, disorient the speaker, or even disrupt the proceedings. One incident reported in the press involved a number of religious fanatics who jumped up from their seats to cry, "You will not touch our faith!"[26] Such outbursts are extremely unusual. Believers prefer to wait until the question-and-answer period after a lecture to ask difficult questions. They seek to embarrass the speaker and, if possible, neutralize the effect of his remarks. In addition to posing questions, they often attempt to debate the speaker, presenting their views and rebutting his. While some speakers become flustered and respond either with inanities or invective, resourceful lecturers can turn challenges into propaganda lessons. For example, one atheist lecturer, asked why older and more experienced people continued to believe in God, responded with a question of his own:

"Tell me, how many years has your cathedral been in existence?"
"Two hundred."
"And how many years has your school been standing?"
"Not very many; it was built only after the Soviets came to power."
"Well, there you have it. If the school had been standing the same number of years as your cathedral, there would probably be no believers in your village today. . . ." [27]

Not all lecturers are so adroit. Many are simply unable to deal with tricky questions.

Defects and shortcomings in the atheist lecture program are pervasive and deeply rooted. The entire effort has two apparently contradictory objectives. On the one hand, it must be militant and vigorous, "taking the offensive" (nastupatelnaya), the Soviets say. On the other hand, it must avoid insults to the feelings of believers. Lecturers are urged to seek a balance between these two aims, but are seldom able to find it. Most of them resort to excessively formal, pedantic language or else appeal to their listeners with "cheap sensationalism." Thus, many lectures are dismissed as "uninteresting," "dry," or "lacking in color." The lecturers responsible for them are accused of "abstract, ideological sermonizing" or "wandering along a barren course." [28] More often, however, lecturers are criticized for excessive militancy. The Central Committee resolution of November, 1954, criticized "attacks upon the clergy and believers who perform religious rites," [29] and dozens of articles published since then have echoed this theme. Even the slogans advertising atheist lectures are tendentious and offensive. Such titles as "Religion—the Enemy of Good Health" or "The Harm Done by Religious Holy Days" naturally deter believers from attending these sessions.[30] The more sophisticated and responsible ideological officials clearly recognize the self-defeating character of this verbal brutality, but they have not succeeded in imposing their will on all propagandists. The offensive style and content of most lecture propaganda continues to antagonize believers, hindering the cause of atheism. It is hardly surprising that when Soviet cartoonists seek to depict a bad lecturer, they almost invariably select an atheist lecturer.[31]

In endeavoring to deal with these problems, the Party has adopted a number of changes. It has improved its recruitment and training programs for atheist propagandists, and it has devised new ways of presenting atheist messages to believers. The major changes are four in number:

First, the ideological authorities have sought out teachers, physicians, and scientists to conduct antireligious work. Members of these professions are likely to have the communications skills and temperament needed for propaganda work. Schoolteachers and faculty members of institutions of higher learning (who now constitute a majority of lecturers) should be particularly adept at lecturing and at handling questions.[32]

Second, the Party is attempting to expand and improve its training programs. In order to acquire greater expertise, lecturers have begun to specialize in one or another facet of atheist work. Some concentrate on questions of Christianity, others on Islam, and still others on the propaganda of science.[33] By improving the knowledge and skills of some, while dropping others from the program, the Party should be able to raise the level of lecture propaganda.

Third, ideological authorities have begun to arrange series of lectures on various aspects of religion and atheism. These are known as "lecture cycles." Over a twelve-month period, lecturers examine a number of important questions, dealing with a new subject each month. According to its advocates, this approach provides "a step-by-step exposition of the basic principles of a scientific understanding of the world and social phenomena." [34] It permits local atheists to present, gradually and systematically, the official doctrine on religion and atheism. It is particularly helpful in establishing contact with believers. By beginning with lectures on purely scientific subjects, then moving gradually into questions dealing with religion and atheism, the speaker can overcome some of the psychological barriers believers erect against atheist propaganda. Indeed, a major objective of the lecture cycle is to induce believers to expose themselves to antireligious materials.[35]

Finally, there has been some effort to do away with crude and offensive lecture titles and to avoid unnecessary insults to religious people during the lectures themselves. Some atheist organizers have gone to great lengths to deal with this problem and, if possible, to attract believers. One Moscow club even combines antireligious lectures with a fashion show.[36] How enduring the new approach is remains to be seen.

Meetings with Former Believers

Specially arranged evenings at which local citizens meet with former believers are said to be one of the most effective forms of antireligious work. These evenings are usually given such titles as "Why I Broke with Religion" or "Why We Ceased to Believe in God." They consist of discussions with former clergymen, church officials, students in ecclesiastical academies and seminaries, and rank-and-file believers, people who for one reason or another have renounced religion. They explain the reasons for their earlier belief in God and then describe their conversion to atheism. The theory behind such meetings is clear: believers, it is thought, will be more receptive to someone who has shared their experiences and their values. The speaker's experiences make it easier for him to establish rapport with the audience. His "inside knowledge" and familiarity with church dogmas strengthen his credibility, and the fact that he has given up religion makes him valuable from the Party's point of view. One atheist has suggested that, "When a clergyman or priest breaks with religion, the effect on a believer is like that of an exploding bomb." [37] While the effect is seldom so dramatic, the speeches of apostates have won considerable favor among professional atheists. In the words of a leading authority,

The vivid and striking stories of those who, from their own personal experience became convinced of the falsity of religious morality, the contradictions of the "holy" books, and found in themselves the strength to tear off their religious fetters—such stories produce a great impression on those who are present, force believers to ponder over their own religious convictions and give rise to doubt about the veracity of these convictions.[38]

Party and Knowledge Society organizations in some areas carry out a vigorous program of recruiting and training former believers. Indeed, the revelations of such people are regarded as such a powerful propaganda weapon that recordings of their speeches are played to workers in particularly remote areas.[39]

The evidence, however, is ambiguous. While the remarks of former clergymen may have the impact of "an exploding bomb" on some believers, others will reject the apostate or cling even more tightly to their beliefs. The more cynical believers—just how many is unclear—apparently argue as follows: "First he deceived us and took money for it. Now he'll deceive the atheists for money. He's not worth a kopek." [40] The problem is a difficult one, and we shall return to it.

Debates

An antireligious measure that has aroused a good deal of controversy among Soviet propagandists is the "Evening for Believers and Nonbelievers." This is a public debate with antireligious specialists on one side and clergymen and rank-and-file believers on the other. Representatives of each side present their views and are given an opportunity to refute the views of their opponents. Members of the audience are encouraged to participate; they may ask questions, offer criticism, or simply present their own observations on some point being disputed.

The practice has been subjected to vigorous attacks. It has been condemned as outmoded and counterproductive, totally unsuited to present-day conditions. In the immediate postrevolutionary period, when the Party's position was weak, debates were a valuable, almost indispensable form of propaganda. Atheists were in a minority, and the great mass of the population was familiar with religious doctrine. Debates therefore afforded atheists an opportunity to challenge religion publicly; they were, so to speak, provided with "equal time." By "smashing the arguments of the preachers," propagandists "brought a new word to the people and explained the fundamentals of the scientific, materialist world-view." But now that only a minority of Soviet citizens are religious, public debates provide the *clergy* with "equal time." To grant ministers a public platform today gives them access to the population and facilitates the spread of religious ideology.[41]

Other considerations support critics of public debates. Most obviously, the atheist may lose the debate. The religious spokesman may be particularly skilled, the atheist particularly inept, or the audience particularly hostile to the atheist. In any event, the contest will only discredit the propagandist, his message, and the Party itself. Moreover, a debate is a sophisticated intellectual exercise, and few listeners are able to comprehend diametrically opposed views on the same subject. In addition, debates are an inefficient instrument of propaganda. The atheist cannot devote his full attention to a thorough and systematic presentation of the problem, but must, as one commentator has put it, respond to the "gossip of the priests' casuistry which, without fail, will divert him from the theme." [42]

These arguments appear to have been effective. Public debates on issues of religion and atheism, which were beginning to come under attack toward the end of the Khrushchev era, are rarely held any more.

"Miracles without Miracles"

One of the most unusual measures employed in the struggle against religion is the staging of specially selected physics and chemistry experiments. The scientists, students, and professional atheists who perform them seek to debunk and ridicule religious dogma. They "unmask the intrigues of the clergy," exposing ministers and priests as charlatans who have for centuries deceived the people into believing miracles possible.[43] The simple scientific demonstrations, usually performed during an "Evening of Miracles without Miracles," demonstrate that the phenomena that clergymen have for centuries explained as "miraculous" are readily explained by the laws of science. The allegedly miraculous event is reproduced for the audience, and it is the visual experience that gives this technique its special impact.

The range of experiments is limited to simple, though sometimes dramatic, demonstrations. (Some are so easily performed that children repeat them at home in front of their religious parents.)[44] Audiences are invited to study "holy water" under a microscope, to see that it does not differ from ordinary water and that it contains bacteria. Physiologists demonstrate the use of hypnosis, suggestion, and autosuggestion to ridicule "miracle healings" of diseases of the central nervous system.[45] Usually, however, such evenings deal with the most important miracles of the Orthodox Church: (1) the so-called "renovation of icons" (the process by which seemingly decrepit icons are made to shine, apparently by Divine intervention), (2) making icons or religious images "weep" or "bleed," (3) the spontaneous ignition of candles, or (4) the transformation of water into wine and wine into the blood of Christ.

The most frequently performed experiment is aimed at debunking the first of these "miracles," the apparently magical process by which icons regain their luster. The audience is asked to examine a darkened icon before it is brought on stage. It is then moistened with a special solution, whereupon it becomes bright. The person in charge explains to those who are present that he has simply taken a mixture of alcohol, liquid ammonia, and pure turpentine. When an old icon or oil painting is rubbed with a cloth containing the solution, it becomes "renovated." Alcohol and turpentine wash away the dirt, and liquid ammonia removes the upper layer of paint, which has generally faded and become worn.[46]

Some Soviet experts have expressed misgivings about the utility of arranging such evenings. They argue that people today do not really accept traditional teachings about miracles. Before the Revolution, "when there were many ignorant people in our country, . . . it was easy enough for the 'servants of god' to take advantage of them." But today "such 'miracles' are a rare phenomenon." [47] They are increasingly irrelevant both to clergymen and to believers. Moreover, the performing of physics and chemistry experiments sometimes has become an end in itself. Some propagandists are more interested in entertaining themselves and their audiences than in "unmasking" religion. "Not infrequently," a leading commentator has written, "propagandists resort to showing 'interesting tricks' which have nothing to do with atheist propaganda." [48]

Even if the propagandist performs his task responsibly and skillfully, the audience may reject his antireligious message. The use of science, even graphic demonstrations, will not automatically make an impact on people with a nonscientific frame of mind. Some people accept religious miracles as an article of faith; "after all," they argue, "He is God!"—and their belief is hardly susceptible of scientific examination or refutation.[49]

Discussions of Literary Works

The atheist movement has devised a number of antireligious measures involving discussion of literary works. Some are simple, while others are far more elaborate. They occasionally contain elements of theater, sometimes, it must be said, resembling the theater of the absurd.

In its most elementary form, this approach features a propagandist who reads atheist materials to a group. These materials can be quite varied, from belles lettres, poetry, and drama to items from the daily press or scientific journals. Newspapers seem to be the principal source. One typical exhortation to atheists reads as follows:

Carry newspapers, comrade agitator, to your shop, brigade or group; acquaint your listeners with the articles. Let the incontrovertible documents and facts about the crimes of the sectarians and priests reach the mind and heart of everyone who is misled, who still believes the clergy.[50]

The technique is a simple and easy to understand form of atheist propaganda. Moreover, it can be conducted anywhere, in a factory or farm during a work break, in field camps, in dormitories or in the home, and it requires little or no preparation. This measure is appropriate for audiences of less well-educated persons, housewives, and members of sects forbidden (on religious grounds) to read books or newspapers. Readings are usually arranged over an extended period of time, and propagandists seek to draw their listeners into a discussion of each reading. Because few believers are willing to discuss their religious beliefs publicly with an atheist, the subject of religion usually is introduced slowly and indirectly. Propagandists first read works of fiction or other items that do not have an obvious antireligious bent. They then shift gradually to stories touching on religious themes. Only then will they examine books and articles directly criticizing religion.[51]

The practice of reading aloud has come under increasing challenge as educational levels rise and the network of mass communications expands into more remote areas. Many propagandists question the continued use of this approach, criticizing it as "formalistic" and arguing that it "has long since outlived its day." "A propaganda measure which has proved itself in one era," they maintain, "may turn into pure formalism in another."[52]

Nonetheless, because some people who would not otherwise be exposed to antireligious messages do receive some exposure, the practice is not likely to be abandoned in the near future.

A more sophisticated version of such encounters is the "readers' conference." Organized under the guidance of a librarian, it involves discussion of a book or articles on any subject. When the work or works selected deal with religion and atheism, the readers' conference can become a vehicle for mass atheist propaganda. The conference can serve not only to propagandize antireligious literature but often is "transformed into a serious discussion of the tasks of atheist upbringing, of the need to combat religious survivals and superstitions." [53]

An unusual and sometimes bizarre variation on this practice is known as the "literary trial." Unlike their real-life counterparts, such "trials" involve mock hearings at which characters in works of fiction, "inveterate religious persons," are "tried" and found "guilty" of one or another misdeed. [54] The literary trial is a kind of readers' conference; participants are called upon to read and evaluate a work of literature. But at a literary trial, participants assume formal roles as judge, jury, prosecutor, and witnesses. This play-acting has stimulated a great deal of controversy. Opponents argue that literary trials are more farcical than serious and serve only to degrade the propagandist and his message. To quote one critic,

The comrades who organize "literary trials" do so in order to make antireligious work more interesting and effective. However, one wants to ask: why make a farce out of such a serious undertaking as the discussion of a book? Who needs this? The faithful would not go to see such a comedy; and if they would, their reaction to such a trial can hardly be expected to be positive. It is easy to "condemn" the convictions of a person, especially when he exists only in the pages of a book. But would it benefit the living believer? [55]

The practice seems only to degrade participants and embarrass spectators. Because the potential for gains on the atheist front is so clearly outweighed by costs in time, manpower, and "good will," there is little likelihood that this measure will be retained.

Other Measures

A number of other antireligious practices can also be considered forms of mass oral propaganda. Some are used widely, while others are employed only in a small number of communities. Most of these measures closely resemble those that we have already described. However, two of them are sufficiently distinctive and widely used to warrant our attention. These are "atheist quizzes" and religious show trials.

A number of communities now arrange public contests, "atheist quizzes," in which participants answer a moderator's questions on religion and atheism. These affairs, which are particularly well suited to reaching young people, are instructive both for the contestants and for the audience. Participants, of course, are expected to prepare diligently for a quiz. But the spectators, too, are exposed to the antireligious messages of each question and answer. Questions are selected with a view toward maximizing the educational value of the contest. Rather than test the knowledge of the participants on some of the more arcane aspects of religion or atheism, organizers try to suit questions and answers to the needs of mass antireligious propaganda.[56] Regardless of how well or badly individual contestants do, the Party almost inevitably wins.

A far more heavy-handed propaganda device is the show trial. These are arranged in many localities and usually are given extensive publicity. While such trials are essentially coercive measures, and hence beyond the scope of this study, they serve a significant propaganda function as well. They help to "expose the obscurantist nature" of religious teachings,[57] "expose the 'holiness' and 'infallibility' of clergymen,"[58] and "unmask" the "antisocial activities" of excessively fervent believers. The court proceedings are well attended, and the trial or excerpts from it usually are broadcast over the radio and published in local newspapers. Local residents may even be organized to attend broadcasts of the court proceedings, for example, by assembling in the town square to hear the broadcast over loudspeakers.[59]

Concluding Remarks

None of the mass oral propaganda measures seems to work very well. It has proved extremely difficult to attract believers to them, and if they do attend, they almost always react negatively. Audiences at antireligious functions consist typically of nonbelievers; according to one survey, only about 15 percent of those who attend are believers.[60] Another study has revealed that only 2 percent of the religious population ever attend any atheist affair.[61] Most believers scrupulously avoid these measures. Some regard attendance at "meetings of the impious" as sinful, while others simply seek to avoid offensive and disagreeable encounters.[62] The end result, as former Central Committee Secretary Leonid Ilyichev once observed, is that atheist measures usually reach only those "who have already been liberated from religion." Ilyichev underscored his concern by quoting (perhaps apocryphally) a clergyman from Sverdlovsk.

Antireligious propaganda does not bother us. The atheists work with the atheists in the clubs and we work with the believers in the church. . . . The atheists do not come to us, and the believers do not go to the clubs. We do not interfere with each other.[63]

"Here is a testimonial to our antireligious propaganda," Ilyichev concluded. "One cannot but agree with it."

Even when religious citizens are exposed to mass propaganda measures, they react with indifference, amusement, scorn, or outright hostility. Their reaction is understandable, for the propaganda is ill-conceived and clumsily executed. Some measures that were emphasized in the past are now regarded as inappropriate or harmful, but not all of these have been abandoned. The approaches that have been retained do not offer much more promise than those that have been rejected.

Evidence from the recent past, however, suggests that persistent criticism of mass oral propaganda techniques is having an effect. Ideological authorities have acknowledged the errors and shortcomings of mass measures and have begun to make certain improvements. More important, they have begun to focus their energies on a radically different approach. This approach, which involves personal, face-to-face conversations with individual believers, offers considerably more promise of success than the tactics we have discussed so far. It is to this technique that we now turn.

7 Individual Work

The foreign defenders of religion assert that any attack on religion is an insult to the feelings of believers and a violation of the freedom of conscience. But this is completely untrue. Not every piece of advice to a person that he change his opinion in some way or even his behavior need be insulting to him. Let us imagine the following case. You are walking along the road and meet a man who asks you how to get to some village or other. You calmly explain to him that he is going in the wrong direction and that he must go in the opposite direction and describe in detail how to get there. Surely there is nothing insulting in explanations of this sort?

Selskaya zhizn, March 10, 1972

. . . is it appropriate for one who is studying, say, psychology, to make a visit to a stranger's house and observe therein how the family talks, takes its meals, quarrels, makes up, or watches television? No, and such an idea would scarcely come into one's head. A visit to a church is also a tactless invasion of the inner world of a group of people. Such an act would offend their feelings. . . .

Uchitelskaya gazeta, November 12, 1973

Ideological specialists have long recognized that believers avoid antireligious functions. Only recently, however, have they begun to mobilize the resources needed to reach these people. Part of this new emphasis involves arranging atheist lectures at times and places that are convenient for housewives, pensioners, and others who have always remained outside the influence of mass measures.[1] But such efforts are still more the exception than the norm. Mass antireligious propaganda continues to be conducted primarily at industrial enterprises, where it does not influence those who "need" it most. To reach these people, the Party has devised an elaborate and far-reaching program of "individual work."

Individual work, which involves direct, face-to-face discussions between atheists and individual believers, is not an entirely new technique. Even the League of the Militant Godless, whose primary responsibility was to organize mass atheist measures, encouraged its members to propagandize on a personal level. A decision adopted in 1926 obliged each member of the League to work with his family and friends, while a resolution of the League's Second Congress (1929) directed local units to select and train the most promising propagandists to conduct individual work. By and large, however, these demands were ignored. Few atheists were qualified (or felt themselves qualified) to do the job, and the League regarded work with individuals or small groups as a luxury it could not afford. To be sure, the *antireligiozniki* did devote greater attention to individual work in the years immediately preceding World War II. Special commissions on individual propaganda were even set up by some of the local Godless cells. But most of these were only paper organizations, and the value of individual work continued to be underrated until the Khrushchev era.[2]

In 1960, the Party Central Committee called for the "wide-scale" use of individual forms of propaganda, "in order to reach every Soviet person, to promote his ideological growth, and to struggle concretely and practically against vestiges of capitalism in people's minds."[3] This demand has been implemented vigorously. In the decade since it was promulgated, individual work has become one of the most widely used forms of antireligious propaganda. Hundreds of thousands of atheist agitators have been recruited and trained, and they are now working in virtually every city, town, and village of the USSR.

Much as the Narodniki a century ago went directly to "backward" peasants in an attempt to awaken them politically, the Party today has mobilized its cadres to persuade "misguided" believers of the virtues of scientific atheism. Although the available evidence suggests that today's propagandists and agitators are no more successful than were their Narodnik predecessors in the nineteenth century, professional atheists are confident that the future will bring dramatic success.

They argue that changes in Soviet society have made individual work increasingly relevant as an instrument of atheist propaganda. Religious belief is no longer determined by general social factors, such as poverty and exploitation. Today it is essentially an individual response to individual circumstances. In order to combat religion, then, it is necessary to concentrate on the distinctive characteristics of each individual believer.[4]

The advantages of individual work are clear. Most important, it exposes believers to propaganda messages they would otherwise avoid. Moreover, these messages can be adapted to each individual. No two believers are alike; the character and intensity of their religious views, as well as their openness to atheist propaganda, vary considerably. Individual work minimizes the problem of *shablon* (stereotyped thinking), which is so pervasive in other areas of antireligious propaganda. The atheist can experiment with various approaches and styles, emphasizing whatever seems to have the greatest impact on "his" believer. He can present his own views, while challenging and criticizing the believer's arguments.

Individual work also permits extended and (it is hoped) close contact with a particular believer. While lecturers speak to an audience they have never met before and will never see again, the atheist conducting individual work will continue to have contact with "his" believer. Indeed, continuity is possible even if the believer moves. When this happens, atheists are supposed to contact the appropriate Party or Komsomol organization in the city he moves to and report on the progress they have had in working with him.[5]

Finally, individual discussions can be conducted anywhere and at any time—during work breaks, on the way to or from work, or whenever an opportunity is present. Even such an inconsequential event as a thunderstorm can provide the resourceful agitaton with an opportunity to combat religion. Because some believers apparently still regard thunder, lightning, and other natural phenomena as manifestations of the anger and strength of God, merely providing an elementary science lesson can serve an antireligious purpose.[6]

Recruiting and Assigning Atheist Agitators
In theory, it is the responsibility of every Party member and every conscientious citizen to conduct individual work with believers. "Each atheist should be an active atheist" is a theme repeated endlessly. Atheists are constantly urged to challenge the religious beliefs of their friends and neighbors, "to struggle for each person," "to free [believers] . . . from their religious prejudices," "to rouse them from their religious sleep," according to the more colloquial language of the Soviet press.[7] A typical exhortation reads as follows:

Every communist, wherever he works, whatever his occupation, has at his disposal one or another means for combating religion. The responsibility of the communist is to be a militant atheist, an active fighter for the purity of Soviet socialist ideology, for the complete eradication of religious prejudices and superstitions.[8]

If all atheists would only conduct individual work with religious relatives, it has been suggested, "the clerics would have a bad time of it. Religious prejudices would soon be removed from every corner of our daily life." [9]

But few citizens, including Party members, respond to the call. While a Communist is in theory a militant materialist, he is in practice a man with many responsibilities and interests. Most Party members are unable or unwilling to spend time in lengthy, complicated, and often frustrating discussions with believers. Indeed, only 10 percent of all atheists try to convert their own religious relatives, and an even smaller percentage voluntarily work with other believers.[10] Most atheists remain passive, preferring to leave antireligious propaganda to those with professional skills and training.

While the authorities continue to encourage all atheists to volunteer their efforts (two *Pravda* correspondents have complained about "the ingrained prejudice" that atheist work "supposedly is the obligation only of specialists in this field"), they have also taken steps to professionalize the corps of atheist agitators.[11] Dissatisfied with the number of volunteers (and with their performance as well), local Party organizations have begun to assign Communists and Komsomols to conduct individual work with believers. They try to find people with "businesslike qualities" and "experience in life," people who "enjoy great authority" among their fellow workers.[12] Because many believers regard religion as the only source of morality, atheists who are designated to perform individual work must be above reproach morally. (Anyone assigned to individual work simply because he is an atheist will find it difficult to gain the respect of "his" believer and may even reinforce the latter's attachment to religion.)[13]

The people assigned to conduct individual work, like those engaged in other forms of antireligious propaganda, tend to be schoolteachers, students, librarians, doctors, nurses, pensioners, and former believers or clergymen. The overwhelming majority, upward of 80 percent, are schoolteachers.[14] Of all professional groups in the USSR, they are probably best suited by temperament and training to succeed in this work. As a Smolensk specialist has put it, teachers have "pedagogical tact, the ability to deal with people and enjoy the population's respect and authority." [15] In rural areas, where religious beliefs and practices are most widespread, schoolteachers constitute virtually the entire intelligentsia. Moreover, because they are likely to have had some background in antireligious propaganda (the "Fundamentals of Scientific Atheism" course was made obligatory for students in pedagogical institutes in 1964), they represent a natural choice for conducting individual work.

The process by which atheists are assigned to particular believers is sometimes random and arbitrary; at other times it is carefully planned and implemented. The problem involves not only a lack of competent, trained cadres but also official disagreement on certain basic questions. Perhaps the most crucial unresolved question is whether or not the atheist should know the believer to whom he is assigned. Some ideological authorities say that individual work should be conducted only by the believer's friends or relatives, while others (emphasizing that it is a task for professionals) advocate that a complete stranger be assigned to each believer.[16] The advantages and disadvantages of each point of view are clear. Friends and/or relatives are likely to be familiar with the believer's religious views, as well as the kinds of arguments to which he or she might be vulnerable.

But friends and relatives may be *too* close to the believer. Both believer and atheist would probably find individual work totally out of keeping with their previous relationship. Neither would want to jeopardize this relationship by introducing such a contentious subject. A stranger, on the other hand, will have to invest time getting to know the believer before he can introduce the issue of religion. But, if he is an accomplished worker or professional, he should be able to win the respect of the believer without much difficulty. His status as an authority figure, more a respected colleague than an intimate friend, should be an asset when he begins to challenge the believer's religious notions.

Those conducting individual work should know, or should get to know, not only the believer but his family, friends, and neighbors as well. They can play a major supporting role, providing the agitator with pertinent information and at the same time serving as his agent in dealing with the believer. (It may, of course, be necessary to conduct a certain amount of individual work with these other people in order to obtain their cooperation.) The proper approach has been described succinctly by an experienced agitator: ". . . you begin discussions with those around the believer, and then gradually establish contact with the believer himself." [17] The atheist will try, step by step, to develop a close relationship with the believer and engage him in conversation about his religion and the merits of scientific atheism.

The assignment of an agitator can be done in such a way as to encourage rapport and effective communication. Whenever possible, female atheists are chosen to work with religious women, and older atheists are mobilized to work with middle-aged and elderly believers. Although no evidence has been cited to support this view, it is widely accepted that a female atheist can, more readily than a man, "find a common language" with a religious woman.[18] It is equally widely believed, this time with a good deal of corroborating evidence, that younger atheists find it almost impossible to gain the respect of older believers. Young people conducting individual work tend to be presumptuous, impatient, and disrespectful. In their desire to "unmask" or refute religious doctrines that a believer may have accepted for decades, they usually manage only to amuse or anger him.[19] A careful choice of cadres is particularly important in dealing with Moslems, because Islam lays great stress on respect for the elderly. Indeed, a leading authority on Islam has suggested that those who conduct individual work among Moslems be of the same nationality and speak the same language as the believer. Otherwise, he argues, the believer might feel that the atheist is simply criticizing Islam while remaining silent about his own religion.[20]

Whatever the merits of this logic, the lack of trained personnel (women, older atheists, and people capable of conducting work among Moslems) has meant assigning atheists who are not always well suited to work with "their" believers.

The establishment of friendly relations with a believer is designed to do more than merely set the stage for future discussions of religion. It is thought to have an antireligious impact in and of itself. The prevailing view is that religious people are basically lonely, even if they seem to have friends. The friendship of an atheist agitator is regarded as somehow more genuine and meaningful than the friendship of fellow believers. According to the official logic, contact with an atheist helps to undercut a believer's need for religion by making him more secure. It has a healthy, "socialist" influence on him, *automatically* prodding him toward atheism. If he can establish roots on earth, Soviet authorities claim,

. . . the believer will feel that he is not alone, that his fate is not a matter of indifference to his associates: he will understand that he has genuine friends around him, to whom he can bare his soul, share his thoughts and doubts, tell what he has stored up within himself during the years of religious life.[21]

This line of reasoning reveals a striking misconception of religious people and has led the atheist movement to waste a good deal of energy. Religious people are viewed as lonely and sullen, almost desperate to unburden themselves of their doubts and anxieties. Despite the implausibility of this view, and despite the lack of evidence to support it, it remains one of the principal theoretical underpinnings for individual work.

Communicating with the Believer

Questions of religion are supposed to be introduced gradually and indirectly, while the atheist attempts to gain the believer's respect and affection. The agitator is advised to observe his new companion and, when appropriate, to offer advice or assistance. A helpful word, "simple human attention at the right moment," is said to be "of far greater influence than an official invitation to listen to the next talk." [22] Those assigned to conduct individual work are encouraged to "penetrate deeply into the 'trivial matters' in the life of every family" to whom they are assigned.[23] By demonstrating solicitude, they can win the believer's trust and through this trust can reduce people's reliance on the clergy. Thus, if there has been a death in the family, the agitator can provide aid and comfort.[24] (It seems not to have occurred to the antireligious authorities that bereaved families might appreciate the efforts of a priest as well.) At other times, too, agitators will stop off at a believer's home under various pretexts. "In agitation, as in medicine," one atheist has commented, "it is necessary not only to treat illnesses, but, more important, to prevent them." [25] While the agitator is supposed to demonstrate that he is a devoted friend, his principal responsibility is to watch the believer, to deter him from going to church, or practicing his religion in any other way.

Precisely when to turn the discussion toward religion requires sensitivity and good timing. While some atheists can sense when the time is right, others have never acquired this skill. There are even agitators who deal only with noncontroversial matters until the believer (perhaps wavering in his faith and seeking reinforcement for his growing doubts) introduces the topic of religion.[26] Because this rarely happens, the atheist usually has to take the initiative.

When he sees what he regards as an opening, he will begin to probe his companion's religious beliefs. At first he will encounter resistance, no matter how much time and effort he invested in the early stages of the relationship. For a while, precisely how long is unclear, the agitator's arguments are likely "to bounce off his [the believer's] consciousness like peas off a wall." [27] The believer will defend his own views, while criticizing those of the atheist. (Indeed, some believers even try to convert the atheists assigned to work with them.)[28] Their recalcitrance, it is said, will eventually be eroded; few people can remain impervious to the repeated questioning and pointed observations of a skilled atheist. A breakthrough and a victory for scientific atheism are inevitable. As one propagandist has described the process,

. . . you speak with people and it seems that you argue something pretty well, but they do not agree with everything you have said. The next time you approach the very same question from another side; you find new, more convincing facts. You return again and again to the same doubts which the believers retain . . . the results of such discussions are telling.[29]

Thus, the psychological and intellectual defenses of all but the most fervent believers can be worn down. A different "key" is required to reach each of these people, and it is the agitator's task to find it.

Problems

There is an immense, perhaps unbridgeable, gap between the theory of individual work and the way it is actually conducted. The system distresses agitators and infuriates believers.

The very fact that an agitator has been assigned to "enlighten" or "reeducate" him is likely to alienate a believer and make him impervious to the atheist's arguments. Nadezhda Krupskaya pointed out in 1928 that "Only when a worker feels that he is not regarded as an object of agitation, but [rather] as a comrade . . . will he be open to persuasion."[30] While her point is no less valid today, her advice has been ignored. It does not take long for most believers to become aware that they have been sought out. Once they recognize the artificiality of the relationship, they turn their backs on their new "friends."[31] While their unreceptiveness is a source of concern to the atheist movement, it is sometimes dismissed with the observation that believers' minds have been "clouded by religion." The point is crucial, however; just as religious people try to avoid mass atheist measures, they try to avoid agitators assigned to them. As one specialist in individual work has put it, "The whole problem with our work is that believers do not seek us . . . but . . . [instead] we must seek them out."[32]

In order to succeed, the atheist must pursue and prod the believer; but that is precisely what infuriates religious people. They tend to be troubled by the agitator's initial approach and become increasingly resentful as he tries to develop a more intimate relationship. Extended contact with an atheist agitator eventually leads to an open challenge, an unwanted assault on someone's cherished beliefs. The agitator may strive to be a teacher, but his students are almost always unwilling to "learn."

Establishing contact with religious people is awkward and difficult, involving problems not encountered by propagandists specializing in other areas. Those who explain foreign policy decisions, agitate for increased economic productivity, or denounce crime and alcoholism can be vigorous, even combative, with their audiences. They need not be concerned about insulting drunkards, criminals, imperialists, or other evildoers. Professional atheists, on the other hand, have to be more discreet, for religious people cannot (or should not) be handled rudely.[33] Books and articles aimed at practitioners constantly caution against impatience, urging respect for the believer's feelings. "Hit-and-run attacks," "storming," "crash methods," "drill-sergeants' tactics," and "cavalry charge methods" are to be assiduously avoided.[34]

Individual work has been described as "a ticklish affair"; "one careless step, and everything is ruined."[35] But not all propagandists who are involved in it have the requisite tact or patience. There cannot be many who are as foolish as the Udmurt atheist who visited a believer's house and announced: "I have come to conduct antireligious propaganda with you."[36] But most atheists underestimate the intellectual abilities or emotional involvement of religious people. Out of naïveté, incompetence, or impatience, they often set out to destroy "their" believer's religious views with a single conversation. This "primitivism," as it is termed by more sophisticated authorities, does far more harm than good. Not only does it alienate the believer at whom it is directed, but it serves to discredit scientific atheism in general. An assault on someone's religious convictions is likely to stir deep-seated passions. If they are ever to be undermined, the job must be done with patience and tact.[37]

Given these circumstances, it is understandable that few atheists volunteer for individual work. Some feel awkward about approaching strangers and establishing an artificial relationship. Others regard people's religious beliefs as their private affair. Still others consider themselves inadequately trained to take on believers in a one-to-one situation; they prefer the security of the podium and the lectern. Many who try to conduct individual work do the job badly and, having been rebuffed, become disconsolate or angry. They either withdraw into apathy and thereafter ignore their antireligious responsibilities or else resort to name-calling and "primitivism." [38]

While Party organizations would prefer to assign only well-trained and experienced propagandists to conduct individual work, a lack of qualified cadres makes this impossible. It has been necessary to resort to makeshift arrangements, using people unfamiliar with the theory and practice of antireligious propaganda. They are enrolled in special training programs, are aided by more experienced atheists in preparing for talks, and are closely supervised and controlled until they achieve a certain level of competence. But they are seldom good enough to do well.

They are encouraged to learn about religious doctrines and practices and to develop their communications skills as well. Only through careful and systematic study can an atheist understand the psychology of religious belief, or, as it has been termed, "the stratagems with which the clergy entangle people's minds." [39] And only by practicing the art of persuasion can he develop the skills needed to succeed with "his" believer. Formal class work is therefore supplemented by practical work, lectures, conferences, correspondence courses, and exposure to specialized publications. The journals *Agitator* and *Nauka i religiya* regularly carry methodological advice for atheists, and the Institute of Scientific Atheism has compiled a handbook for local agitators to follow. They outline the principal theme for each discussion, suggest specific questions and answers, and recommend literature for study prior to each talk.[40]

Still, most atheists involved in individual work continue to be woefully lacking in formal training. Very few have more than a superficial understanding of religion, atheism, or propaganda. Students enrolled in

training course are usually assigned to work with believers before complet-
ing the basic course, when they are hardly likely to be polished propagandists. In fact, only a small proportion of atheists who complete one of the
various training programs are capable of conducting individual work. Most
lack the knowledge, skill, or self-confidence needed to succeed.[41]

Effectiveness

Individual discussions, which would seem to offer a particularly effective
vehicle for challenging people's religious views, have not, in fact, proved
very useful. We have already dealt with some of the problems confronting
the atheist agitator, but there are other reasons for doubting the efficacy of
this approach. We will examine four of these. Our remarks are offered here
in outline form only; the question of the effectiveness of the antireligious
effort in general is treated in Chapter 8.

First, while professional atheists are enthusiastic about the potential
value of individual work, they do not yet know which believers are most
likely to yield to it. According to one school of thought, individual work is
most appropriate for those who resist mass propaganda measures most
vigorously. Because these believers are especially stubborn, they can be
persuaded to change their views only through intensive, extended discussions. A second group of atheists takes the opposite position, arguing that
individual work be directed primarily at those who are wavering in their
faith. Because the convictions of these believers are far from firm, they
would seem to be particularly susceptible to resocialization through
personal attention. Adherents of the former view try to convert the leaders
of local religious organizations and, with their help, persuade others in the
congregation to renounce their convictions. The second group focuses its
attention on the less committed believers, the so-called "reserves." [42]
Neither approach seems to work very well. Indeed, the uncertainty
surrounding the very purpose and applicability of individual work has
probably limited its effectiveness.

Second, because religious beliefs are among the most intimate and
deep-seated aspects of a person's makeup, it seems likely that they would be
among the least susceptible to change. It is extremely difficult to modify a
person's belief on any matter. And, according to Western social scientists,
the task becomes even more difficult when especially salient beliefs are
involved. Therefore the Soviet assumption that intensive efforts at persuasion, even if continued over a protracted period of time, are bound to
undermine a believer's religious notions is open to serious challenge.

A third reason for doubting the effectiveness of individual work involves the very nature of religious belief. Religious people accept some things on faith, and what someone accepts on faith does not lend itself to rational dispute. There is no common ground between faith and reason that will permit the atheist to persuade someone of the groundlessness of faith. "Our pet device," one atheist has written, "is to point to the Bible's contradictions and absurdities." But, he added,

It has been brought to us more than once that even aptly noted contradictions do not shake the foundations of faith. After all, faith rests not on reason, but on feelings, on emotions. Man believes because he wants to believe. He sees in religion what he wants to see! Once several years ago I conscientiously set forth all the "contradictions" for Auntie Varya. She answered me with words from the Bible: "The foolishness of God is wiser than wisdom turned away from or turned against God!" [43]

"Just try to argue with that!", he concluded with obvious exasperation. The incident he reported is not an isolated case. Indeed, it seems to be typical.

The fourth reason for questioning the utility of individual work is more difficult to define. Soviet writings on antireligious tactics, which usually are rich in details of approach, emphasis, and rebuttal, are curiously incomplete when they describe successes in individual work. The fact that they say so little about the actual conversion mechanism makes one wonder about their authenticity. Two examples will make this clear. The first describes a young woman who joined a religious group.

Having learned of this, the director of the local school . . . began to conduct talks with her about the achievements of Soviet science, about interesting books and films, about the best people in the collective farm and the district. The teacher told the girl many times about how science explains the origin of life on earth, about the structure of the universe, about the development of human society, about unusual natural phenomena.

In order to extend the girl's knowledge, [the agitator] . . . acquainted her with atheist literature, showed her step by step how she erred, tried to reveal the true face of those who were deceiving her.

And then a turning-point came. Now [the young woman] . . . has become one of the most advanced workers in the collective farm. . . . [44]

The second example involves another woman belonging to a community of Seventh-Day Adventists.

One of the workers from the Department of Propaganda and Agitation of the district party committee resolved to change her views: he held many discussions with her on the contents of biblical writings. The first time she talked reluctantly: each of the atheist's arguments was given a "hostile reception." Then, under the pressure of irrefutable scientific data, and also having discovered the blindness and contradictions of the "holy scriptures" themselves, she . . . became more reasonable. . . . Eventually, she broke with religion. . . . [45]

These descriptions are strikingly unilluminating. They fail to come to grips with the key issue of *how* the conversions actually occurred, and give rise to a number of unanswered questions. Should success be attributed to the introduction of some crucial fact or argument or to the cumulative impact of discussions that may have gone on for years? Does conversion involve a gradual erosion of religious belief, or do believers suddenly and dramatically renounce their views? Is it necessary to introduce new facts, or does success lie in constant repetition of the same message? When does "the pressure of irrefutable scientific data," with which most believers are already familiar, produce a loss of faith? How can some believers acknowledge contradictions in the Bible or Koran while still retaining their belief in God? Atheists who record their experiences merely note that they cited certain arguments whose validity was so overpowering that the believer's resistance collapsed. Why this happens only sometimes, or whether it happens at all, is not clear.

The fact that so little is said about the dynamics of the transition from religiousness to atheism can be interpreted in a number of ways. (1) It may mean that atheist agitators are not sufficiently knowledgeable about psychology and learning theory to understand, much less explain, how the believer is transformed into an atheist. (2) It may mean that the agitator has deluded himself, believing that he has succeeded when, in fact, he has not. (3) There may be an element of conscious deception. When writing for other agitators, whom he presumably wishes to inspire, he may exaggerate his successes. (4) It may be that the believer, growing weary of the atheist's harangue, will feign agreement with him or her. By pretending to have rejected religion, he can rid himself of an omnipresent, importunate, and unwanted "friend."

Whatever the reasons, the fact remains that accounts of successful individual work do not ring true. They seem almost fictional. The improbable scenarios belong more to the realm of socialist realism than to the real world. Experience with individual work has been disappointing at best, and one wonders whether it can ever fulfill the hopes of its supporters.

8 An Assessment

... despite all the efforts by theologians to preserve religion and to keep
the people's consciousness the prisoner of fancy, the laws of the development of human society doom religion to destruction. Sooner or later reason
will finally triumph over ignorance.

Sovetskaya Rossia, March 1, 1972

We have lived through the epoch of the suppression of the masses; we are
now living through the epoch of the suppression of the individual in the
name of the masses.

Evgeny Zamyatin (1919)

Any attempt to assess the Soviet effort to eradicate religion involves a
number of problems. First, the available sources are often unreliable: some
are tendentious, others are uninformed, while still others are deliberately
misleading. Official Soviet commentaries tend to be superficial and biased,
describing isolated events in ambiguous language. Survey data gathered in
one area of the USSR are sometimes presented, without warrant, as
representative of conditions elsewhere. Similarly, refugee accounts and the
observations of Westerners who have visited the USSR are often flawed.
Many are excessively cynical and hostile, while others are too credulous
and naïve. Commentators are sometimes so anxious to condemn or laud
Soviet policy that they fail to analyze carefully all the evidence or even
notice that certain data are lacking.

Second, it has proved difficult to devise an unambiguous definition of
religiousness. Church attendance and participation in religious rites are not
always an expression of religious convictions. What is to some an indicator
of religiousness may be to others simply a family or national tradition.
Soviet studies indicate that more people perform religious rituals, celebrate
religious holy days, and hang icons in their homes than attend church
services, pray to God, or believe in an afterlife. Only some of these citizens
are religious; others are uncertain about their religious views, and some
may even be atheists. Many people, for example, participate in religious
rites "to be on the safe side," because "it is the custom," or because of
parental pressure.[1] They may combine religious and secular rituals, e.g.,
baptizing an infant and also taking part in secular ceremonies celebrating
the birth of a child, or getting married both in church and in a wedding
palace. People in particularly remote areas may even combine modernity
with pagan ritual. The Ulchey (one of the most backward nationalities in
the USSR) sometimes place a red star or some other modern Soviet emblem

at gravesites, but they also leave fragments of a sled or skis for the souls of the deceased to use in the afterlife.[2]

Finally, it is difficult to establish a causal link between the Party's antireligious programs and the decline of religious belief among citizens of the USSR. While the fact that religion has lost much of its hold on the population cannot be denied, it may have nothing to do with the efforts of the atheist movement. The experience of other societies suggests that industrialization, urbanization, and scientific and educational progress may themselves bring about a secularization of life.[3] If the industrial revolution does not actually require secularization, it certainly seems to stimulate trends in that direction. Because noncommunist countries without any official atheist movement have witnessed a decline in religiousness, we cannot automatically attribute the decline of religion in the USSR to such a movement. Even if the Party had made no effort to combat religious belief, social and economic progress over the past half century might well have undermined the church's influence.

Assessing the contribution of atheist propaganda to the overall antireligious effort involves additional problems. Two are particularly important.

1. *The presence of other antireligious weapons.* It is very difficult to isolate the influence of propaganda, because it is often combined with coercion or the threat of coercion. Indeed, the Party's antireligious efforts are a classic example of what has been termed "coercive persuasion."[4] Violence and the threat of violence have helped to reduce people's outward commitment to religion and may thereby have undermined their religious beliefs as well. At the very least, instances of job loss, dismissal from a university, public ridicule, and the application of other kinds of coercive measures obviously deter people from professing religious beliefs. Moreover, many clergymen have been executed or imprisoned since the Revolution, and most of the others have suffered from official harassment. The government has interfered with the recruitment of new clergy and has placed severe restrictions on those who remain.[5] These measures have, of course, limited the church's access to the masses.

2. *The unreliable character of success indicators.* The four kinds of evidence generally used to demonstrate the effectiveness or ineffectiveness of propaganda—responsive action, participant reports, observer commentaries, and indirect indicators—are not well suited to assessing Soviet atheist propaganda.[6] While it is easy to find pertinent materials, their value is often questionable.

The Soviet media describe countless instances of people renouncing religion, allegedly in response to atheist propaganda. In addition, both believers and atheists regularly pay tribute in the press to the power of antireligious propaganda. Various indirect indicators, such as the closing of churches or a reduction in the number of church weddings, are also cited by Soviet authorities as evidence of successful propaganda. But there are serious problems of source credibility; at the very least, the evidence cited is generally susceptible of more than one interpretation. The link between propaganda messages and individual responses is usually only asserted and is almost never demonstrated. Indeed, one sometimes wonders if the link has not been invented. Extravagant claims of instantaneous conversion are implausible at best and sometimes border on the absurd.

After Yuri Gagarin's first flight in space, for example, one believer is said to have remarked: "Now I am convinced that god is science, is man! Yuri Gagarin overcame all the faith in heavenly power that I had in my soul." [7] Another believer is said to have reacted similarly to a discussion with an atheist: "I believed in the power of god for many years, but now I am convinced that it is not god, but man, who is the master of science and is capable of such miracles." [8] Still another believer, having read for the first time a Soviet criticism of the Bible, allegedly was moved to declare: "I heard from my parents . . . that the Bible is a holy book . . . and . . . I felt reverence for it; but now, having heard extracts from it, I have lost this sense, and I see nothing holy in it; it is simply a book of fairy tales and fiction." [9] Accounts of this kind strain the credulity of the reader. In fact, they give rise to doubts about more modest claims that might otherwise have seemed credible.

Soviet efforts to devise quantitative indexes of successful propaganda have not been successful. Ideological specialists traditionally have sought merely to fulfill quantitative plans for the publication or presentation of antireligious propaganda, and even now an increase in the number of atheist articles or measures is usually interpreted as evidence of more effective propaganda.[10] While this approach is obviously inappropriate (to identify exposure with effectiveness is at best dubious), it is widely practiced. Similarly, a reduction in the number of people who attend church or celebrate holy days, or the closing of a certain number of churches, may be attributed to effective propaganda, even if this has been brought about by official pressure and intimidation.[11]

In 1960, the Party Central Committee criticized those who were "preoccupied with the outward aspect of propaganda," and demanded instead that indoctrinational efforts be judged by their results.[12] Party organizations throughout the country discussed the Central Committee's criticism and echoed its demands. One provincial party secretary put the matter colorfully: ". . . you judge the hunter not by the number of shots, but by the number of squirrels he brings down." In evaluating propaganda, he explained, "we should look not at the number of lectures delivered or at the number of those listening to them; we should consider first of all whether we have convinced people, [see] what kind of imprint our lectures have left on their minds. . . ." [13]

A decade of discussion and criticism has not ended the practice. As recently as 1971, *Kommunist Tadzhikistana* reminded its readers that the effectiveness of an atheist's work cannot be measured by the number of lectures or talks he gives. If quantitative indicators are to be a valid guide in judging propaganda, the newspaper pointed out, the atheist should count "the number of people he has released from religious fetters, the actual number he has helped liberate from the harmful influence of the church." [14] While this suggestion has some merit, it also involves problems. Perhaps most important, it would not yield very impressive figures. As a Moscow atheist has observed, "we gauge the number of atheist measures by the hundreds, but victories in the struggle for man by ones and tens." [15]

How Many People Are Religious?

Religious belief and behavior clearly have not disappeared from the USSR. However, inasmuch as no comprehensive statistics on church membership are published by either religious or secular authorities, it is not possible to determine precisely how widespread religious views are today. The last official nationwide survey of religious belief (included in the 1937 census) was never made public, apparently because it revealed the presence of too many believers.[16] Since that time, leading academic specialists on atheism have recommended that such a study be undertaken once again.[17] Nothing has come of their proposals. In fact, the Chairman of the USSR Council of Ministers' Council for Religious Affairs has defended the absence of census questions dealing with religion as "one of the conditions for ensuring freedom of conscience in the USSR." [18]

There has been some empirical research into the nature and extent of religious belief in the past decade, but the published results frequently are of questionable value. While some studies are methodologically sound, others are completely unscientific. The sampling procedures and interview schedules that are used are not always made clear, and when they are, they often fall short of methodological rigor. Many of the studies appear to serve more of an inspirational than an informative function, and even the most scholarly Soviet literature on religion usually contains an element of propaganda. Because Westerners cannot carry out their own empirical research in the USSR, any effort to gauge the strength of religion there must be highly tentative.

Soviet studies usually count as religious only those who claim to be "convinced believers," sometimes ignoring a group of at least equal size who are agnostic or who waver in their faith. Moreover, not everyone is honest in talking with a pollster. Given the nature of the topic and the sanctions available to the Soviet authorities, people's answers to questions about their religious beliefs should be treated as highly suspect. Thus, the Western analyst must be concerned with the possibility of disingenuousness on the part of both the pollster and the respondent.

According to the estimates of Soviet scholars, between 15 and 30 percent of the total population believe in God.[19] Sample surveys published during the last decade are roughly consistent with these estimates, although a wide range of results has been reported. In general, surveys indicate that the incidence of religious belief is far greater in the countryside than in urban areas. Polls of urban dwellers show an incidence of 10 to 20 percent, while in rural districts, perhaps a third of the population are believers.[20] Thus a 1967 poll of Kazan citizens eighteen years of age and older showed that 21 percent of those questioned believed in God, while a 1970 survey of Pskov revealed that only 12 to 13 percent of the city's residents considered themselves believers.[21] The most comprehensive study of religion in rural areas (conducted in 1965–1967 in the Voronezh countryside) found 12 percent of the population to be "convinced believers," while another 16 percent expressed belief in "some kind of supernatural forces." [22]

Table 8.1   Estimated Number of Believers (1964)

Religious Group	Number
Russian Orthodox	35,000,000
Moslems	15,000,000
Old Believers	5,000,000
Evangelical Christian Baptists	4,000,000
Roman Catholics	3,500,000
Lutherans	900,000
Jews	500,000
Calvinists	90,000
Mennonites	10,000
Total	64,000,000

Source: Paul B. Anderson, testimony before the Subcommittee on Europe, Committee on Foreign Affairs, U.S. House of Representatives, 88th Congress, Second Session, *Recent Developments in the Soviet Bloc*, Part I (January 27–30, 1964), pp. 100–101.

The most authoritative Western estimate has been advanced by Paul B. Anderson, a leading Western student of religion in the Soviet Union. Anderson suggested in 1964 that approximately 64 million Soviet citizens, or 28 percent of the population, could be classified as religious. Table 8.1 gives his estimate of the size of the major religious groups found in the Soviet Union.

Why Religion Remains

Many factors stimulate or reinforce religious belief. Ten are particularly important in helping to offset the Party's atheist efforts.

1. To some extent, the Soviet leadership has deliberately sought to preserve religion in the USSR. This argument can take two forms, both of which rely heavily on intuition and surmise. On the one hand, it can be argued, the regime has had to exercise restraint despite its hostility to religion. It has feared alienating the vast numbers of citizens who profess faith in God. Organized religion, particularly the Orthodox Church, has invariably approved official initiatives at home and abroad, and the regime finds its support useful. Moreover, according to this point of view, antireligious excesses would be costly in terms of international good will. Because the presence of religious organizations and citizens serves the Party's interests, then, there is reason to believe that there has been a measure of official tolerance.

On the other hand, some who point to official indulgence of organized religion have seen this support as basically pernicious. This line is associated most closely with the Albanians. According to these sources, the Soviets' desire to preserve religion in the USSR has become "an irrational passion of the revisionists," one which has "penetrated deep" into their "ideological arsenal." Echoing Marx and Engels on the role of religion under capitalism, the Albanians accuse the Soviet authorities of using religion as "holy water with which to sprinkle [their] demands and satisfy the reactionary forces," and as an "opium for the working masses." [23] "Like the Pope," one accusation reads, "Brezhnev and his company preserve religion as a means of 'calming' the souls of the people they rule." At the same time, they promote rivalries within Soviet society and thereby keep their enemies divided. The Party thus is able "to separate the people . . . from the acute problems of the time, to leave them confused politically and to educate them with the concepts of Christian subordination in order to further facilitate the domination and the oppression of the people." [24] By nourishing several churches, the CPSU can keep Soviet society "as ideologically confused and heterogeneous as possible," and thus promote "the return of the revisionist cliques to capitalism." [25]

While the Albanian claims clearly are exaggerated, the available evidence does indicate a certain level of official tolerance of religion. While it has varied over time, and continues to vary from denomination to denomination, this support has contributed to the continued existence of religious beliefs and practices.

2. Many people turn to religion to escape from their personal or family burdens. Overwhelmed by the dreariness of their lives, concerned about "everyday difficulties, painful experiences, and misfortunes in their personal lives," they seek relief in the church's promise of future bliss.[26] This process was manifested most dramatically during World War II. The extraordinary suffering that Soviet citizens experienced during the war stimulated a revival of religious feelings. As two leading authorities have pointed out,

. . . the war brought grief to millions of families which suffered heavy losses, experienced suffering and disaster, the horror of the Hitler regime in temporarily occupied territories. The bitter taste of losses, concern for the fate of relatives, the breakdown in customary forms of daily life—all these changes gave the sectarians an opportunity to significantly consolidate their position.[27]

But while war provides the most dramatic example, it is nonetheless true that anyone who is downcast, insecure, troubled, or frightened may seek in religion a release from his burdens.

3. It is also clear that certain individuals are particularly attracted to religion for psychological and emotional reasons. While Soviet scholars are only beginning to explore the psychology of religious belief, there is already considerable evidence that some people are more susceptible than others to the appeals of religion.[28] For example, many are attracted to the emotional side of religion, i.e., its rituals, ceremonies, and music. In view of this, Leonid Ilyichev, Khrushchev's principal adviser on ideology, once remarked,

. . . the church, especially in the provinces, still attracts people by the pomp and beauty of religious ceremonies. . . . The music of Mozart, Tchaikovsky, Beethoven, and other composers is often performed during ceremonies . . . more and more attention is devoted to choir music. Architecture and painting are widely used to intensify the emotional effect of religion. Orthodox hierarchs say that the person praying in a temple ". . . satisfies his religious mood . . . and his aesthetic feelings in the splendor of the temple and the beauty of the service." [29]

Besides the aesthetic and emotional elements, there are also intellectual and moral dimensions to religion's appeal. Religion satisfies some people's innate need for answers to unanswerable questions. The less educated, who lack the scientific knowledge necessary to refute religious teachings and who are more readily satisfied with a nonscientific conception of nature, are particularly apt to become religious. Perhaps most important, the "positive content" of religion, "which plays upon the age-old aspirations of men . . . toward good, justice, and equality of opportunity," contributes to its appeal.[30]

4. Contact between believers and nonbelievers is inevitable, and this too helps to keep religion alive. Religious persons cannot be kept in isolation from the rest of society; with any protracted contact, there is always a possibility that they will infect others with "bourgeois prejudices." This process is manifested most powerfully, but not exclusively, within families where children receive religious training from their parents or grandparents. Studies have shown that more than a third of Soviet schoolchildren have close and frequent contact with relatives who are believers. Moreover, they indicate that the overwhelming majority of those who believe in and/or practice religion have been believers from childhood. Some children are said to acquire religious habits and beliefs "almost literally with their mother's milk." [31] Surveys conducted in Kiev and Voronezh, for example, found that between 80 and 93 percent of all believers grew up in families that taught them to believe in God.[32]

This phenomenon, of course, is not confined to relations within individual families. Any contact with religious persons can stimulate a religious response. In the countryside, the fact that male believers largely are elderly people helps to make their religious views attractive. (Elderly men tend to be the most respected people in the village, particularly in the Moslem areas of the USSR.) Moreover, members of some denominations, e.g., the Baptists and some of the smaller Protestant sects, place particular emphasis on proselytizing. Seventh-Day Adventist leaders, for example, have encouraged those of their followers who are employed at hospitals (mainly nurses and orderlies) to engage in "medico-missionary" work. They seek to persuade patients that they can be healed only through belief in God, linking efforts to save the patient's life with a program to save his soul.[33]

5. These remarks suggest a fifth factor influencing the longevity of religion—the activities of ministers and churches. Unlike other vestiges of the past, religion has an organizational base in its various churches and clergymen. These "religious cadres" are said to have at their disposal large

sums of money and vast quantities of literature, which they use to transform their potential influence into an active, aggressive, militant force, securing new converts and combating antireligious efforts.[34]

Even the physical presence of churches, with their attractive architecture, icons, and frescoes, apparently helps to bring out religious feelings. They stimulate in some citizens the same excitement and reverence that the original architects, builders, artists, and parishioners felt. In fact, Soviet commentators have complained of a certain "church bias" in sightseeing tours arranged for Soviet (as well as foreign) tourists. The problem is exacerbated by the failure of most tour guides to mention "the reactionary role played by those who supported the temple." [35]

6. Support for religion comes from foreign sources, too. Thus, religious themes are said to occupy "a prominent place in the arsenal of imperialist propaganda." [36] Radio broadcasts in Russian and other languages of the USSR, it is claimed, are supplemented by the use of tourists and other illegal channels. Some religious groups in the USSR, particularly the Baptists, Jehovah's Witnesses, and Seventh-Day Adventists, apparently tape Western broadcasts for future group listening. In addition, tourists from the West and from Israel are said to smuggle religious items into the USSR for the purpose of illegal distribution. Charges of this sort are relatively common and invariably emphatic.[37] Thus, a high-ranking police official declared in 1969,

Tens of thousands of publications that propagandize religion are prepared in the USA, Britain, the FRG and other countries in Russian and other languages of the peoples of the USSR and are sent to our country through various channels. . . .

In addition to radio broadcasts and the smuggling into the USSR of literature propagandizing religion, numerous foreign centers make the maximum effort to acquire "their own people" among believers and attempt to set believers among the citizenry against the agencies of Soviet rule.[38]

7. A seventh factor that helps to explain the high incidence of religious views in certain parts of the country is the fact that these lands were absorbed long after the Bolshevik Revolution. Religion is comparatively strong in the Baltic States, in Moldavia, in western Belorussia, and in the Ukraine, because the people there "were only comparatively recently liberated from social and national oppression and from the church." "Socialist transformations" in these areas are of recent vintage, and as a consequence, "religious vestiges" abound.[39]

8. In addition, religious survivals are continually nourished by *other* survivals of the past. Soviet analysts suggest the existence of a symbiotic

relationship, as religious and nonreligious vestiges stimulate and reinforce one another. As a consequence, religious tendencies are intensified by seemingly unrelated flaws in Soviet society. In particular, religious survivals are said to be reinforced by "bourgeois nationalism" and other "outdated national traditions" that are still observed by many citizens. They serve as a "nutritive medium" for one another, inasmuch as some churches regard themselves as "custodians of national distinctiveness and culture."[40] The strong links between Catholicism and Lithuanian nationalism, between Islam and Arab or Turkic nationalism, and between Judaism and the state of Israel suggest the significance of this factor. Moreover, religion seems to have exhibited greater powers of endurance in areas where "feudal" or "patriarchal" attitudes are present. Strong religious communities still exist in Central Asia and Siberia, where male-dominated, highly organized societies developed rigid religious patterns that mirrored and reinforced systems of socioeconomic organization.

Similarly, alcoholism contributes to the perpetuation of religion.[41] When drunkenness diminishes a man's control over himself and his environment, he may become dependent on the church for moral sustenance, or, more likely, his family may turn to the church in their despair.[42] To the extent that excessive drinking, "bourgeois nationalism," and other vestiges of the past persist, the problem of religious survivals will remain and be exacerbated.

9. One of the more unusual Soviet explanations for the continued existence of religion, somewhat puzzling at first glance to a Westerner, hinges on the collective's role in people's lives. Empirical studies indicate that the great majority of the faithful are people who are isolated from production collectives and from official sociopolitical activities. They have not, either by design or by chance, been exposed to the salubrious influence of "advanced socialist ideology," and are therefore more apt to retain their "backward" views. Particularly relevant here are housewives, pensioners, and the disabled, who spend much of their time alone, but the proposition can also be applied to cleaning women, painters, tailors, waiters, and others. Working alone, or not working at all, these people stand apart from collective influence and control. They do not take part in the "communal, social, political, and cultural life of the country," and as a consequence some of them turn to the church for companionship or recreation. Moreover, antireligious activists seldom conduct individual work with persons who live and work in relative seclusion.[43]

The proposition that social isolation stimulates an inclination toward religion can also be applied to children. According to a Soviet study, religious beliefs and behavior tend to be more characteristic of children who are "isolated from the life of the class and school." [44] However, it is difficult to determine whether the children's isolation helped to produce religiousness or, more likely, whether their deviant views and behavior, reinforced by parental demands, caused them to avoid any organized school activities that might have threatened their religious values.

10. One additional factor should be mentioned, if only because Soviet atheists underscore it so emphatically. They frequently argue that religion continues to exert an influence over a portion of the citizenry because of past and present deficiencies in the antireligious program. Thus, where atheist propaganda is weakest, religious belief and behavior remain widespread, and clergymen may even find additional converts.[45]

While acknowledging that this argument is, to a degree, valid, we should not accept it uncritically. Substantial evidence can be cited to show that antireligious propaganda is only marginally effective. Nonetheless, it may be true that more sophisticated propaganda in the past would have resulted, and in the future will result, in a diminution of religious belief.

Major Problems

Soviet antireligious propaganda has been subjected to criticism for more than half a century. Even its most ardent supporters point to major shortcomings and errors, and authoritative sources acknowledge that it "still does not fully correspond to the demands of the present day." [46] While some of the problems appear to be minor, others are of basic importance. Indeed, the available evidence strongly suggests that the antireligious effort is fundamentally unsound.

Fifty years ago, Lenin criticized Soviet attempts at atheist propaganda as "boring and dry." [47] The passage of five decades has not brought much improvement. "Life changes," one commentator has remarked, "but the methods of propagandists remain the same." [48] According to an article in the Party's principal ideological journal, antireligious propaganda has hardly changed at all since Lenin's time.[49] It is criticized regularly for being "inaccurate," "primitive" and "formal." [50] Atheist propagandists tend to be uninterested, unskilled, and uninformed, and their efforts remain unsophisticated, inadequate, and unwelcome.

The most critical problems are the following:

1. Atheist propaganda seldom reaches believers. Perhaps the most significant problem is the fact that atheist propaganda seldom reaches believers.

Religious people try to avoid atheist messages, and Party workers often do not even bother to coax them into attending propaganda sessions.[51] Moreover, lectures and other mass measures are confined principally to the larger cities and provincial centers. Propagandists are reluctant to visit the remote areas of the country, and Party members who reside in the countryside are relatively unconcerned with religion. Thus, those persons who are most apt to be religious (rural dwellers in the smallest and most isolated villages) are least apt to be exposed to propaganda. Residents of the most out-of-the-way communities literally do not see atheist propagandists for years on end.[52] (See Figures 8.1 and 8.2.)

What is more, propaganda measures are organized in such a way that believers find it easy to avoid them. Most lectures and discussions are held in clubs, agitation points *(agitpunkty)*, or houses of political enlightenment *(doma politicheskogo prosveshcheniya)*. Few believers take the initiative to visit these places, and, as one atheist put it, "you couldn't drag a lassoed believer" to one of them.[53] There has been some effort to attract believers to antireligious meetings, by sending them invitation cards, personally inviting them, or arranging discussions at the believer's home.[54] But unless this movement grows markedly, atheist propaganda will continue to be a colloquy in which only atheists participate.

2. Faith is seldom undermined by reason. The Party assumes, without justification, that faith can always be undermined by reason. To quote one ideological official, "Reason is the enemy of religion." [55] The official argument is simple: there is no rational basis for belief in God, and everything in nature can be explained by science. Just as medieval theologians long ago devised elaborate proofs of the existence of God, Soviet ideologists today continually prove that God does not exist. Their task is to explain the "errors," "misconceptions," and "delusions" of religious believers, replacing an "antiscientific religious world-view" with a "scientific, Marxist-Leninist world-view."

But it is extremely difficult, perhaps impossible, for an atheist to persuade someone of the groundlessness of faith. By its very nature, faith is not susceptible to attack on logical grounds. Thus, articles and lectures stating that Soviet cosmonauts did not see God during their flights elicited a predictable response from believers. After one such article in the antireligious magazine *Nauka i religiya*,

. . . letters began to pour in, accusing the journal, and at the same time all scientific atheist propaganda, of ignorance, of being unfamiliar with the commonly known truth that it is impossible to see God, since he is an incorporeal being. . . . [This] served as a basis for "catching" atheists with a crude, oversimplified understanding of religious dogma. . . .[56]

Figure 8.1   Lord! Send at least one antireligious lecturer to our district!
Source: Krokodil, No. 6 (1960).

Figure 8.2   The appearance of the atheist lecturer before the people.
Source: Krokodil, No. 26 (1962).

Scientific truths are not necessarily incompatible with religious belief; many people feel that there is more to life than the laws of science.[57] Educated people, even those with advanced scientific training, can, and do, believe in God.

Atheist propaganda pays insufficient attention to the real reasons underlying religious belief. Although scholarly studies provide insights into the believer's thoughts and behavior, they do not provide a full understanding of religion. To understand why people are religious requires an appreciation of the psychological, aesthetic, and emotional satisfaction derived from faith. A Writers' Union official, addressing a conference of atheist specialists, went to the heart of the problem.

If we base antireligious propaganda only on the data of archeology, history, and medicine, only on material excavations or on the success of doctors in curing various diseases, we will be unable to conquer religion before we can conquer the diseases themselves. . . . [Religiousness] is a feeling, and you cannot fight it without instilling a counterfeeling.[58]

But the need to understand religion as a feeling, and not just a collection of outdated or wrong ideas, is not widely recognized.

To be sure, the authorities have demonstrated some awareness of the emotional and aesthetic appeal of religion by devising a system of secular holidays and customs. Even here, however, the Party's efforts have been clumsy and unimaginative. The new affairs are usually dry, boring, and artificial, and they do not appeal to believers. Until the Party is able and willing to provide an outlet for the hopes, needs, doubts, and fears that are now expressed as religious belief, it cannot hope to undermine religion.

Professional atheists tend to be prisoners of their own ideological bias; they can only express puzzlement and frustration when religious people refuse to accept the logic of scientific atheism. Soviet discussions of antireligious propaganda indicate that this feeling of exasperation is widespread. The truth of antireligious propaganda "is obvious only to us atheists," one prominent scholar has remarked. "Religion has its own 'logic.' "[59] It is difficult, another atheist has observed, to destroy religious views, even by "what would seem to be the most irrefutable logic."[60] Faith itself makes a believer virtually immune to rational argument, and the propagandist almost always "runs up against the blank wall of misunderstanding."[61] For most believers, "emotion prevails over reason," for people's critical faculties are seldom applied to their faith. They "blindly accept religious doctrine and do not try to interpret it from the position of reason." Indeed, "they frequently react negatively to the atheist's attempts to liberate them from their religious delusions."[62] Believers, then, are seen as "biased people," who do not accept, and who actively oppose, atheist propaganda.[63]

3. Confusion and apathy in the antireligious movement are widespread. Confusion and apathy among atheists are a major barrier to the movement's success. No one, whether atheist or believer, can ever be quite certain of official policy. Higher authorities often provide cadres with conflicting guidelines, and they permit, or secretly encourage, practices that are nominally prohibited. Whether the resulting contradictions in policy are a sign of Machiavellianism, or instead represent uncertainty and conflict at a higher level, is unclear. But they definitely hinder the struggle against religion.

Atheists have found it particularly difficult to satisfy demands for a proper balance of coercion and persuasion in combating religion. The problem is one of extremes: atheists tend to be either too militant or not militant enough. Some are overzealous. They declare war on religion, promise to eliminate it "with one stroke," and resort to "voluntarism," "subjectivism," and "hare-brained scheming." They make use of "administrative measures," discharging believers from their jobs, prohibiting church services, and interfering with pilgrimages to holy places.[64] This approach understandably angers believers and tends to reinforce their religious convictions.

Other officials are not aggressive enough. Whether guided by conviction, rationalization, or lack of interest, they do nothing to achieve the Party's atheist objectives. Some believe that religion will die out without any assistance from the Party. Others misinterpret the Constitutional guarantee of freedom of conscience, not realizing that it is supposed to "protect atheists from the pretensions of religious people and to protect believers themselves from the arbitrariness of the clergy." [65] Still other atheists are simply apathetic; they do not regard religious belief as a significant problem and think it a waste of time to combat it.

Indifference to the problem of religion is extremely widespread. Few of the individuals or institutions responsible for conducting atheist propaganda do their work enthusiastically, and most atheists combat religion perfunctorily or not at all. Newspapers, youth organizations, and school-teachers, as well as Party propagandists and agitators, usually ignore the question, confining their antireligious efforts to the eve of religious holy days. Ordinary workers are far more concerned about their wages or the problems of alcoholism and crime, and Party members, even those responsible for ideological work, are not interested in the religious views of those with whom they work.[66] In fact, in some areas of the country, Party bodies do not discuss questions of atheism for years on end.[67]

4. Propagandists lack knowledge and skill. To be effective, antireligious propagandists require enthusiasm, knowledge, and skill. But not many atheists have the proper credentials, and fewer still volunteer their services. Most propagandists are Party members or Komsomols who have been assigned to atheist work. The younger ones tend to be too inexperienced and aggressive, while their older colleagues, who have the advantage of maturity and experience, usually have too little formal training.

To be sure, formal training is not necessarily an asset. The knowledge acquired through the system of atheist schools, seminars, and lectures is seldom adequate to the needs of effective propaganda. Critics of the program have charged that graduates "are often ignorant of the most elementary questions of religion and are totally unfamiliar with the 'scriptures.' " [68] Moreover, those who have taken courses frequently find it difficult to apply their classroom learning. Their knowledge tends to be too esoteric, and they are given only the most rudimentary training in the art of persuasion.

Until recently, Soviet ideological specialists assumed that the success of atheist work depended primarily on the conviction, persistence, and tenacity of the propagandist, rather than on his knowledge of religion and atheism or his ability to communicate his views to a believer.[69] Most university graduates who have studied scientific atheism are said to be better equipped to challenge a neo-Kantian, whom they presumably will never meet, than an ordinary believer.[70] Equally important, they usually find it difficult to communicate their views to the faithful. Lacking skill and self-confidence, speakers often read their lectures to an audience "without so much as raising their eyes from their texts" and then quickly leave the hall.[71] Some have such an exaggerated conception of the debating skills of believers that they refuse to confront them.[72]

Much of the academic work done on religion and atheism, especially the literature atheist activists rely on, is of inferior quality. Serious, scholarly treatment of the subject has traditionally been discouraged, and commentators have generally had to conform to rigid ideological demands. To be sure, this observation is not as apt today as it was two decades ago. The period since the November, 1954, Central Committee resolution has witnessed a considerable improvement in the standards of antireligious scholarship, as the recruitment and training of atheist cadres has received increased attention. For example, the series *Voprosy nauchnogo ateizma*

(Problems of Scientific Atheism), published since 1966 by the Institute of Scientific Atheism, includes a good deal of sophisticated and "relevant" research. But despite these and certain other volumes produced by better-trained young historians and social scientists, "scientific atheism" has not yet risen to the level of other academic disciplines. Bright and creative young people continue to be drawn to other specialties, and the field has been left primarily to hacks and *agitprop* functionaries. What is more, most scientists, philosophers, psychologists, and other academic specialists still do no want to be propagandists; neither do writers, artists, or playwrights.[73]

The atheist movement, then, has created problems for itself. Its major figures are highly dogmatic, and their protégés are given little opportunity to develop sensitivity and balance. The scientific study of religion has thus remained a relatively backward sector of intellectual life. Moreover, strict controls over the publication of religious materials have made it difficult for scholars and propagandists to obtain even the most basic sources. "In order to wage a serious offensive against religion," a Soviet history teacher has written, "we must know its dogma thoroughly from primary sources, and not from popular pamphlets." [74] But the appropriate primary sources are in short supply. New editions of the Bible and the Koran are published only occasionally, and then in very limited numbers.[75] In fact, many of the available copies are distributed abroad as gifts, leaving few for believers, scholars, and propagandists in the USSR. Propagandists must rely on popularized treatments in the press or on more specialized (but nonetheless superficial) journals such as *Nauka i religiya* and *Agitator*. This in turn makes it difficult for them to master their subject and to deal with the probing questions often asked by believers.

5. Antireligious propaganda is seldom relevant to the life of the typical believer. In 1960, the Party Central Committee observed that propaganda was "detached from life, from the practice of communist construction." It was said to lack "concreteness and purposefulness" and was often of an "abstract, purely elucidative nature." [76] The charge is no less true today. Much of the propaganda effort is directed toward the remote past. Lecturers condemn the excesses of medieval popes, the horrors of the Inquisition, the political opposition of the clergy during the early years of Soviet rule, and other events remote from the lives of believers. Despite substantial changes in religious dogma and church life under the Soviet regime, propagandists repeat the same old arguments in the same old way, apparently oblivious or indifferent to their effect on believers.[77]

A good deal of propaganda deals with isolated and aberrant happenings, described in sensational and/or vulgar language. Atheist films, for example, depict such phenomena as crucifixions, murders, starvation, and cases of severe mental derangement. It is difficult to see how descriptions of crimes committed by religious persons (including religiously inspired murders) or reports of bizarre happenings can help undermine religious beliefs, and Soviet specialists are coming to recognize this. Widespread use of such materials, the editors of *Nauka i religiya* have observed, "confuses nonbelievers and outrages believers." [78] This sort of propaganda is not merely ineffective but often is counterproductive, reinforcing, rather than undermining, a believer's notions.

Atheist propaganda frequently attacks the wrong targets. Propagandists often focus on an instance of unseemly behavior by a minister and imply, or state outright, that such behavior is characteristic of all clergymen. They direct their criticism toward individual believers and ministers, rather than toward religious belief as such. Church leaders are denounced for their "hypocrisy, abuse of confidence, striving for material gain, indifference toward socially useful work, and unreliability," [79] while individual believers are attacked for their fanaticism and the harm they bring to others. The clergy are said to exploit other people's religious feelings for their own gain, while rank-and-file believers are regarded as unfortunate victims of these zealots.[80]

If, as appears likely, this approach is designed to produce a rift between religious leaders and ordinary believers, it has not been successful. Even if a congregation rejects its minister (and propaganda attacks seldom have this result), members of the congregation almost always retain their religious convictions.[81]

The conclusion seems inescapable that atheist propaganda is misconceived, misdirected, and clumsy. Those responsible for formulating and implementing antireligious policies base their efforts on an unsophisticated view of the task they face, and they lack much of the information needed to devise a more effective program. There has been little effort to explore the psychology of religious belief or the dynamics of persuasion and opinion change. Ideological specialists have little understanding of the influence of propaganda on people's moods, feelings, and behavior.[82] Few Western studies dealing with social psychology have been translated into Russian, and until the very recent past, Soviet scholars and propagandists have ignored this literature. While some useful research has been done in the last decade by sociologists, psychologists, and ethnographers, most of the scholarly work in the field of scientific atheism deals with antireligious efforts during the first years of the Soviet regime or with the history of religion. The utility of such material in the struggle against religion today is at best problematical.[83]

Soviet empirical research into the effectiveness of atheist propaganda lends support to this conclusion. Although few studies have been published, and the evidence they provide is somewhat ambiguous, most investigations indicate that antireligious propaganda is not persuasive. This argument cannot be accepted uncritically, however. Three considerations suggest the need for caution in interpreting the data.

First, statements made by respondents are open to challenge, because they may have been exacted by pressure. Soviet analysts claim that believers who report being unmoved by antireligious propaganda are often not telling the truth. They are said to be following the instructions of clergymen anxious to prove that religious belief is impervious to atheist propaganda.[84] Second, polling procedures are seldom made clear. The sources do not reveal how the samples were selected. They indicate neither the wording of the questions nor the criteria for assigning respondents to one or another category. Third, and perhaps most important, the results of some of the most comprehensive studies of propaganda effectiveness have not been published. Whether the findings of these inquiries reinforce or conflict with the results of those that have appeared in print is not known. Given what we know about atheist propaganda, however, it is likely that these studies reflect official disappointment with the ineffectiveness of the program.[85]

In one poll of believers exposed to atheist propaganda, only 15 percent of those questioned said that they "consider atheist propaganda effective." Still fewer, only 10 percent, of those questioned in a second poll were impressed; they said that antireligious propaganda "gave rise to serious doubts" about their faith. Another 40 percent acknowledged that it had a marginal effect, but 42 percent said it had "no influence whatsoever" on them.[86] Other researchers have come up with comparable results.

While most surveys of audience reaction emphasize the ineffectiveness of atheist propaganda, some studies have yielded contradictory findings. Polls of former believers suggest that propaganda *can* play a role in changing people's attitudes toward religion. Approximately half of those questioned in one survey said their conversion was stimulated, at least in part, by atheist lessons at school, discussions with individual atheists, and antireligious radio broadcasts. A smaller number pointed to the influence of newspapers, magazines, and books.[87] A second study of former believers in another area of the country showed a similar pattern. Respondents ranked discussions with atheists highest, followed by antireligious literature, lectures, radio, films, and television.[88] Thus, even though propaganda seldom influences believers, it sometimes does, especially if it is conducted skillfully.

Pertinent Findings of Western Research

Western social scientists have devoted a great deal of attention to the processes of communication, opinion formation, and opinion change. By applying some of their conclusions to the USSR, we may be able to shed additional light on the successes and failures of Soviet antireligious propaganda.

Differences between the Soviet and American environments are, of course, very pronounced, particularly in the area of religion. The CPSU has a near-monopoly on the means of communication; it controls the mass media and the publishing industry, assigns lecturers and speakers, determines what they shall say, and when they shall say it. The few church publications that the Party permits to be printed appear in small editions. Because the regime places strict limits on the printing or mimeographing of theological works, many must be copied by hand and are thus not widely accessible. Moreover, the Soviet media adhere to a single line, describing religion as "bad" and atheism as "good." In contrast, American churches have ample opportunity to publish, propagandize, and communicate with the masses. Various points of view on the subject of religion are presented in books, journals, and the mass media, and individuals have easy access to those in which they are interested.

But if differences between the Soviet and American settings are extensive, they certainly are not all-encompassing. Soviet citizens clearly are not isolated from religious influences. While "religious propaganda" is prohibited by law, religious persons interact with each other and with nonreligious persons. Individuals in the USSR can be exposed to religious messages in the family, through friends and colleagues, or, of course, at church. They are, like their American counterparts, subjected to cross-pressures. Although the two environments are far from identical, an understanding of persuasive communications in the West may help us assess Soviet antireligious propaganda.

One of the basic conclusions of Western research is that persuasive mass communications function far more frequently as an agent of reinforcement than as an agent of change. Because of the mediating influence of selective exposure, selective perception, selective interpretation, and selective retention, people exposed to a particular message rarely modify their opinions to a significant degree. In general, when a message is inconsistent with an individual's cognitive structure, it will be ignored, rejected, or distorted so as to inhibit conflict or anxiety. This finding, valid in most situations, is particularly relevant for communications on subjects that are important to an individual. When an attitude or opinion is crucial to a person, he is highly resistant to any kind of persuasion.[89] The implications of these findings for Soviet antireligious efforts are clear. Inasmuch as religious beliefs are among the most intimate and deep-seated aspects of a person's make-up, it seems likely that they would be among the least susceptible to change.

In observing that strongly held attitudes are less susceptible to change than weakly held ones, we are also saying that opinion change is possible. Behavior and ideas sometimes can be altered. Soviet authorities claim that religious beliefs can, and will, be changed through the dissemination of atheist propaganda and cite case studies to "prove" that the systematic communication of antireligious messages guarantees success. But both the general argument and the illustrations are extremely implausible. Case studies never explain how a particular believer was converted to atheism; they only assert that conversion has occurred "under the pressure of irrefutable scientific evidence," that people, when exposed to the "truth," recognize and accept it. No evidence is presented suggesting that they want to change. In fact, Soviet specialists readily acknowledge that believers conscientiously avoid both propaganda and propagandists. As one atheist has remarked,

Once they have scented an emotional or ideological "incursion" on their religious feelings and convictions, believers often retreat, as it were, into a blind "emotional defense" which is scarcely vulnerable to logical proofs or arguments.[90]

If this is true, and there is no reason to doubt it, the dissemination of antireligious propaganda would seem to be a fruitless exercise.

It is far more believable, though of course conjectural, to see reports of apostasy as examples of what Herbert Kelman has called "compliance." [91] A believer, like any other citizen, probably will adopt behavior that promotes his own psychological and physical security. Faced with what he regards as constant badgering, he may express agreement with the atheist agitator or propagandist—simply in order to be left alone—while not changing his belief in any way.

It is conceivable, of course, that an individual might internalize the official position on religion, particularly if he is exposed to atheist propaganda at an early age. There is considerable evidence suggesting that mass communications are effective in creating attitudes among people who were not previously in favor of or against some point of view. Communications on matters about which an audience has no preexisting opinions are said to be capable of "inoculating" audience members, that is, "rendering them more resistant to later communications or experiences suggesting a contrary view." [92] This suggests that antireligious propaganda aimed at young children can be a powerful force. Thus, it probably is easier to bring up a child as an atheist than it is to persuade an adult believer to change his views.

If, however, a child has already been given religious instruction by his family before he reaches school age, it may be impossible to influence him with atheist propaganda. There is reason to believe that children accept the views of adults who are near to them more readily than they accept the lessons of schoolbooks.[93] If this is so, we could argue that children who are exposed to religion before they begin school have already been "inoculated" *against* antireligious propaganda. Because religious views are apt to be particularly salient to religious persons, it is unlikely that children with religious parents or grandparents will face their first school lesson in atheism tabula rasa.

Western social scientists have also discovered that personal, face-to-face communication is a powerful instrument of opinion change, particularly when operating in conjunction with the mass media.[94] Allowing for certain obvious differences between East and West, it appears that the Soviet Union has its own "opinion leaders" and "two-step flow of communications." The Soviet system provides specially trained opinion leaders—propagandists, agitators, and political information specialists *(politinformatory)*. Unlike their American counterparts, they are assigned explicit communications responsibilities. The messages they transmit to believers (in lectures, discussions, etc.) are identical with the messages distributed through the mass media; thus, person-to-person influences reinforce the influence of the media. Moreover, while a believer can ignore the mass media and avoid mass antireligious measures, he has less opportunity to ignore the atheist who is assigned to "reeducate" him. Thus, it would appear that conversations between atheist agitators and individual believers are ideally suited to bring about opinion change. Certainly, individual work is regarded by officials and propagandists alike as the most effective way to influence believers. The atheist can present his case slowly and fully; he can challenge and give a detailed critique of any of the believer's doubts. He can adjust his approach, timing, and style to the "needs" of the believer.[95]

However, one additional factor should keep us from applying too readily to the USSR the findings about opinion leadership in America. In discussions between American opinion leaders and other citizens, it is not the opinion leader who introduces the special topic. The ordinary citizen customarily initiates the conversation and points it toward the question that interests him. Influence is exerted, then, only after the ordinary citizen requests assistance.[96] In the words of one authority, "The opinion leader . . . is not an agitator, anxious to arouse discussion; rather, others urge him to share his sound judgments with them." [97] While personal contact enjoys distinctive advantages in comparison with other forms of communication, it loses much of its efficacy when the opinion leader tries to thrust his views onto his fellow conversationalist. Personal relationships based on mutual trust facilitate communication; information comes from a reliable source in a straightforward, nonpurposive manner.[98] If, however, the atheist is perceived not as a friend but as an agent preaching a repugnant doctrine and intent on undermining and destroying a person's most precious beliefs, opinion change is unlikely to be produced. Personal contact is likely to be perceived as hostile communication, to be studiously avoided.

Concluding Remarks

The Communist Party regards religion as an unfortunate, undesirable, and outdated relic of the past. Belief in God is said to encourage "privatization and withdrawal," making people less willing to fulfill their political, social, and economic obligations. More generally, religion is thought to impede official efforts to control and manipulate the citizenry. As a leading Western sociologist has observed, "From the standpoint of a system that desires total commitment and loyalty, even a compartmentalization of worldly political and otherworldly nonpolitical attachments is intolerable." [99]

The possibility that religious values might lead to beliefs and conduct supportive of the Soviet system is seldom acknowledged. Religious people are seen as deluded and desperate for help, and the fact that they do not realize it is taken as evidence of their confusion. The Party considers itself duty bound to aid believers, both for their benefit and for society's. According to Marxist-Leninist doctrine, history demands that religion disappear, and the Party has mobilized vast resources in order to accelerate this "inevitable" process. The methods by which it prods believers to renounce their religious beliefs have been the subject of this study.

The drive to create an atheist society has not lost its significance during the half-century of Soviet power. Indeed, the Soviets argue, the battle against religion has assumed even greater importance as the day of the ultimate communist society draws near. According to authoritative spokesmen, atheist propaganda now involves not merely the "propagandizing of godlessness" but also the inculcation of "communist ideals into the conscience of the masses." [100] The regime, that is, is determined not only to uproot religion but fundamentally to restructure people's value-systems. As a result, the term "scientific atheist propaganda" has increasingly come to replace the expression "antireligious propaganda" in the past decade.[101]

What is more, the Party has continued to mold Marxism-Leninism into a more and more elaborate "secular religion." Although the official value system is alleged to be completely free of religious or metaphysical overtones, it is, in fact, permeated with religious and quasi-religious symbols. The substitution of new secular ceremonies and holidays for their religious counterparts is only one example of this; other parallels are equally striking. Thus, History, the Party, or (at times) the Supreme Leader have served as the functional equivalent of God's will on earth. Similarly, the writings of Marx, Engels, and Lenin have become, in a very real sense, sacred texts, and their apocalyptic teachings are remarkably similar to those of St. Augustine. The "red corners" that can be found in factories, schools, and even private homes today serve much the same function that small shrines did in tsarist times, while the Orthodox Church's veneration of holy relics has been transformed into veneration of the bodily remains of Lenin (and, for a time, of Stalin).[102]

Indeed, Communist rule in the USSR displays many of the traits of a state religion; the Party has imposed a new orthodoxy in place of the one taught before the Bolshevik Revolution. The regime functions as a church in the sense that "it is the institutionalization of belief. It is the organization that bears and propagates the faith." The very mode of official thinking and discourse is religious: it involves "unquestionable truths, the proper profession of faith, the observance of liturgical rigor in the formulae of belief and ritual." [103] A priesthood, a hierarchy, a missionary spirit, a doctrine made into a dogma, "fervor, dogmatism, fanaticism, dedication, atonement, and martyrdom"—all these characteristics of universalistic religions are also major features of Party rule over the past five decades.[104]

Like other universalistic faiths, the Party has endeavored to impose a set of strict moral teachings on the population. It has sought to uphold the people's faith and morals and has developed sophisticated instruments to inculcate and enforce the official dogma. The regime's principal moral teachings—requiring sobriety, honesty, respect for authority, avoidance of sexual incontinence, and concern for the welfare of others—are not very different from those of other faiths. The "Moral Code of the Builder of

Communism," incorporated into the 1961 Party Program, resembles the ethical teachings of most of the world's great religions.[105]

Policy toward religion has always been governed by several crucial considerations. The Party has been particularly concerned about the danger of any alternative source of authority. It has found many church teachings and practices harmful, and it has been anxious to mobilize the energies of the population to achieve certain social and economic goals. In trying to refashion the political culture of the Soviet people, then, the Party has been guided by what might be termed "a passion for unanimity." [106]

Over the fifty-five years of Soviet power, the regime has sought to achieve six antireligious objectives:

1. To destroy the political and economic strength of the church. It has been basically successful in this effort. If the church retains any political influence today, it is almost always used to support the CPSU's foreign and domestic policies.

2. To limit the church's access to the citizenry, especially to children. The regime has, in the main, succeeded in this area as well. The separation of church and state, the separation of the church from the schools, the rejection of any "social mission" on the part of the church, and the ban on "religious propaganda" have served to curb church influence to a substantial degree.

3. To induce people not to attend church. The Party has been fairly successful in this quest. It has closed large numbers of churches, prevented others from being built, and has made citizens, except for the elderly and the intrepid, feel awkward or apprehensive about being seen in church. Freedom of religion is little more than a legal fiction; "people are not only strongly discouraged from religious participation, they are also deprived of adequate facilities for it." [107]

4. To induce people not to celebrate religious holy days or perform religious rituals. The Party has been only moderately successful in this endeavor. Religious celebrations tend to be more private than church attendance, and certain rituals can be disguised as a family or national tradition. As a result, more people take part in religious ceremonies than attend religious services.

5. To convince religious believers that their views are "wrong." The Party has been very unsuccessful in achieving this objective. While some citizens have renounced their religious convictions as a result of atheist propaganda, they are few in number. The range, intensity, and frequency of criticisms of atheist measures suggest that the effort has been virtually useless, and sometimes even counterproductive. Large numbers of citizens continue to believe in God, and the Soviet contention that believers are merely ignorant old women does not really come to grips with the strength of religion. As Maurice Latey has observed, the same argument has been made for half a century, which means that each new generation of the elderly provides a new generation of churchgoers.[108]

6. *To mold citizens into militant atheists and New Soviet Men.* This effort has been an almost total failure. Most people are simply uninterested in religion, and very few are anxious to take on the responsibility of becoming atheist propagandists.

The Communist Party, then, has been successful in achieving only some of its goals. It has dealt successfully with problems that it considered urgent, primarily because it was willing to combine propaganda with coercion and the threat of coercion. But the Soviets have been less successful in gaining the more far-reaching objectives they have sought through indoctrinational programs. Persuasion, it seems, is far less effective on the "religious front" than more vigorous measures. It is not surprising, therefore, that the Party has decided once again to supplement its socialization efforts with greater use of the criminal law and intensified pressure on religious believers. Soviet citizens may be unresponsive to atheist propaganda, but they cannot avoid the law.

The antireligious program has also involved heavy costs, of which two are especially important. First, atheist efforts have been destructive, perhaps more destructive than the authorities realize. Both believers and atheists have expressed concern that the erosion of religious belief has given rise to a moral vacuum in Soviet society. Religion traditionally has served as an important mechanism of social control, and neither "scientific atheism" nor the Moral Code of the Builder of Communism has been able to replace it.[109] Many churches teach the virtues of hard work, respect for law and order, and avoidance of excessive drinking, promiscuity, and other harmful practices. The experience of churches in other countries—and in the USSR as well—demonstrates that religion can be socially progressive and an asset to the secular authorities. The Soviet belief that modernization requires secularization has made it impossible to exploit this asset fully.

Second, and far more important, antireligious efforts have stimulated dissent and in some instances transformed dissent into political opposition. Many religious citizens have expressed intense resentment at the closing of churches and the dissemination of propaganda they regard as inherently offensive. Those who are treated especially harshly for their religious beliefs are apt to develop profoundly hostile feelings toward the political system.

While the Party has been willing to accept these costs, one wonders if the costs might not outweigh the gains. As early as 1928, Anatolii Lunacharskii, who was then Minister of Education, said, "Religion is like a nail; the harder you hit it, the deeper it goes into the wood." [110] The remark was a perceptive one. Antireligious propaganda, it would appear, is at best an exercise in futility and self-deception, and at worst an instrument that stimulates and reinforces the religious convictions it aims to destroy.

Why, then, do the Soviets continue to urge believers to renounce their religious convictions? The answer is by no means clear, and we can only suggest the most tentative of hypotheses.

First, the ideological authorities may not be completely aware of the shaky premises on which the atheist program rests. They seem to operate on the assumption that man is infinitely malleable, or, as Raymond Bauer has put it, that people are essentially "plastic." [111] But socialization involves more than a one-way flow of influence from the Party to the masses. In fact, it is a complex process in which "societal 'screens' interfere to mitigate the effect of society's efforts." Many forces can and do "intervene to foil ideological designs." [112]

Second, it may be that, while atheist propaganda is irrelevant to the believer, it is highly functional to the atheist and to the Party. The propagandist may feel that he is participating in an important project by combating a doctrine the regime defines as alien.[113] By inducing propagandists to identify their goals with those of the Party, the leadership stimulates the enthusiasm of its cadres and keeps the official ideology "revolutionary" and "relevant."

A third explanation, while not incompatible with the first two, is perhaps the most plausible of all. Atheist propaganda may be no more than a harmless ritual that is performed today only because it has always been performed, and because any alternative policy involves considerable risks. The costs of terror are too great, and the leadership lacks either the patience or the confidence to see if religious belief will die out by itself. When "historical inevitability" has failed, there is nothing left but rhetoric.

Appendix 1 Geographical Distribution of Religious Denominations in the USSR

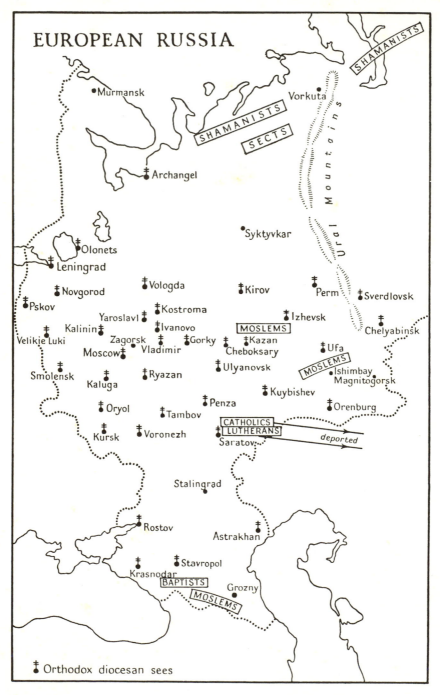

EUROPEAN RUSSIA

SHAMANISTS

•Murmansk

Vorkuta

SHAMANISTS

SECTS

Ural Mountains

‡ Archangel

•Syktyvkar

‡Olonets
‡Leningrad

‡Vologda   •Kirov   Perm   ‡Sverdlovsk

‡Novgorod

•Pskov

‡Kostroma   ‡Izhevsk

Yaroslavl‡   MOSLEMS

Kalinin‡   ‡Ivanovo   ‡Ufa

Velikie Luki   Zagorsk   ‡Gorky   ‡Kazan   MOSLEMS

Moscow‡ Vladimir   Cheboksary   •Ishimbay

Smolensk   ‡Ulyanovsk   Magnitogorsk

Kaluga   ‡Ryazan   ‡Kuybishev

•Oryol   ‡Penza   ‡Orenburg

‡Tambov

Kursk   •Voronezh   CATHOLICS
                        ‡LUTHERANS   deported
            Saratov•

Stalingrad•

‡Rostov
            Astrakhan‡

‡Stavropol
•Krasnodar
        BAPTISTS   Grozny
            MOSLEMS

‡ Orthodox diocesan sees

Figure A1.1
Source: Walter Kolarz, *Religion in the Soviet Union* (New York: St. Martin's Press, 1961), p. 79.

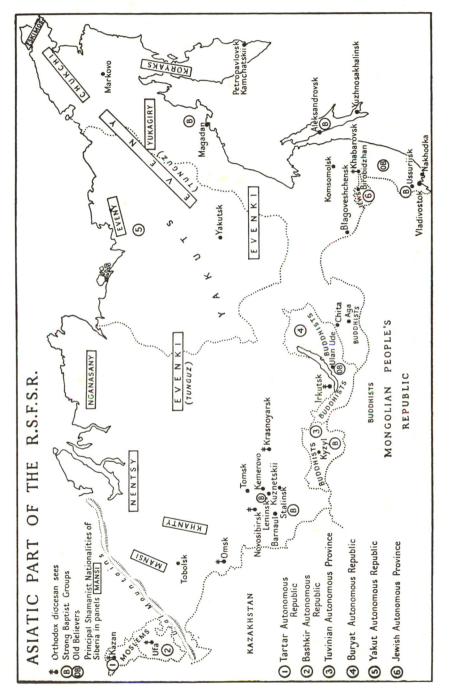

Figure A1.2
Source: Ibid., p. 85.

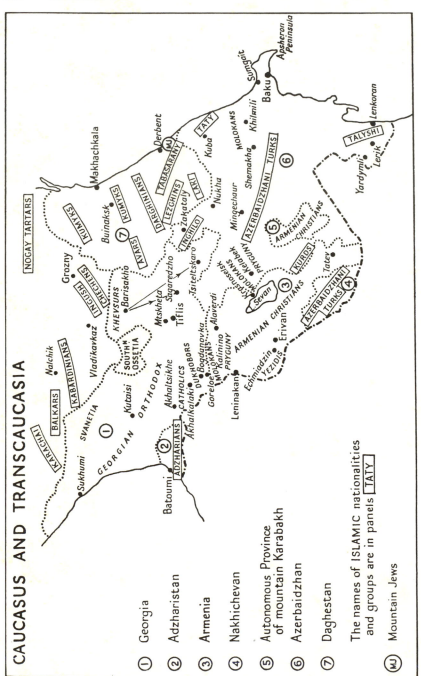

Figure A1.3
Source: Ibid., p. 98.

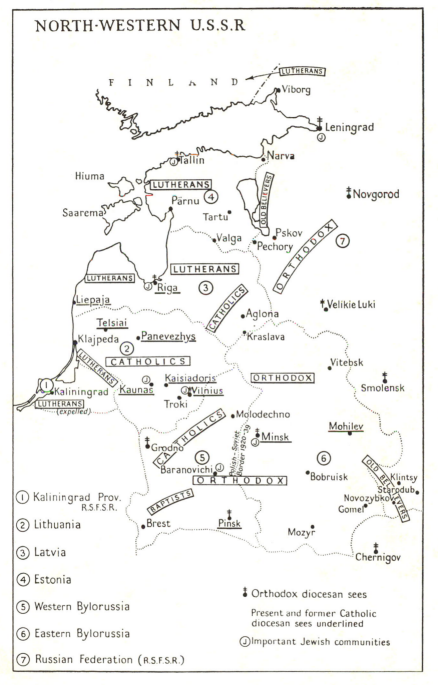

NORTH·WESTERN U.S.S.R

① Kaliningrad Prov. R.S.F.S.R.

② Lithuania

③ Latvia

④ Estonia

⑤ Western Bylorussia

⑥ Eastern Bylorussia

⑦ Russian Federation (R.S.F.S.R.)

‡ Orthodox diocesan sees

Present and former Catholic diocesan sees underlined

ⒿImportant Jewish communities

Figure A1.4
Source: Ibid., p. 205.

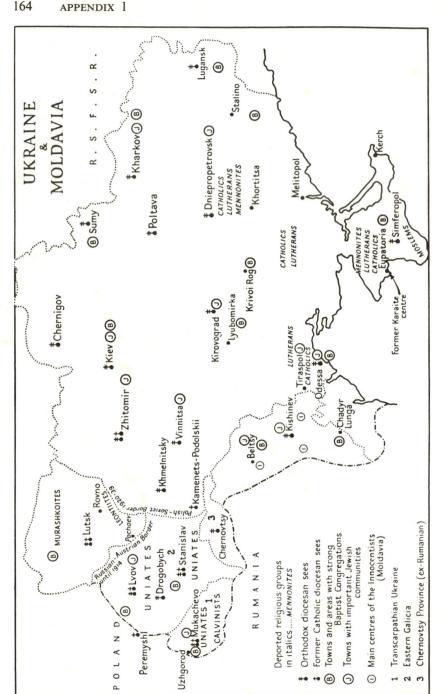

Figure A1.5
Source: Ibid., p. 307.

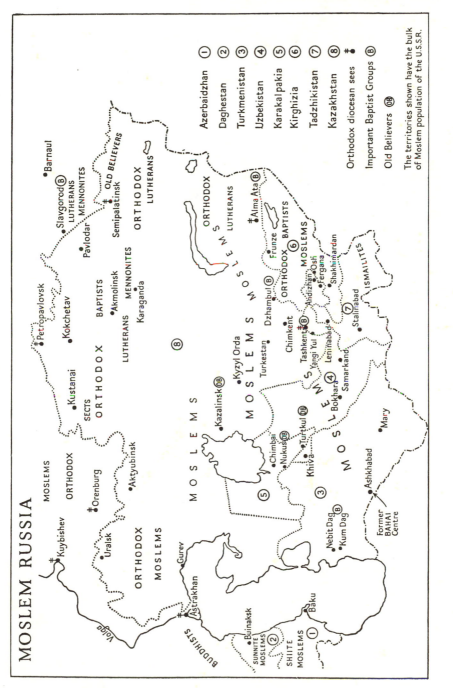

Figure A1.6
Source: Ibid., p. 403.

Appendix 2   Rules of a Typical Atheism Club*

1. The atheism club is a mass voluntary organization, setting as its goal the active ideological struggle against religion and religious holidays and rites.

2. Citizens who have reached the age of 18 and who accept the rules of the club are eligible for membership.

3. A member of the atheism club must

    a. Take part in conducting active antireligious propaganda.

    b. Regard intolerantly all manifestations of religious prejudices in production and in daily life; combat the performance of religious rites and the holding of religious holidays; draw people away from attending church;

    c. Constantly broaden his mental outlook in the area of scientific atheism;

    d. Serve as a personal example at production and in daily life.

4. A member of the club keeps a personal account, in which all his concrete activities in propagandizing atheism among the population and in drawing people away from church are recorded.

5. On the recommendation of the general meeting, members of the club who have done the most service in combating religion and who have performed active work are to be awarded the title "Honored Member of the Atheism Club."

6. In conducting its work, the atheism club makes use of various techniques: lectures, cycles of discussions, thematic evenings, discussions, the showing of films, etc. It is the club's task to provide active participation in these measures for a broad circle of workers, primarily those people who have been under the influence of the church.

7. The club is located in the reading room of the House of Culture.

8. The club organizes sections for practical work: (a) scientific-atheist propaganda, (b) work among women, (c) work among schoolchildren, (d) the organization of mass-cultural measures, (e) informational.

9. The task of the scientific-atheism section is to develop broad atheist propaganda, raise the quality of scientific-atheist evenings, lectures, discussions, and other forms of work which are conducted, improve the activities of libraries in the area of scientific-atheist propaganda.

* Adopted at a meeting of the Danilov Atheism Club, October 20, 1959. *Source:* "Ustav danilovskogo kluba ateistov," *Nauka i religiya,* No. 5 (1960), pp. 75–76.

10. The section for work among women has as its chief task the atheist enlightenment of women and individual work among them.

11. The basic task of the section for work among schoolchildren is to intensify atheist propaganda in school and extraschool institutions, drawing schoolchildren into the ranks of active propagandists of scientific atheism.

12. The section for mass-cultural measures organizes the struggle with religious rites and holidays by means of opposing them with healthy, interesting, and instructive rites and holidays.

13. The informational section gathers material connected with the activities of churchmen and sectarians in the city of Danilov, and regularly informs the members of the club with regard to it.

14. Members of the club gather for meetings at least once every two months to hear speeches by members of the club on questions of scientific atheism and to discuss practical tasks in antireligious work in the city.

15. A bureau of 5 to 7 persons is selected to lead the club's activities.
   The bureau selects from its ranks a chairman and a secretary.
   The bureau meets 1 or 2 times per month.
   The bureau of the club has the right: (a) to give tasks to members of the club and to check up on the execution of these assignments; (b) to accept new members into the club; (c) to place before the general meeting the question of finding out which members of the club do not justify the confidence of the club, and are not conducting any work according to the club's rules.

16. Activists—organizers of scientific-atheist measures—are selected to conduct practical work in enteprises, academic institutions, and cultural institutions through public, Komsomol, and trade union organizations.

17. The chief practical task of the club is to expose the reactionary, antiscientific and antisocial nature of religious ideology and to tear believers away from religious fanaticism.

Appendix 3 Suggested Themes for Lectures on Scientific Atheism*

1. K. Marx, F. Engels, and V. I. Lenin on Religion.

Questions: Dialectical and historical materialism, the philosophical basis of scientific atheism. Religion as a fantastic reflection of reality. The classics of Marxism-Leninism on the social role of religion. The revolutionary struggle of the proletariat for socialism and communism; the social basis of Marxist atheism.

2. Marxism-Leninism, the Ideological Basis of Scientific Atheism.

Questions: The Marxist understanding of religion. Marxism-Leninism on the social and epistemological roots of religion. Religion and atheism—opposed systems of views of the world, society, and man. The struggle against religion; the struggle for true happiness on earth.

3. The Attitude of the CPSU and Soviet State Toward Religion, the Church, and Believers.

Questions: The scientific bases of the policies of the Communist Party and the Soviet state toward religion. Bourgeois and Marxist-Leninist conceptions of freedom of conscience. The efforts of the Communist Party in overcoming religious vestiges in people's consciousness.

4. The Construction of Communism and the Elimination of Religious Vestiges.

Questions: V. I. Lenin on the tasks of Marxist militant atheism. The successes of communist construction in the USSR—a prerequisite for the elimination of religious ideology. Criticism of the efforts of priests and theologians to reconcile Christian ideology with communism. The Program of the CPSU on the tasks of atheist upbringing of the workers in the period of the expanded construction of communism.

5. Russian Orthodoxy and Modernity.

Questions: Russian Orthodoxy, a variety of Christianity. Contemporary Russian Orthodoxy and morality. The attitude of Russian Orthodoxy toward communism. The Russian Orthodox cult and its modernization.

6. Criticism of the Ideology and Activity of Contemporary Christian Sectarianism.

* *Source:* "Primernaya tematika lektsii po nauchnomu ateizmu," *Nauka i religiya*, No. 10 (1967), pp. 90–93. Prepared by the scientific methodology council for the propaganda of scientific atheism under the administration of the All-Union "Knowledge" Society, together with the Moscow House of Scientific Atheism.

Questions: The classics of Marxism-Leninism on the features of sectarian religious ideology. Sectarian organizations in the USSR. Features of their dogma, cult, organization, and sermons.

7. Baptism and Modernity.

Questions: The Baptist religion, one trend in Christianity. Features of Baptist organization and cult. The attitudes of the Baptist religion toward the ideals of communism. The attitude of Baptists toward contemporary natural science. Features of atheist work among Baptist sectarians.

8. Adventism and Modernity.

Questions: Adventism, one trend in Protestantism. The cult, church organization, forms, and methods of missionary work. The antiscientific character of the ideology of Adventism. The reactionary nature of Adventists' views that the world will soon come to an end.

9. The Vatican, Its Ideology and Policies.

Questions: The social demagogy of the Catholic Church. Catholicism's use of Thomist philosophy in the struggle against science. Catholicism's adaptation to contemporary conditions. The Twenty-First Ecumenical Council and the tendency toward "renewal" in contemporary Catholicism.

10. Criticism of the Ideology of Contemporary Islam.

Questions: The class character of Islamic ideology. The bankruptcy of efforts to "reconcile" Islam with contemporary science. The irreconcilability of Islamic ideology with the theory and practice of communist construction. The opposition of communist morality and the moralizing of Islam.

11. The Moral Code of the Builder of Communism and Religious Moralizing.

Questions: Sources of religious morality. The perversion of moral norms common to all mankind by religious morality. Criticism of religious precepts and doctrines. Our epoch, the epoch of the triumph of communist morality.

12. Scientific and Religious Images of Man.

Questions: The bankruptcy of religious "teachings" about man and his place in the universe. Scientific views of the origin of man. What is the essence and purpose of man?

13. The Mortality and Immortality of Man.

Questions: Criticism of religious conceptions of the immortality of the soul. Scientific views of man's psychic activity. On the true immortality of man.

14. Religious and Atheist Interpretations of the Meaning of Life.
Questions: The purpose, goal, and meaning of life. The bankruptcy of religious views on the meaning of life. The Marxist understanding of the meaning of human life.

15. The Significance of Faith in Man's Life.
Questions: The characteristics of religious faith. Communist conviction and religious faith. Faith and knowledge. The role of faith and conviction in man's life.

16. Science and Religion on Moral Feelings.
Questions: Criticsm of theological teachings on moral feelings. Religion's negative influence on moral feelings. What is a "moral miracle"?

17. Religion and Women.
Questions: The attitude of religion toward women. Religion, the family, and women. Socialism liberates women. Women will not build communism through religion.

18. What Is the Bible?
Questions: The books of the Bible; the work of people. Does the Bible contain the truth? Must one live according to the Bible's morality?

19. Scientific Convictions and Religious Faith.
Questions: The religious world-view, a crude form of idealism. The smashing of religious views of the world by science. The struggle of science and religion in contemporary conditions. The atheist significance of contemporary scientific and technological achievements.

20. Religion and the Conquest of Space.
Questions: Criticism of the cosmological proof of the existence of God. Scientific views on the origin of the universe. The atheist significance of man's conquest of space.

21. On Nonreligious Holidays and Ceremonies.
Questions: The role of religious ceremonies and holidays in the preservation of religious vestiges. The ideological-educational significance of new nonreligious holidays and ceremonies. A glorious future *(shirokuyu dorogu)* for new ceremonies and traditions.

22. Propagandizing Scientific Atheism in School.

Questions: The scientific-atheist upbringing of schoolchildren, a most important task of the schools. The atheist upbringing of schoolchildren through instruction in natural and social sciences. The atheist upbringing of schoolchildren through extracurricular activities.

Notes

Abbreviations used in notes

CDSP   *Current Digest of the Soviet Press*
JPRS   Joint Publications Research Service
NiR   *Nauka i religiya*
RICDA   *Religion in Communist Dominated Areas*
VNA   A. F. Okulov et al. (eds.), *Voprosy nauchnogo ateizma,* 12 Vols.

Chapter 1, pp. 1–21

1. Karl W. Deutsch, "Social Mobilization and Political Development," *American Political Science Review,* Vol. 55, No. 3 (September, 1961), p. 494. See also Samuel P. Huntington, *Political Order in Changing Societies* (New Haven: Yale University Press, 1968), pp. 32–33; Manfred Halpern, "Toward Further Modernization of the Study of New Nations," *World Politics,* Vol. 17, No. 1 (October, 1964), p. 173; Robert C. Tucker, *The Marxian Revolutionary Idea* (New York: W. W. Norton and Co., 1969), p. 109.

2. Aristotle, *Politics* (New York: Random House, 1943), Book VIII, Chapter 1, p. 320.

3. Leon Trotsky, *Literature and Revolution* (Ann Arbor: University of Michigan Press, 1960), p. 256.

4. "Kto ne rabotayet, tot ne yest," *Kommunist,* No. 14 (1960), p. 21.

5. Yu. Frantsev and Yu. Filonovich, "Filosofskii kamen," *Izvestia,* September 19, 1965, p. 5.

6. Frederick C. Barghoorn, *Politics in the USSR,* 2nd Ed. (Boston: Little, Brown and Co., 1972), p. 88.

7. See Richard E. Dawson and Kenneth Prewitt, *Political Socialization* (Boston: Little, Brown and Co., 1969), pp. 125–126.

8. Barghoorn, op. cit., p. 110. See also Gayle Durham Hollander, *Soviet Political Indoctrination* (New York: Praeger Publishers, 1972), p. 11.

9. Waldemar Gurian, "Totalitarian Religions," *Review of Politics,* Vol. 14, No. 1 (January, 1952), p. 10.

10. Donald Eugene Smith, *Religion and Political Development* (Boston: Little, Brown and Co., 1970), p. 6.

11. Jesse D. Clarkson, *A History of Russia,* 2nd Ed. (New York: Random House, 1969), p. 368; Thomas Fitzsimmons et al., *USSR* (New Haven: HRAF Press, 1960), p. 137; Hans Braker, "The Muslim Revival in Russia," in Erwin Oberlander, et al. (eds.), *Russia Enters the Twentieth Century* (New York: Schocken Books, 1971), p. 183; Gerhard Simon, "Church, State and Society," in ibid., pp. 199–235; John Shelton Curtiss, *Church and State in Russia, 1900–1917* (New York: Columbia University Press, 1940).

12. Karl Marx, "Marx Arnoldu Ruge," in K. Marx and F. Engels, *Sochineniya,* 2nd Ed. (Moscow, 1962), Vol. 27, p. 370.

13. Karl Marx, "K kritike Gegelevskoi filosofii prava, vvedeniye," ibid., Vol. 1, p. 415.

14. Karl Marx, "Kapital," ibid., Vol. 23, p. 188.

15. Walter Kolarz, *Religion in the Soviet Union* (New York: St. Martin's Press, 1961), p. 2; Ye. Mayat, "Formirovaniye i razvitiye massovogo ateizma v SSSR," *Politicheskoye samoobrazovaniye,* No. 11 (1972), p. 88.

16. A. F. Okulov, "Za glubokuyu nauchnuyu razrabotku sovremennykh problem ateizma," *VNA,* No. 1 (1966), p. 13. See also Z. Balevits, "Nastupatelnost ateizma," *Sovetskaya Latvia,* June 16, 1972, p. 2.

17. N. A. Gorbachev, "K voprosu o predmete teorii nauchnogo ateizma," *VNA,* No. 1 (1966), p. 86.

18. T. Saidbayev, "Chemu uchit koran?", *NiR,* No. 5 (1966), p. 22.

19. See *Voprosy istorii KPSS,* No. 10 (1966), p. 11.

20. N. Gubanov, "Krainost—plokhoi pomoshchik," *Selskaya zhizn*, March 10, 1972, p. 3.

21. Robert V. Daniels, "Fate and Will in the Marxian Philosophy of History," *Journal of the History of Ideas*, Vol. 21, No. 4 (October–December, 1960), pp. 538–552. Quotation on p. 545.

22. N. Lobkowicz, "Karl Marx's Attitude Toward Religion," *The Review of Politics*, Vol. 26, No. 3 (July, 1964), pp. 319, 320.

23. See Bohdan R. Bociurkiw, "Lenin and Religion," in Leonard Schapiro and Peter Reddaway (eds.), *Lenin: The Man, the Theorist, The Leader* (New York: Frederick A. Praeger, 1967), pp. 107–134.

24. See Smith, op. cit., pp. 11, 85–86, 119.

25. For other definitions of the term, see Gerald J. Bender, "Political Socialization and Political Change," *The Western Political Quarterly*, Vol. XX, No. 2, Part I (June, 1967), pp. 370–407; Fred I. Greenstein, "A Note on the Ambiguity of 'Political Socialization': Definitions, Criticisms and Strategies of Inquiry," *The Journal of Politics*, Vol. 32, No. 4 (November, 1970), pp. 969–978.

26. Gabriel A. Almond, "Introduction: A Functional Approach to Comparative Politics," in Gabriel A. Almond and James S. Coleman (eds.), *The Politics of the Developing Areas* (Princeton: Princeton University Press, 1960), pp. 27–28.

27. See "Istochniki i podbor materialy dlya besed," *Agitator*, No. 16 (1960), p. 37.

28. Herbert Hyman, *Political Socialization* (Glencoe, Ill.: The Free Press, 1959), p. 17.

29. See, e.g., "Ateist—vsegda v nastuplenii," *Kommunist Tadzhikistana*, January 19, 1971, p. 1. For a more general discussion of political socialization in the USSR, see Robert Sharlet, "A Conceptual Framework for Mass Political Socialization in Soviet Political Development," in Roger E. Kanet and Ivan Volgyes (eds.), *On the Road to Communism* (Lawrence, Kans.: University Press of Kansas, 1972), pp. 47–59.

30. Jermy R. Azrael, "Communism, Religion and the Churches," *Problems of Communism*, Vol. XI, No. 5 (September–October, 1962), p. 55.

31. Gurian, op. cit., p. 4.

32. See, e.g., S. Simkus, "Mesto ateizma v sisteme kommunisticheskogo vospitaniya," *NiR*, No. 8 (1967), p. 19; V. Yevdokimov, "Konkretnyye sotsialnyye issledovaniya i ateizm," *NiR*, No. 1 (1968), pp. 24–25; M. I. Lensu et al., "Differentsirovannyi podkhod v ateisticheskoi vospitanii," *VNA*, No. 9 (1970), p. 134.

33. V. Garadzha, "Istina—odna," *Izvestia*, January 27, 1972, p. 5.

34. "Karl Marx i religiya," *VNA*, No. 5 (1968), p. 13.

35. Gubanov, op. cit., p. 3.

36. N. Obraztsova, "Ne 'rab bozhii,' a chelovek," *Kommunist Tadzhikistana*, March 23, 1972, p. 2.

37. "Improve Atheistic Training," *Leninskoye znamya*, November 21, 1969, in JPRS No. 49,536, p. 103.

38. N. Tarasenko, "My—ateisty," *Pravda*, April 2, 1972, p. 3.

39. Obraztsova, op. cit., p. 2.

40. Gorbachev, op. cit., p. 84. See also V. I. Stepakov, "V. I. Lenin o putyakh formirovaniya novogo cheloveka," *Voprosy filosofii*, No. 3 (1970), p. 9.

41. Balevits, op. cit., p. 2.

42. Ibid.; Obraztsova, op. cit., p. 2.

43. V. A. Mezentsev, "O sochetanii kriticheskogo i positivnogo v individualnoi rabote s veruyushchimi," in N. I. Gubanov et al. (eds.), *Individualnaya rabota s veruyushchimi* (Moscow, 1967), p. 62.

44. E. Z. Bairamov, "Osobennosti individualnoi raboty sredi posledovatelei islama," ibid., p. 114; M. Suzhikov and O. Segizbayev, "Religiya i natsionalynyye otnosheniya," *Partiinaya zhizn Kazakhstana*, No. 1 (1970), pp. 75–76.

45. See, e.g., Yu. A. Rozenbaum, "Otdeleniye tserkvi ot gosudarstva v SSSR," *Sovetskoye gosudarstvo i pravo*, No. 3 (1972), p. 58.

46. See, e.g., V. Loginov, "Babka Marfa i ateisty," *Sovetskaya Rossia*, January 6, 1972, p. 3.
47. A. Pavlov, "Iegovism kak on yest," *Sovetskaya Kirgizia*, August 13, 1970, p. 3; A. Doyev, "Sluzhiteli mraka," *Sovetskaya Kirgizia*, January 12, 1972, p. 3; M. Morozov, "Raspyatoye doveriye," *Sovetskaya Belorussia*, April 23, 1972, p. 4.
48. E. I. Lisavtsev and S. I. Nikishov, "Rukovodyashchaya rol partiinykh organizatsii v sisteme ateisticheskogo vospitaniya," *VNA*, No. 9 (1970), p. 88; N. Ashirov, "Izmeneniye sotsialnykh pozitsii," *NiR*, No. 4 (1971), pp. 37–41; N. Ashirov, "Modernizatsiya nravstvennykh predpisanii," *NiR*, No. 6 (1971), pp. 40–44.
49. E. Filimonov, "Mnogolikoye sektanstvo," *Trud*, December 30, 1971, p. 2.
50. L. Sytenko, "Vsedobryi, bez anafemy . . . ," *Komsomolskaya pravda*, November 1, 1969, p. 2.
51. A. Chertkov, "Schastye podlinnoye i mnimoye," *Moskovskaya pravda*, February 29, 1972, pp. 2–3; Lisavtsev and Nikishov, op. cit., p. 88.
52. Tarasenko, op. cit., p. 3.
53. *Sputnik ateista*, 2nd Ed. (Moscow, 1961), p. 13.
54. V. A. Smirnov, "Issledovaniye religioznogo obryada kreshcheniya sredi rabochikh," *VNA*, Vol. 5 (1968), p. 92.
55. V. Smirnov, "Voinstvuyushchii, neprimirimyi," *Komsomolskaya pravda*, October 13, 1971, p. 2.
56. N. Ashirov, "Izmeneniya v kulte," *NiR*, No. 9 (1971), p. 15.
57. Yu. Safronov, "Avtoritet ateista," *Izvestia*, November 12, 1971, p. 3; "Rech tov. G. Aliyeva," *Bakinskii rabochii*, March 14, 1972, p. 3.
58. K. Vimmsaare, "The 22nd Party Congress on Problems of Scientific-Atheist Propaganda," *Kommunist Estonii*, No. 5 (1962), in JPRS No. 16,032.
59. Ye. F. Muravyev and Yu. V. Dmitriyev, "O konkretnosti v izuchenii i preodolenii religioznykh perezhitkov," *Voprosy filosofii*, No. 3 (1961), pp. 67, 68; L. Ilyichev, "Formirovaniye nauchnogo mirovozzreniya i ateisticheskoye vospitaniye," *Kommunist*, No. 1 (1964), p. 30; T. Mering, "Konkretno o samom vazhnom," *NiR*, No. 4 (1968), p. 43.
60. M. K. Tepliakov, "Metodika i rezultaty izucheniya religioznosti selskogo naseleniya," *VNA*, Vol. 4 (1967), pp. 133–134. For a somewhat different scheme, see N. Krasnikov, "Blizhe k zhizni—blizhe k uspekhi," *NiR*, No. 12 (1965), p. 5.
61. J. Kichanova, "Vo imya cheloveka," *Izvestia*, December 19, 1965, p. 5.
62. Vimmsaare, op. cit.; I. A. Galitskaya, "Izucheniye kanalov vosproizvodstva religioznosti v novykh pokoleniyakh—odno iz trebovanii sistemy ateisticheskogo vospitaniya," *VNA*, Vol. 9 (1970), p. 76.
63. See the remarks of Yu. P. Zuyev in "Yubileinyye sessii," *VNA*, Vol. 5 (1968), p. 355.
64. A. Snechkus, "Vazhneisheye usloviye vospitaniya novogo cheloveka," *Kommunist*, No. 4 (1962), p. 50.
65. See P. N. Fedoseyev et al., *Obshchestvo i religiya* (Moscow, 1967), p. 470; P. Kolonitskii, "V. I. Lenin o kornyakh sotsialnoi sushchnosti religii," *Agitator*, No. 19 (1969), p. 51.
66. Karl Marx, *Critique of the Gotha Programme* (New York: International Publishers, 1938), p. 8.
67. Safronov, op. cit., p. 3.
68. I. D. Pantskhava (ed.), *Osnovyye voprosy nauchnogo ateizma* (Moscow, 1962), p. 337.
69. "Razum—oruzhiye!", *Komsomolskaya pravda*, December 26, 1970, p. 2.
70. V. I. Lenin, "A. M. Gorkomu," *Sochineniya*, 4th Ed. Vol. 35, pp. 89–90.
71. See Zvi Gitelman, "The Jews," *Problems of Communism*, Vol. XVI, No. 5 (September–October, 1967), pp. 92–101; Lionel Kochan (ed.), *The Jews in Soviet Russia Since 1917* (London: Oxford University Press, 1970); Yehoshua Gilboa, *The Black Years of Soviet Jewry* (Boston: Little, Brown and Company, 1971).
72. *Iudaizm bez prikras* (Kiev, 1963), pp. 86, 96.
73. A. Osipov, *Katekhizis bez prikras* (Moscow, 1963), pp. 276, 281.

74. See Kolarz, op. cit., p. 176.

75. Ibid., pp. 336–347. On the dissident movement among Soviet Baptists, see Michael Bourdeaux, *Religious Ferment in Russia* (London: The Macmillan Company, 1968). On the dissident movement within the Orthodox Church, see William C. Fletcher, *The Russian Orthodox Church Underground* (New York: Oxford University Press, 1971).

76. Kolarz, op. cit., p. 38.

77. Ibid., p. 131.

78. Ibid., pp. 425–431.

79. See *Voprosy istorii KPSS*, No. 10 (1966), p. 11.

80. A. Okulov, "Ateisticheskoye vospitaniye," *Pravda*, January 14, 1972, p. 3.

81. I. D. Pantskhava, "Vvedeniye," in I. D. Pantskhava (ed.), *Konkretnoso-tsiologicheskoye izucheniye sostoyaniya religioznosti i opyta ateisticheskogo vospitaniya* (Moscow, 1969), p. 4.

82. See L. Burkhanov, "Vsegda v nastuplenii," *Kommunist Tadzhikistana*, October 25, 1969, p. 2.

83. Robert C. Tucker, *The Marxian Revolutionary Idea* (New York: W. W. Norton and Co., 1969), p. 105.

84. R. Danilchenko, "Vse nachinayetsya s semi," *Uchitelskaya gazeta*, April 4, 1972, p. 2. See also Rozenbaum, op. cit., p. 61.

85. L. A. Filippov, "O voinstvuyushchem materializme i ateizme," *Voprosy filosofii*, No. 3 (1972), p. 67.

86. Ibid. See also "Slovo ateista," *Sovetskaya Latvia*, September 12, 1970, p. 1; Kh. Magidov, "Ateisticheskoye vospitaniye v shkolakh Dagestana," *Vospitaniye shkolnikov*, No. 1 (1972), p. 37.

87. Nancy Whittier Heer, *Politics and History in the Soviet Union* (Cambridge, Mass.: MIT Press, 1971), p. 112.

88. See, e.g., "Ateisticheskoye vospitaniye," *Pravda*, August 18, 1971, p. 1.

89. William C. Fletcher, "Religious Dissent in the USSR in the 1960s," *Slavic Review*, Vol. 30, No. 2 (July, 1971), pp. 299–300.

90. Gubanov, op. cit., p. 3. See also B. Ramm, "Vospityvat voinstvuyushchikh ateistov," *Uchitelskaya gazeta*, January 29, 1972, p. 2; V. Tancher, "Ateisticheskoye naslediye i sovremennost," *Pravda Ukrainy*, August 31, 1971, p. 2.

91. A. Belov and A. Shilkin, *Moskovskaya pravda*, May 20, 1972, p. 2. See also Balevits, op. cit., p. 2.

92. P. Dmitrenko, "Umeniye ubezhdat," *Pravda Ukrainy*, May 28, 1970, p. 3; "Vospityvat ubezhdennykh ateistov," *Prepodavaniye istorii v shkole*, No. 1 (1972), p. 4.

93. A. I. Rogov, "Ateisticheskiye radioperedachi," *VNA*, Vol. 9 (1970), p. 309; L. Burkhanov, op. cit., p. 2. See also P. P. Mishutis, "Opyt sozdaniya sistemy ateisticheskogo vospitaniya v Litovskoi SSR," *VNA*, Vol. 1 (1966), pp. 218–219.

94. See Gubanov, op. cit., p. 21.

95. Quoted in V. I. Lenin, "Chto delat?", *Sochineniya*, 5th Ed., Vol. 5, p. 380.

96. L. Ilyichev, "K novomu podemu ideologicheskoi raboty," *Kommunist*, No. 14 (1960), p. 35; M. Rusakov, "Informatsiya—vazhnyi instrument rukovodstva," *Partiinaya zhizn*, No. 14 (1969), pp. 35–38. See also Aryeh L. Unger, "Politinformator or Agitator: A Decision Blocked," *Problems of Communism*, Vol. XIX, No. 5 (September–October, 1970), pp. 30–43.

97. William H. E. Johnson, "Education," in George B. deHuszar et al., *Soviet Power and Policy* (New York: Crowell, 1955), p. 222.

Chapter 2, pp. 22–46

1. Harvey Fireside, *Icon and Swastika* (Cambridge, Mass.: Harvard University Press, 1971), p. 34. Lenin was, however, willing to exploit differences among religious communities. From 1903 until the end of the 1902s, for example, the Bolsheviks encouraged "sectarianism" in an effort to undermine the authority of the Russian Orthodox Church. See Bohdan R. Bociurkiw,

"Lenin and Religion," in Leonard Schapiro and Peter Reddaway (eds.), *Lenin: The Man, the Theorist, the Leader* (New York: Frederick A. Praeger, 1967), pp. 111–116.

2. Fireside, op. cit., p. 25.

3. Ibid., p. xiv.

4. Ibid., p. 25.

5. Ibid., p. 167.

6. For a discussion of this concept, see Edgar H. Schein, *Coercive Persuasion* (New York: W. W. Norton and Co., 1961).

7. "Law and Freedom of Conscience" (July 14, 1917), in Robert Paul Browder and Alexander F. Kerensky (eds.), *The Russian Provisional Government, 1917* (Stanford, Calif.: Stanford University Press, 1961), Vol. 2, pp. 809–810.

8. For the texts of these decrees, see Boleslaw Szczesniak (ed.), *The Russian Revolution and Religion* (Notre Dame, Ind.: Unversity of Notre Dame Press, 1959), pp. 28–33. See also Joshua Rothenberg, "The Legal Status of Religion in the Soviet Union," in Richard H. Marshall, Jr., et al. (eds.), *Aspects of Religion in the Soviet Union, 1917–1967* (Chicago: University of Chicago Press, 1971), p. 63.

9. Szczesniak, op. cit., pp. 36–37.

10. See M. Kogan, "Yakhve teryayet priverzhentsev," *Sovetskaya Moldavia*, July 7, 1966, p. 3.

11. Bociurkiw, op. cit., p. 124; Michael Bourdeaux, *Religious Ferment in Russia* (London: Macmillan and Co., 1968), p. 5.

12. For the text of the decree, see Szczesniak, op. cit., pp. 34–35. See also Robert Conquest, *Religion in the USSR* (New York: Frederick A. Praeger, 1968), p. 14.

13. "Tov. Kalinin o protsessakh tserkovnikov," *Izvestia*, August 6, 1922, p. 1.

14. John Shelton Curtiss, *The Russian Church and the Soviet State* (Boston: Little, Brown and Co., 1953), pp. 61–105; Nicholas S. Timasheff, *Religion in Soviet Russia, 1917–1942* (New York: Sheed and Ward, 1942), pp. 26–27; Rothenberg, op. cit., pp. 68–69.

15. Zvi Gitelman, "The Communist Party and Soviet Jewry: the Early Years," in Marshall, op. cit., p. 334.

16. For a discussion of the annihilation of the Catholic hierarchy, see Walter Kolarz, *Religion in the Soviet Union* (New York: St. Martin's Press, 1961), pp. 197–200.

17. See Alexandre Benningsen and Chantal Lemercier-Quelquejay, *Islam in the Soviet Union* (New York: Frederick A. Praeger, 1967); Alexander G. Park, *Bolshevism in Turkestan, 1917–1927* (New York: Columbia University Press, 1957), pp. 204–248; Kolarz, op. cit., pp. 400–447.

18. Kolarz, op. cit., p. 412.

19. N. A. Smirnov, *Ocherki istorii izucheniya islama v SSSR* (Moscow, 1954), p. 145.

20. Quoted in V. Kandidov, "Put dukhovnyi svobody," *NiR*, No. 8 (1969), p. 7.

21. Conquest, op. cit., pp. 69–70.

22. V. I. Lenin, "Doklad o partiinoi programme," *Sochineniya*, 4th Ed., Vol. 29, p. 151; I. V. Stalin, "Deklaratsiya o sovetskoi avtonomii Dagestana," *Sochineniya*, Vol. 4, p. 396, and "Doklad o sovetskoi avtonomii Terskoi oblasti," ibid., p. 402.

23. Kolarz, op. cit., p. 408.

24. Bociurkiw, op. cit., p. 126.

25. See V. Zybkovets, "Put sovetskogo ateizma," *NiR*, No. 9 (1967), p. 13. See also V. Timafeyev, "Ne takticheskii priyem, a postoyannaya liniya," *NiR*, No. 1 (1968), p. 4.

26. F. Garkavenko (ed.), *O religii i tserkvi* (Moscow, 1965), p. 63.

27. Donald W. Treadgold, *Twentieth Century Russia*, 2nd Ed. (Chicago: Rand McNally and Co., 1964), p. 251; Warren B. Walsh, *Russia and the Soviet Union* (Ann Arbor, Mich.: University of Michigan Press, 1958), pp. 425–426.

28. William C. Fletcher, *A Study in Survival* (New York: The Macmillan Company, 1965), p. 16.

29. Kolarz, op. cit., p. 416.

30. Fireside, op. cit., p. 31.

31. Vladimir Gsovski, "Separation of Church from State in the Soviet Union," in Alex Inkeles and Kent Geiger (eds.), *Soviet Society* (Boston: Houghton Mifflin Co., 1961), p. 417.

32. Cited in Nicholas S. Timasheff, "The Anti-Religious Campaign in the Soviet Union," *The Review of Politics*, Vol. 17, No. 3 (July, 1955), p. 335.

33. Bohdan R. Bociurkiw, "The Shaping of Soviet Religious Policy," *Problems of Communism*, Vol. XXII, No. 3 (May–June, 1973), p. 43.

34. Fletcher, op. cit., p. 19.

35. Nicholas V. Riasanovsky, *A History of Russia* (New York: Oxford University Press, 1963), p. 634; Paul Anderson, *People, Church and State in Modern Russia* (New York: Macmillan, 1944), pp. 81–82.

36. Kolarz, op. cit., p. 40.

37. Quoted in Treadgold, op. cit., pp. 251–252.

38. Curtiss, op. cit., pp. 160–161.

39. Anderson, op. cit., pp. 81–82.

40. Kolarz, op. cit., p. 41.

41. Fletcher, op. cit., p. 22.

42. Kolarz, op. cit., pp. 384, 409; Gitelman, op. cit., p. 331.

43. Fletcher, op. cit., p. 27.

44. Ibid., p. 24.

45. Ibid., p. 32; Curtiss, op. cit., pp. 175–195.

46. Timasheff, *Religion,* op. cit., pp. 39–40; Treadgold, op. cit., p. 350; G. V. Vorontsov, "Stroitelstvo sotsializma v SSSR i massovoi otkhod trudyashchikhsya ot religii, *VNA*, Vol. 4 (1967), p. 54.

47. Kolarz, op. cit., p. 417.

48. Ibid., p. 413.

49. Gsovski, op. cit., p. 417.

50. Curtiss, op. cit., p. 233.

51. Rothenberg, op. cit., pp. 72–80. Quotation on p. 79.

52. Curtiss, op. cit., p. 193. See also Kolarz, op. cit., pp. 413, 463.

53. Eugene Lyons, *Assignment to Utopia* (New York: Harcourt, Brace and Co., 1937), pp. 212–213.

54. *KPSS v resolyutsiyakh i resheniyakh Sezdov, konferentsii i plenumov TsK* (hereafter cited as *KPSS*), 7th Ed. (Moscow, 1954–1960), Part II, p. 19.

55. I. V. Stalin, "Pismo A. M. Gorkomu," *Sochineniya*, Vol. 12, p. 172.

56. *KPSS*, op. cit., p. 671. See also Jesse D. Clarkson, *A History of Russia* (New York: Random House, 1961), p. 641.

57. Curtiss, op. cit., pp. 272–273.

58. Fireside, op. cit., p. 37.

59. See Conquest, op. cit., pp. 29, 73, 83; Kolarz, op. cit., pp. 46–47, 422.

60. Kolarz, op. cit., p. 48.

61. Fletcher, op. cit., p. 97.

62. Timasheff, "The Anti-Religious . . . ," op. cit., p. 329; Curtiss, op. cit., pp. 290–297.

63. See Conquest, op. cit., pp. 74, 102.

64. See *Antireligioznik*, No. 5 (1939), p. 18.

65. Clarkson, op. cit., p. 686; Curtiss, op. cit., pp. 292–297; Walsh, op. cit., pp. 524, 526; Fireside, op. cit., p. 175.

66. Conquest, op. cit., p. 38; Fireside, op. cit., p. 179; Clarkson, op. cit., p. 710; Curtiss, op. cit., p. 304.

67. Conquest, op. cit., pp. 74–76.

68. Bohdan R. Bociurkiw, "The Uniate Church in the Soviet Ukraine: A Case Study in Soviet Church Policy," *Canadian Slavonic Papers*, Vol. VIII (1965), pp. 89–113.

69. Joshua Rothenberg, "Jewish Religion in the Soviet Union," in Lionel Kochan (ed.), *The Jews in Soviet Russia Since 1917* (New York: Oxford University Press, 1970), p. 174; Yehoshua A. Gilboa, *The Black Years of Soviet Jewry, 1939–1953* (Boston: Little, Brown and Company, 1971), pp. 187–225, 293–310.

70. Conquest, op. cit., p. 13.

71. *KPSS,* op. cit., Part I, pp. 420–421.

72. *Sputnik ateista* (Moscow, 1961), 2nd. Ed., p. 450.

73. Kandidov, op. cit.

74. *Sputnik ateista,* op. cit., p. 450.

75. *KPSS,* op. cit., p. 551. See also V. I. Lenin, "O znachenii voinstvuyushchego materializma," *Sochineniya,* 5th Ed. Vol. 45, pp. 23–33.

76. *Sputnik ateista,* op. cit., pp. 447–449; Clarkson, op. cit., p. 572. For a criticism of such "superficial" and "vulgar" propaganda, see I. Mindlin, "Ateisticheskoye nasledoyve N. K. Krupskoi," *Kommunist,* No. 12 (1965), p. 120.

77. P. N. Fedoseyev et al., *Obshchestvo i religiya* (Moscow, 1967), p. 461; A. Sternin, "Pomoshchik ateistov," *Agitator,* No. 19 (1967), p. 63; Curtiss, op. cit., pp. 202–203; B. N. Konovalov, "Soyuz voinstvuyushchikh bezbozhnikov," in *VNA,* op. cit., p. 65, footnote 2. See also A. A. Valentinov, *The Assault of Heaven* (London: Boswell Printing and Publishing Co., 1925), pp. 97–113.

78. *Kratkii nauchno-ateisticheskii slovar* (Moscow, 1964), p. 524.

79. See Konovalov, op. cit., pp. 66–69; Joan Delaney, "The Origins of Soviet Antireligious Organizations," in Marshall, op. cit., pp. 103–129.

80. Konovalov, op. cit., p. 73.

81. Ibid., p. 90.

82. Fedoseyev et al., op. cit., p. 463; *Kratkii nauchno-ateisticheskii slovar,,* op. cit., p. 523.

83. Konovalov, op. cit., p. 69; Zybkovets, op. cit., p. 14.

84. Fedoseyev et al., op. cit., p. 460, footnote 10; N. P. Andrianov and V. V. Pavliuk, "Kulturnaya revolyutsiya v natsionalnykh respublikakh i razvitiye ateizma mass," in *VNA,* op. cit., p. 172.

85. Walsh, op. cit., p. 426; Curtiss, op. cit., pp. 211–212.

86. Clarkson, op. cit., p. 641; I. Zhernevskaya and L. Laskina, "Kazanskaya ploshchad, dom 2 . . . ," *NiR,* No. 11 (1967), p. 17.

87. Matthew Spinka, *Christianity Confronts Communism* (New York: Harper and Brothers, 1936), pp. 112–113.

88. Curtiss, op. cit., p. 255; Zhernevskaya and Laskina, op. cit., p. 18.

89. Paul Babitsky and John Rimberg, *The Soviet Film Industry* (New York: Frederick A. Praeger, 1955), p. 117; Bertram W. Maxwell, "Political Propaganda in Soviet Russia," in Harwood L. Childs (ed.), *Propaganda and Dictatorships* (Princeton: Princeton University Press, 1936), p. 72.

90. Babitsky and Rimberg, op. cit., pp. 165–166.

91. See Poster No. 101 in Maurice Rickards, *Posters of Protest and Revolution* (New York: Walker and Co., 1970).

92. A. J. Mackenzie, *Propaganda Boom* (London: The Right Book Club, 1938), p. 98.

93. Conquest, op. cit., p. 23. I have altered the phrasing of the quoted remarks to conform more closely to American usage.

94. Konovalov, op. cit., pp. 76–78; Anderson, op. cit., p. 118.

95. Curtiss, op. cit., p. 251.

96. Fireside, op. cit., p. 43.

97. G. Kelt, "Svyataya svyatykh—chelovek!", *Komsomolskaya pravda,* August 15, 1965, p. 4.

98. See Curtiss, op. cit., pp. 246–259. Quotation on p. 259.

99. Cited in J. de Bivort de la Saudee, *Communism and Anti-Religion* (London: Burns Oates and Washbourne, Ltd., 1938), pp. 49–50.

100. Cited in Gsovski, op. cit., p. 423.

101. Babitsky and Rimberg, op. cit., p. 181.

102. *Sputnik ateista,* op. cit., pp. 457–458.

103. See *Bolshaya sovetskaya entsiklopediya,* 2nd Ed. (Moscow, 1949–1958), Vol. 2, p. 512.

104. Babitsky and Rimberg, op. cit., pp. 201–202, 208.

105. Kolarz, op. cit., p. 194; Conquest, op. cit., p. 93.

106. "O krupnykh nedostatkakh v nauchno-ateisticheskoi propagande i merakh yeyo ulushcheniya," *Voprosy ideologicheskoi raboty* (Moscow, 1961), pp. 61–65.

107. "Ob oshibkakh v provedenii nauchno-ateisticheskoi propagandy sredi naseleniya," *Pravda,* November 12, 1954.

108. See Donald A. Lowrie and William C. Fletcher, "Khrushchev's Religious Policy, 1959–1964," in Marshall, op. cit., pp. 131–132 and the sources cited therein.

109. Joan Delaney Grossman, "Khrushchev's Anti-Religious Policy and the Campaign of 1954," *Soviet Studies,* Vol. XXIV, No. 3 (January, 1973), p. 375.

110. Bohdan R. Bociurkiw, "Church-State Relations in the USSR," in Max Hayward and William C. Fletcher, *Religion and the Soviet State: A Dilemma of Power* (New York: Frederick A. Praeger, 1969), p. 96.

111. Kolarz, op. cit., p. 71.

112. Nikita Stuve, *Christians in Contemporary Russia* (New York: Charles Scribner's Sons, 1967), pp. 296–297.

113. Bohdan R. Bociurkiw, "Religion in the USSR After Khrushchev," in John W. Strong (ed.), *The Soviet Union Under Brezhnev and Kosygin* (New York: Van Nostrand Reinhold Co., 1971), pp. 133, 151.

114. Bourdeaux, op. cit., p. 14.

115. Ibid., p. 5.

116. Ibid., p. 13; Bociurkiw, "Church-State Relations . . .," op. cit., p. 98.

117. This body, more properly called the Council for the Affairs of Religious Cults, was established in January 1966 under the USSR Council of Ministers. From 1943 until 1966, its responsibilities were carried out by two separate bodies: a Council for the Affairs of the Russian Orthodox Church and a Council for the Affairs of Religious Cults. For details, see Rothenberg, op. cit., pp. 83, 96–97.

118. Bourdeaux, op. cit., p. 16.

119. Rothenberg, op. cit., pp. 87–91.

120. William C. Fletcher, *The Russian Orthodox Church Underground, 1917–1970* (New York: Oxford University Press, 1971), pp. 256–261. Quotation on p. 257.

121. *NiR,* No. 6 (1964), p. 78. See also Yu. Aleksandrov, "Mestnyye sovety i zakonodatelstvo o kultakh," *Agitator,* No. 13 (1966), pp. 58–59, and Fletcher, *A Study in Survival,* op. cit., pp. 60–62.

122. D. Konstantinov, "The Results of Soviet Persecution of the Orthodox Church," *Bulletin* (Munich), Vol. XII, No. 5 (May, 1965), pp. 42–43.

123. *Ugolovnyi kodeks RSFSR* (Moscow, 1966), p. 78.

124. L. Ilyichev, "Formirovaniye nauchnogo mirovozzreniya i ateisticheskoye vospitaniye," *Kommunist,* No. 1 (1964), p. 30. See also G. Z. Anashkin, "O svobode sovesti i soblyudenii zakonodatelstva o religioznykh kultakh," *Sovetskoye gosudarstvo i pravo,* No. 1 (1965), p. 41.

125. Anashkin, op. cit., p. 41. See also Yu. Rimaitis, "Mestnyye sovety i zakonodatelstvo o religioznykh kultakh," *Sovetskaya Litva,* March 27, 1969, p. 2.

126. See N. Shtuchnaya, "Lisheniye roditelskikh prav," *Sovetskaya yustitsiya,* No. 7 (1971), p. 15. See also the sources listed in Fletcher, *The Russian Orthodox Church Underground, 1917–1970,* op. cit., p. 233, footnote 14.

127. Struve, op. cit., p. 330.

128. Leonid F. Ilyichev, cited in ibid., p. 327.

129. Fletcher, *The Russian Orthodox Church Underground, 1917–1970,* op. cit., p. 260; Struve, op. cit., p. 305; Bourdeaux, op. cit., p. 13.

130. See, e.g., Paul B. Anderson, "The Orthodox Church in Soviet Russia," *Foreign Affairs,* Vol. 39, No. 2 (January, 1961), p. 299; Rothenberg, "The Legal Status . . . ," op. cit., pp. 89, 93.

131. A. Sukontsev, "Slugi dyavola," *Pravda,* April 14, 1968, p. 6.

132. Anashkin, op. cit., p. 41.

133. "Podstrekateli," *Izvestia,* October 18, 1969, p. 6.

134. N. Miroshchnichenko, "Who Can Be Called An Atheist?", *Komsomolskaya zhizn,* No. 13 (1963), in *RICDA,* Vol. II, No. 26, pp. 205–206; A. Olshauskas, " 'Reshitelnyye mery' tseli ne dostigayut," *NiR,* No. 6 (1963), pp. 72–73.

135. Kelt, op. cit., p. 4.

136. Ibid. See also L. N. Mitrokhin, "O metodologii konkretnykh issledovanii v oblasti religii," in V. N. Fokin et al. (eds.), *Sotsiologiya v SSSR* (Moscow, 1966), Vol. 1, p. 311.

137. *NiR,* No. 10 (1961), p. 91.

138. I. V. Stalin, "Beseda s pervoi amerikanskoi rabochei delegatsiei," *Sochineniya,* Vol. 10, p. 133.

139. See William C. Fletcher, *Religion and Soviet Foreign Policy* (New York: Oxford University Press, 1973).

140. See P. Kurochkin, "Politicheskaya orientatsiya," *NiR,* No. 4 (1969), pp. 48–52; M. Mchedlov, "Nauchnyye osnovy ateisticheskoi raboty," *Kommunist,* No. 4 (1969), p. 74.

141. "Pozdravleniye predsedatelya soveta ministrov SSSR Nikity Sergeyevicha Khrushcheva patriarkhu Moskovskomu i vseya Rusi Aleksiyu," *Zhurnal Moskovskoi Patriarkhii,* No. 12 (1962), p. 5.

142. In fact, the authorities simultaneously pursue two seemingly contradictory policies: "the progressive strangulation of organized religion and . . . the 'sovietization' of religious groups and their exploitation for [secular] purposes . . ." Bociurkiw, "Lenin and Religion," op. cit., p. 129.

143. Merle Fainsod, *How Russia is Ruled,* Rev. Ed. (Cambridge, Mass.: Harvard University Press, 1963), p. 110; Gsovskii, op. cit., p. 424.

144. William C. Fletcher, *Nikolai* (New York: The Macmillan Company, 1968), pp. 184–202.

Chapter 3, pp. 47–65

1. K. Fitisenko, "V borbe za cheloveka," *Sovetskaya Kirgizia,* August 15, 1970, p. 2; S. V. Koltunyuk and I. G. Sidorkin, "Podgotovka kadrov—vazhnoye zveno sistemy ateisticheskogo vospitaniya," *VNA,* Vol. 9 (1970), p. 173.

2. *Ustav Kommunisticheskoi Partii Sovetskogo Soyuza* (Moscow, 1966), p. 18.

3. D. Sidorov, "Terpimy li religioznyye obryady v semye kommunista?" *Agitator,* No. 6 (1964), pp. 41–42; "Voinstvuyushchiye ateisty," *Sovetskaya Rossia,* March 21, 1969, p. 1; V. I. Yevdokimov, "Mesto ateisticheskogo vospitaniya v sisteme kommunisticheskogo vospitaniya," *VNA,* Vol. 9 (1970), p. 12.

4. Yu. Safronov, "Avtoritet ateista," *Izvestia,* November 12, 1971, p. 3.

5. For a criticism of these councils, see N. Tarasenko and I. Shatilov, "Zaboty ateistov," *Pravda,* July 6, 1969, p. 3.

6. I. Davydov, "Kak my organizuyem lektsionnuyu propagandu," *Sovetskiye profsoyuzy,* No. 8 (1961), p. 32.

7. A. Voss, "Vazhnyi uchastok ideologicheskoi raboty," *Partiinaya zhizn,* No. 15 (1962), p. 24.

8. See the Central Committee resolution, "O merakh po uluchsheniyu raboty Vsesoyuznogo obshchestva po rasprostraneniyu politicheskikh i nauchnykh znanii," *Partiinaya zhizn,* No. 18 (1959), pp. 37–41. There has been little improvement since the resolution was issued.

9. G. Merkurov, *Mass Organizations in the USSR* (Moscow, n.d.), p. 36.

10. Voss, op. cit., p. 24.

11. "O merakh . . . ," op. cit., p. 37.

12. V. Arsyukhin, "Ravnodushiye," *Sovetskya Rossia*, January 14, 1972, p. 3.

13. D. Dotsenko, "Tovarishch Usanov prav!", *Agitator*, No. 2 (1963), pp. 55–56; N. Pecherskii, "Pod zvon kolokolov," *Pravda*, December 13, 1961, p. 3.

14. P. Kolonitskii, "Nekotoryye voprosy propagandy ateizma," *Politicheskoye samoobrazovaniye*, No. 4 (1963), p. 90.

15. I. Korshunov, "Umeniye ubezhdat," *Politicheskoye samoobrazovaniye*, No. 12 (1963), p. 81.

16. Nigel Grant, *Soviet Education* (Baltimore: Penguin Books, 1964), p. 63.

17. In 1970, 50 percent of all urban children and only 30 percent of rural children in the eligible age groups were enrolled in preschool facilities. "Glavnaya zadacha," *Ogonyok*, No. 9 (1971), p. 3, cited in Bernice Madison, "Social Services for Families and Children in the Soviet Union Since 1967," *Slavic Review*, Vol. 31, No. 4 (December, 1972), p. 83.

18. V. Smirnov, "Voinstvuyushchii, neprimirimyi," *Komsomolskaya pravda*, October 13, 1971, p. 2.

19. Ibid; M. A. Shelikhanov, "Ateisticheskoye vospitaniye detei," *Nachalnaya shkola*, No. 10 (1971).

20. See N. I. Boldyrev et al., *Pedagogika* (Moscow, 1968), pp. 276–286; "Teaching Methods Used to Form Atheistic Convictions in Soviet Students," *Sredneye spetsialnoye obrazovaniye*, No. 1 (1966), in JPRS No. 36,058, p. 10.

21. *Russkyi yazyk v nerusskoi shkole*, No. 1 (1966), in JPRS No. 34,804, pp. 7–8.

22. M. I. Lensu et al., "Differentsirovannyi podkhod v ateisticheskom vospitanii," *VNA*, Vol. 9 (1970), p. 147; *Prepodavaniye istorii v shkole*, No. 1 (1972), p. 3.

23. *Prepodavaniye istorii v shkole*, op. cit., p. 4.

24. V. Samsonov, "Pervaya konferentsiya," *NiR*, No. 9 (1966), pp. 67–68; "Ugolok yunogo ateista," ibid., p. 72; "Kak organizovat klub yunogo ateista," *NiR*, No. 2 (1967), pp. 77–78.

25. V. Yakub, "Muzei v shkole," *NiR*, No. 9 (1964), pp. 46–49; V. Yakub, "Vospityvat ubezhdennykh, voinstvuyushchikh ateistov," *Vospitaniye shkolnikov*, No. 5 (1971), pp. 19–20.

26. R. F. Filippova, "Ob effektivnosti ateisticheskogo vospitaniya uchashchikhsya," *Sovetskaya pedagogika*, No. 11 (1971), p. 20.

27. V. Kozhemyako, "Uchitel boretsya za cheloveka . . . ," *Pravda*, July 12, 1964, p. 3; R. Danilchenko, "Vse nachinayetsya s semi," *Uchitelskaya gazeta*, April 4, 1972, p. 2.

28. Ye. Aleshko, "Tlevornyye zerna," *NiR*, No. 3 (1967), p. 64.

29. V. Makarova, "Postavte zaslon, ateisty!", *Uchitelskaya gazeta*, August 23, 1966, p. 4.

30. I. Okunev, "Shkole pora nastupat," *NiR*, No. 12 (1961), pp. 79–80.

31. N. Lagov, "Rastit voinstvuyushchikh ateistov," *Pravda*, March 6, 1964, p. 2; B. Ramm, "Vospityvat voinstvuyushchikh ateistov," *Uchitelskaya gazeta*, January 29, 1972, p. 2; A. Gorelov, "Dokhodit do kazhdogo," *Partiinaya zhizn*, No. 12 (1971), p. 48.

32. V. Loginov, "Babka Marfa i ateisty," *Sovetskaya Rossia*, January 6, 1972, p. 3.

33. *Prepodavaniye istorii v shkole*, op. cit., p. 4.

34. V. Kindrat and S. Martensyuk, "Svyatoye delo vospitatelya," *NiR*, No. 9 (1961), p. 56. See also T. Mering, "Konkretno o samom vazhnom," *NiR*, No. 3 (1969), p. 40.

35. L. Laskina, "Ne iz prazdnogo lyubopytstva," *Uchitelskaya gazeta*, November 12, 1970, p. 2.

36. Henry Chauncey (ed.), *Soviet Preschool Education*, 2 Vols. (New York: Holt, Rinehart and Winston, 1969).

37. B. I. Katagoshchin, "Talks on Religion," *Nachalnaya shkola*, No. 5 (1962), in JPRS No. 20,515, p. 28.

38. Lagov, op. cit., p. 2; S. D. Skazkin et al., *Nastolnaya kniga ateista* (Moscow, 1968), p. 502.

39. *Administration of Teaching in Social Sciences in the USSR* (Ann Arbor: University of Michigan, 1960), pp. 1–35, especially pp. 23–24.

40. Two years earlier the course had been introduced in the Ukraine on an experimental basis. See "Voprosy ateisticheskogo vospitaniya—v povestke dnya zasedaniya ideologicheskoi kommisii pre tsentralnom komitete KPSS," *NiR*, No. 1 (1964), p. 33.

41. N. Sokolov and S. Belous, "Chto znachit byt ateistom," *Sovetskaya Rossia*, July 6, 1966, p. 3.

42. Oleg Moiseyev, "Permskiye razdumya," *NiR*, No. 10 (1966), p. 2.

43. "O meropriyatiyakh po usileniyu ateisticheskogo vospitaniya naseleniya," *Partiinaya zhizn*, No. 2 (1964), p. 23.

44. "Kazhdyi intelligent—propagandist ateizma," *NiR*, No. 2 (1962), pp. 17–18; A. Kozhevnikov, "Zabota ob ateisticheskom vospitanii," *Agitator*, No. 8 (1968), p. 48.

45. Sokolov and Belous, op. cit., p. 3; *Sputnik komsomolskogo aktivista* (Moscow, 1962), pp. 192–197; Koltunyuk and Sidorkin, op. cit., p. 158.

46. Koltunyuk and Sidorkin, op. cit., p. 157; Ye. Blyakher, "Kafedra filosofii: poisk, problemy," *Kommunist Tadzhikistana*, February 12, 1972, p. 2.

47. Sokolov and Belous, op. cit., p. 3; Moiseyev, op. cit., p. 2.

48. "Voprosy . . . ," op. cit., p. 32.

49. V. G. Afanasiev and Yu. A. Petrov, "O dissertatsionnykh rabotakh po filosofii v 1967/68 uchebnom godu," *Voprosy filosofii*, No. 1 (1969), pp. 147, 149; V. G. Afanasiev and Yu. A. Petrov, "O dissertatsionnakh rabotakh po filosofii i sotsiologii v 1968–1969 uchebnom godu," *Voprosy filosofii*, No. 12 (1969), pp. 140–142.

50. *Kratkii nauchno-ateisticheskii slovar* (Moscow, 1964), p. 178; V. Murashova, "U ateistov Moskvy," *NiR*, No. 4 (1968), pp. 31–43; L. Rozhenovich, "Novaya forma v deistvii," in I. Shatilov (ed.), *Zaboty i dela ateistov* (Moscow, 1970), p. 89.

51. S. Kurshakov, "V gorode na Volge," *NiR*, No. 4 (1968), p. 43; Ye. Riumin, "Zhivoye slovo i glubina soderzhaniya," *Agitator*, No. 6 (1967), p. 45.

52. "Obyedinennymi silami," *NiR*, No. 5 (1960), pp. 75–76.

53. P. Melnik, "Usilivayem ateisticheskuyu propagandu," *Agitator*, No. 7 (1962), p. 58; L. Volkov, "Zhiznyu rozhdennyye," *Partiinaya zhizn*, No. 24 (1962), p. 68; *Kratkii nauchno-ateisticheskii slovar*, op. cit., p. 178; Ye. Bondar, "Desyat tysach 'pochemu,' " *Agitator*, No. 23 (1964), p. 40.

54. In 1970, there were 1,114 museums in the country. See *Narodnoye obrazovaniye, nauka i kultura v SSSR* (hereafter *Narodnoye obrazovaniye*) (Moscow, 1971), p. 345.

55. P. Smolin and B. Rzhevskii, "Velikoye ucheniye o razvitii zhivogo," *NiR*, No. 6 (1966), pp. 34–37.

56. A. Medvedeva, "V pskovskikh muzeyakh," *Agitator*, No. 6 (1972), p. 35.

57. N. V. Nosovich and R. F. Filippova, "Nauchno-ateisticheskaya propaganda v kraevedcheskikh muzeyakh," *Yezhegodnik muzeya istorii religii i ateizma*, Vol. VII (1963), (Moscow-Leningrad, 1964), p. 285; A. Mennik, "Nasuchnyye zadachi ateisticheskogo vospitaniya," in Z. V. Balevits et al. (eds.), *Ateizm i religiya* (Riga, 1969), p. 10.

58. "Ateisticheskaya vystavka," *Agitator*, No. 13 (1960), p. 64.

59. Yu. Nikitin, "Antireligioznyi muzei na obshchestvennykh nachalakh," *NiR*, No. 10 (1965), pp. 56–57; I. Matusevichyus, "Dobro pozhalovat," *NiR*, No. 8 (1967), pp. 20–23; *Spravochnik propagandista i agitatora, 1966* (Moscow, 1966), p. 152.

60. *Kratkii nauchno-ateisticheskii slovar*, op. cit., pp. 382–383.

61. Ibid.; M. S. Butinova, "Novaya ekspozitsiya muzeya ('Proizkhozhdeniye religii')," *Yezhegodnik muzeya istorii religii i ateizma*, Vol. VI (1962), pp. 389–415; B. Ya. Ramm et al. (eds.), *Religiya i ateizm na zapade* (Moscow-Leningrad, 1965).

62. Matusevichyus, op. cit., pp. 20–23. See also Kh. Gordon, "Nadezhnyi pomoshchnik," *Agitator*, No. 20 (1966), p. 45.

63. G. Vorontsov, *O propagande ateizma* (Leningrad, 1959), p. 54; A. Dubinin, "Nash opyt ideinogo vospitaniya studentov," *Politicheskoye samoobrazovaniye*, No. 6 (1963), p. 79.

64. Filippova, op. cit., p. 20.

65. "Aktivno vesti ateisticheskoye vospitaniye," *Pravda*, March 2, 1964, p. 2; "V institute nauchnogo ateizma," *Izvestia*, February 19, 1967, p. 6; R. A. Lopatkin, "Na opornykh punktakh instituta nauchnogo ateizma," *VNA*, Vol. 5 (1968), pp. 336–342.

66. See V. Leshan, "Propaganda ateizma," *Partiinaya zhizn*, No. 8 (1972), p. 66. Of the 15,788 people's universities in existence in 1969, only 198 were devoted to the study of scientific atheism. See *Narodnoye obrazovaniye*, op. cit., p. 352.

67. Koltunyuk and Sidorkin, op. cit., p. 160. See also G. Mukvich, "Vazhnoye usloviye ateisticheskogo vospitaniya," *Politicheskoye samoobrazovaniye*, No. 5 (1972), p. 97.

68. M. K. Tepliakov, "Sotsialnyye issledovaniya v sisteme ateisticheskogo vospitaniya," *VNA*, Vol. 9 (1970), p. 119.

69. G. A. Aliyev, *Bakinskii rabochii*, March 14, 1972, p. 3.

70. *Pid Praporom Leninismu*, No. 24 (1970), in JPRS No. 53,088, pp. 67–70.

71. "Rech pervogo sekretarya TsK Kompartii Moldavii tov. I. I. Bodyula na XVI sezde komsomola Moldavii," *Sovetskaya Moldavia*, March 14, 1972, p. 2; *Komsomolskaya zhizn*, No. 23 (1971), p. 24.

72. T. K. Nikolayeva, "Ideologicheskaya rabota i zadachi profsoyuzov," *Klub i khudozhestvennaya samodeyatelnost*, No. 15 (1968), p. 2; I. G. Shlemis et al., *Kulturno-prosvetitelnaya rabota* (Moscow, 1969), p. 372.

Chapter 4, pp. 66–84

1. I. Kryvelev, "Vazhnaya storona byta," *Kommunist*, No. 8 (1961), p. 65; M. Magomedov, "Obychai predkov khranya," *Sovetskaya Rossia*, July 23, 1971, p. 3.

2. B. Vestnikov, "Narod sozdayet traditsii," *NiR*, No. 1 (1964), p. 61. See also S. S. Ostroumov, *Sovetskaya sudebnaya statistika* (Moscow, 1969), p. 24.

3. A. Kozhevnikov, "Ateisticheskoye vospitaniye selskogo naseleniya v sovremennykh usloviyakh," in I. Shatilov (ed.), *Zaboty i dela ateistov* (Moscow, 1970), p. 53.

4. A. Filatov, *O novykh i starykh obryadakh* (Moscow, 1967), pp. 20, 42; P. P. Kampars and N. M. Zakovich, *Sovetskaya grazhdanskaya obryadnost* (Moscow, 1967), pp. 8, 163; "Eto ochen vazhno," in *Torzhestvenno, krasivo, pamyatno!* . . . (Moscow, 1966) (hereafter cited as *Torzhestvenno*), p. 5.

5. V. Dolgova, "Prazdniki, obryady, traditsii," *NiR*, No. 12 (1966), p. 11. See also Kryvelev, op. cit., pp. 68–69.

6. Filatov, op. cit., p. 14.

7. V. Konstantinov, "O tak nazyvayemom rozhdestve Khristovom," *Agitator*, No. 22 (1966), pp. 50–51; S. F. Almazov and P. Ya. Piterskii, *Prazdniki pravoslavnoi tserkvi* (Moscow, 1962). See also Williston Walker, *A History of the Christian Church* (New York: Charles Scribner's Sons, 1959), pp. 154–155.

8. P. Tronko, "Novaya ideologiya—novyye obryady," *Izvestia*, June 2, 1964, p. 6.

9. Kampars and Zakovich, op. cit., pp. 19–21; G. V. Vorontsov, "Stroitelstvo sotsializma v SSSR i massovyi otkhod trudyashchikhsya ot religii," *VNA*, Vol. 4 (1967), p. 51; B. N. Konovalov, "Soyuz voinstvuyushchikh bezbozhnikov," ibid., p. 80.

10. See Walter Kolarz, *Religion in the Soviet Union* (New York: St. Martin's Press, 1961), pp. 31–32; Samuel Harper, *Civic Training in Soviet Russia* (Chicago: University of Chicago Press, 1929), pp. 225–227.

11. I. P. Tsamerian, *Osnovy nauchnogo ateizma*, 2nd Ed. (Moscow, 1962), p. 391; G. Paskel and G. Denisenko, "Ateisticheskaya rabota na sele," *Politicheskoye samoobrazovaniye*, No. 7 (1962), p. 98; O. Shvydak, "Novyye prazdniki i obychai," *Agitator*, No. 22 (1964), p. 48.

12. L. Alekseyeva, *Sovremennyye prazdniki i obryady v derevne* (Moscow, 1968), p. 48; Yu. Feofanov, "Persistently, Flexibly, Intelligently!", *Sovety deputatov trudyashchikhsya*, No. 10 (1960), in *CDSP*, Vol. XII, No. 51, p. 38; Yevgeny Kriger, "Spor prodolzhayetsya," *Izvestia*, December 5, 1959, p. 2.

13. Tronko, op. cit., p. 6.

14. Kampars and Zakovich, op. cit., p. 48.

15. Ibid., pp. 101–102. See also S. Abramov, "Prazdniki v kolkhoze 'Rossia,' " in Shatilov (ed.), op. cit., p. 193.

16. Filatov, op. cit., pp. 97–100.

17. D. Sidorov, "Zhizn podskazyvayem," *Partiinaya zhizn*, No. 6 (1963), p. 50. See also Filatov, op. cit., p. 20.

18. Alekseyeva, op. cit., p. 14.

19. Filatov, op. cit., pp. 44, 45.

20. Ibid., p. 52; Kolarz, op. cit., p. 33.

21. Kampars and Zakovich, op. cit., pp. 29–30.

22. "Rabote sredi zhenshchin—osoboye vnimaniye," *NiR*, No. 1 (1964), p. 37.

23. Ye. A. Karpovskii, "Prichiny sushchestvovaniya religioznykh perezhitkov v SSSR i puti ikh preodoleniya," *Voprosy filosofii*, No. 4 (1964), p. 150.

24. O. Poleshko-Polesskii, "Khoroshiye traditsii," *Partiinaya zhizn*, No. 6 (1963), p. 53.

25. N. Arkhangelskii, "Den semeinogo schastya," in *Torzhestvenno*, op. cit., p. 39. See also N. Semakin and Ye. Bugrov, "Bolshogo schastya tebe, malysh," ibid., pp. 47–48. For photographs of the medals distributed in Leningrad and Kerch, see *NiR*, No. 1 (1964), p. 39.

26. A. Yefremova, "Vsekh interesuyet: a kak v Moskve?", in *Torzhestvenno*, op. cit., pp. 16–17.

27. Filatov, op. cit., pp. 49–50.

28. Semakin and Bugrov, op. cit., p. 45.

29. Yefremova, op. cit., p. 15.

30. V. Kaupuzh, *Izvestia*, October 28, 1971, p. 5; V. D. Kobetskii, "Obryad kreshcheniya kak proyavleniye religioznosti," in I. D. Pantskhava (ed.), *Konkretno-sotsiologicheskoye izucheniye sostoyaniya religioznosti i opyta ateisticheskogo vospitaniya* (Moscow, 1969), p. 167; V. A. Smirnov, "Issledovaniye religioznogo obryada kreshcheniya sredi rabochikh," *VNA*, Vol. 5 (1968), p. 88.

31. T. Sivokhina, "Na 'trekhgorke,'" in *Torzhestvenno*, op. cit., p. 93.

32. Poleshko-Polesskii, op. cit., pp. 53–54. See also Kaupuzh, op. cit., p. 5.

33. G. Gerodnik, "Grazhdanskiye i bytovyye obryady," *NiR*, No. 7 (1962), pp. 48, 49; V. Ranne, "Ateisticheskoye vospitaniye: problemy i zadachy," *Sovetskaya Estonia*, October 9, 1971, p. 3.

34. Kriger, op. cit., p. 2.

35. S. Shchetinin, "Braki v Tartu . . . ," *Izvestia*, May 10, 1959, p. 6.

36. K. L. Yemelyanova, *Pervyi v strane* (Leningrad, 1964); V. Razumov, "Razveyat tuman religioznykh predrassudkov," *Agitator*, No. 16 (1963), pp. 34–35.

37. See, e.g., Sh. Annaklychev, "Pogovorim ob obychayakh," *Turkmenskaya iskra*, September 24, 1971, p. 4.

38. Alekseyeva, op. cit., p. 23.

39. John Shelton Curtiss, *The Russian Church and the Soviet State* (Boston: Little, Brown and Co., 1953), p. 71.

40. Kampars and Zakovich, op. cit., pp. 211, 239–240; Filatov, op. cit., p. 70.

41. Kampars and Zakovich, op. cit., p. 211.

42. A. Saar, "Ob odnom selskom raikome," *Kommunist*, No. 11 (1960), p. 63.

43. Poleshko-Polesskii, op. cit., p. 52.

44. Saar, op. cit., p. 63.

45. Ibid.; Poleshko-Polesskii, op. cit., p. 52.

46. Kampars and Zakovich, op. cit., pp. 175, 190; K. Sharova, "Dorogi otsov—puti synovei," in *Torzhestvenno*, op. cit., pp. 105–111; Kryvelev, op. cit., p. 71.

47. M. Karimov, "Staromu—boi!", *NiR*, No. 10 (1966), p. 54.

48. See Bertram D. Wolfe, *An Ideology in Power* (New York: Stein and Day, 1969), p. 235, footnote 2.

49. Kriger, op. cit., p. 2.

50. See P. Kolonitskii, "Nekotoryye voprosy propagandy ateizma," *Politicheskoye samoobrazovaniye*, No. 4 (1963), p. 91; V. Grigoriev, "Da, byli prazdniki . . . ," *NiR*, No. 6 (1966), p. 51; Kampars and Zakovich, op. cit., pp. 6, 201; Alekseyeva, op. cit., p. 49.

51. Gerodnik, op. cit., p. 51; Kampars and Zakovich, op. cit., p. 234.

52. Filatov, op. cit., p. 20.

53. Gerodnik, op. cit., p. 51. See also Alekseyeva, op. cit., pp. 19, 29.

54. Kampars and Zakovich, op. cit., pp. 202–203; Semakin and Bugrov, op. cit., p. 44.

55. Kamil Faizulin, "Kladbishchenskiye tsitserony," *Izvestia*, August 19, 1961, p. 6.

56. Gerodnik, op. cit., p. 46. See also G. Gerodnik, "Tak v dobryi chas!", *NiR*, No. 7 (1966), p. 33.

57. "Forum ateistov Srednei Azii," *NiR*, No. 5 (1964), p. 16.

58. Gerodnik, "Grazhdanskiye . . . ," op. cit., p. 46; "Ideologicheskii otdel partiinogo komiteta," *Partiinaya zhizn*, No. 24 (1963), pp. 50–51.

59. See I. Dzhabbarov, *Kommunist Uzbekistana*, No. 6 (1971).

60. N. Ashirov, "Izmeneniya v kulte," *NiR*, No. 9 (1971), pp. 16–17.

61. Kampars and Zakovich, op. cit., pp. 229, 237; Tronko, op. cit., p. 6; Ranne, op. cit., p. 2; Kaupuzh, op. cit., p. 5.

62. Kampars and Zakovich, op. cit., p. 237.

63. Kaupuzh, op. cit., p. 5; Gerodnik, "Grazhdanskiye . . . ," op. cit., p. 49.

64. B. Shneidere, "Sovetskiye obryady—partiinoye delo," *NiR*, No. 2 (1969), p. 37; Tronko, op. cit., p. 6.

65. A. Nikolayev, "Ateizm v efire," in Shatilov, op. cit., p. 122; "Podderzhat poleznoye delo," *Sovety deputatov trudyashchikhsya*, No. 8 (1971), pp. 83–85; Kaupuzh, op. cit., p. 5.

66. Kampars and Zakovich, op. cit., pp. 238–239.

67. See H. Kent Geiger, "Changing Political Attitudes in Totalitarian Society: A Case Study of the Role of the Family," *World Politics*, Vol. 7, No. 2 (January, 1956), pp. 187–205; Alex Inkeles and Raymond A. Bauer, *The Soviet Citizen* (Cambridge, Mass.: Harvard University Press, 1959), pp. 210–230.

68. The Party has experienced particular difficulty in developing an effective response to people's personal traumas and crises. Many people in the West have commented on communism's apparent inability to deal, for example, with suffering and grief when a loved one dies. As William C. Fletcher has put it, the Christian doctrine of personal immortality seems to "have a power with which the Communist Party of the Soviet Union cannot compete." William C. Fletcher, *Nikolai* (New York: The Macmillan Company, 1968), p. 139.

69. Tsamerian, op. cit., pp. 391–392.

Chapter 5, pp. 85–103

1. See Steven H. Chaffee et al., "Mass Communication and Political Socialization," *Journalism Quarterly*, Vol. 47, No. 4 (Winter, 1970), pp. 647–659.

2. V. I. Lenin, "S chego nachat?", *Sochineniya*, 4th Ed., Vol. 5, p. 10.

3. F. Oleshchuk, "Propaganda ateizma," *Sovetskaya pechat*, No. 10 (1959), p. 32.

4. Nikolai G. Palgunov, *Osnovy informatsii v gazetakh* (Moscow, 1956). See also D. Shevlyagin, "Neodolimaya sila marksistsko-leninskikh idei," *Pravda*, June 14, 1967, pp. 4–5; A. Shishkov, "Partiya i sredstva massovoi informatsii," *Kommunist*, No. 4. (1970), p. 64.

5. I. Tolkunov, "Problemy nravstvennogo vospitaniya i pechat," *Kommunist*, No. 2 (1967), p. 74.

6. B. Grigorian, "Nauchno-ateisticheskaya tema," *Sovetskaya pechat*, No. 4 (1963), p. 41.

7. P. Yeran, "Za cheloveka—protiv boga," *Sovetskaya pechat*, No. 7 (1961), pp. 23–24; A. Muzafarov, "Bogi ne umirayut sami," *Pravda vostoka*, July 5, 1970, p. 2; M. Kutsenko, "Nauchno-ateisticheskaya tema v gazete," *Sovetskaya Belorussia*, June 26, 1971, p. 2.

8. I. Shatilov, "Novoye u ateistov ryazanshchiny," *NiR*, No. 3 (1968), p. 32.

9. "Prizvaniye zhurnalista," *NiR*, No. 6 (1965), p. 36; N. Sorokovoi, "Nastupayet!", *Sovetskaya pechat*, No. 10 (1962), p. 24.

10. Alexander Osipov, "Otkaz ot religii—yedinstvenno pravilnyi put," *Pravda*, December 6, 1959, p. 4.

11. On the subject of Party infiltration of the church, see Walter Kolarz, *Religion in the Soviet Union* (New York: St. Martin's Press, 1961), pp. 91–92. For a Soviet denial that such tactics are used, see A. Osipov, "Ne po sushchestvu spora," *NiR*, No. 10 (1965), p. 14.

12. *Sovetskaya Latvia*, December 1, 1962.

13. Ibid.

14. See, e.g., "Borba protiv religii—borba za cheloveka," *Politicheskoye samoobrazovaniye*, No. 12 (1963), p. 73; B. Zaikin and Yu. Krasovskii, "Nad gazetnoi stranitsei," *NiR*, No. 6 (1967), p. 95.

15. B. Marianov, "Metodami ubezhdeniya," *Agitator*, No. 4 (1966), p. 46; "Pismo iz redaktsii," *NiR*, No. 3 (1965), pp. 23–26; A. Sulatskov, "Medvezhya usluga ateistam," *NiR*, No. 2 (1968), pp. 94–95; I. Dementieva, letter to the editor, *Izvestia*, February 19, 1969, p. 4.

16. "Publitsistka vysokikh idei," *Sovetskaya pechat*, No. 7 (1964), p. 15.

17. Grigorian, op. cit., p. 41.

18. Ibid.; Oleshchuk, op. cit., pp. 32–33; A. Akliyev, "Bolshe literatury po kritike islama," *NiR*, No. 9 (1965), p. 86.

19. Grigorian, op. cit., p. 41. See also M. Kriukov, "Myuridy poluchayut otpor," *Pravda*, March 29, 1970, p. 2.

20. Cited in Mark W. Hopkins, *Mass Media in the Soviet Union* (New York: Pegasus Publishers, 1970), p. 150.

21. V. Davydchenkov and L. Karpinskii, "Chitatel—gazeta," *Izvestia*, July 11, 1968, p. 5; "Poll of Izvestia Readers," *Nedelya*, March 5–11, 1967, in *CDSP*, Vol. XIX, No. 16, p. 27.

22. *Sputnik ateista*, 2nd Ed. (Moscow, 1961), p. 435.

23. Yu. Feofanov, "Nelzya stoyat v storone . . . ," *Izvestia*, March 15, 1959, p. 3.

24. V. Bukin, "Preodoleniye religioznykh chuvstv," *Kommunist*, No. 2 (1963), pp. 73–74. One character in the atheist film *In Broad Daylight* is said to resemble "a snake crawling out of a crevice." Yu. Lukin, "Boyevoi kinoreportazh," *Pravda*, August 10, 1964, p. 4.

25. G. Prozhiko, "Poprobuyem razobratsya . . . ," *NiR*, No. 1 (1965), p. 79.

26. I. Stepanov, "Protiv lzhi i mrakobesiya," *Partiinaya zhizn*, No. 10 (1963), p. 76.

27. V. Baulin, "Deyaniya 'svyatogo Filina,' " *NiR*, No. 2 (1963), pp. 92–93.

28. I. Bakurinskii, "Kino i nauchno-ateisticheskaya propaganda," *Agitator*, No. 8 (1962), p. 63.

29. See Prozhiko, op. cit., p. 79; Yefim Dorosh, "Dostovernost vzglyada," *Pravda*, March 24, 1967, p. 3.

30. A. Baigushev, "Day Against Night," *Literaturnaya zhizn*, April 9, 1961, in *CDSP*, Vol. XIII, No. 17, p. 14.

31. Ibid.; R. Bakhrakh, "Ateisticheskaya tematika v nauchno-populyarnykh i dokumentalnykh sovetskikh filmakh," *NiR*, No. 5 (1962), p. 14.

32. Baulin, op. cit., p. 92.

33. "Filosofskiye zavety V. I. Lenina," *Kommunist*, No. 5 (1962), p. 41.

34. Baigushev, op. cit., p. 15.

35. L. N. Mitrokhin, "Izucheniye sektanstva v Tambovskoi oblasti," *Voprosy filosofii*, No. 1 (1960), pp. 143–148.

36. Bukin, op. cit., p. 74. See also M. Semenov, "V dolgu pered yunymi zritelyami," *NiR*, No. 9 (1966), p. 77.

37. D. Ugrinovich, "Neobkhodima produmannaya sistema nauchno-ateisticheskogo vospitaniya," *Kommunist*, No. 9 (1962), p. 100.

38. Bakurinskii, op. cit., p. 63. For an example of an atheist film scenario, see Gennadi Koleda and Yazgeldy Seidov, "On ochen khotel zhit," *NiR*, No. 1 (1969), pp. 52–62.

39. "Put k razumu i chuvstvam," *NiR*, No. 3 (1963), pp. 3–7.

40. *Kazakhstanskaya pravda*, October 24, 1971.

41. V. Surkov, "Komandirovka v rai," *Izvestia*, September 26, 1963, p. 4.

42. L. Anufriyev, "K chemu my stremimsya?", *NiR*, No. 2 (1963), p. 67. See also Bakhrakh, op. cit., p. 14.

43. A. Sergeyev, "Nashi probely," *NiR*, No. 10 (1962), p. 71; Prozhiko, op. cit., p. 79.

44. "O meropriyatiyakh po usileniyu ateisticheskogo vospitaniya naseleniya," *Partiinaya zhizn*, No. 2 (1964), p. 24.

45. "Vazhnoye resheniye dolzhno byt vypolneno," *NiR*, No. 6 (1964), p. 92.

46. "Gde dostat diafilm?", *NiR*, No. 12 (1964), p. 88.

47. Bakurinskii, op. cit., p. 63.

48. "O meropriyatiyakh . . . ," op. cit., p. 25; V. Suyarko, "The Children's Movie Theater 'Pioneer,' " *Voiovnichii ateist*, No. 2 (1963), in *RICDA*, Vol. II, No. 13, pp. 99–100.

49. Yu. Babakin, "V selskom dome kultury," *Agitator*, No. 10 (1965), p. 29; "Vesti lyudei v shirokii mir," *Agitator*, No. 9 (1963), p. 34; B. Markin, "Bez boyevitosti," *Agitator*, No. 20 (1965), p. 50.

50. A. Rapokhin, "Gazeta bez bumagi i rasstoyanii," *Agitator*, No. 7 (1972), p. 43.

51. "Ob uluchshenii sovetskogo radioveshchaniya i dalneishem razvitii televidenii," *Partiinaya zhizn*, No. 4 (1960), p. 29.

52. "Tvorcheskiye sily—vypolneniyu reshenii partii," *Pravda*, May 7, 1972, p. 2. See also Hopkins, op. cit., p. 252.

53. "Tvorcheskiye . . . ," op. cit., p. 2; K. K. Yatskevich, "XXIV Sezd KPSS o zadachakh sredstv massovoi informatsii i propagandy v borbe protiv burzhuaznoi ideologii," *Voprosy istorii KPSS*, No. 6 (1972), p. 101.

54. S. Zagoruiko, "Zabota ob uluchshenii partiino-politecheskoi informatsii," *Agitator*, No. 11 (1969), p. 45.

55. See Hopkins, op. cit., p. 239.

56. A. I. Rogov, "Ateisticheskiye radioperedachi," *VNA*, No. 9 (1970), p. 319.

57. G. L. Andreyev et al., "Boyevoye oruzhiye ateisticheskoi propagandy," *Voprosy filosofii*, No. 7 (1964), p. 163. See also A. Oparin, "Propaganda nauchnogo mirovozzreniya i televideniye," *Pravda*, March 21, 1964, p. 2.

58. A. Kozhevnikov, "Ateisticheskoye vospitaniye selskogo naseleniya v sovremnnykh usloviyakh," in I. Shatilov (ed.), *Zaboty i dela ateistov* (Moscow, 1970), pp. 42–43.

59. A. Yakovlev, "Televideniye: problemy, perspektivy," *Kommunist*, No. 13 (1965), p. 71.

60. G. Kazakov, "Finding Programs to Meet Television's Voracious Needs," *Kommunist*, No. 8 (1959), quoted in Wilson P. Dizard, "Television in the USSR," *Problems of Communism*, Vol. XII, No. 6 (November–December, 1963), p. 45.

61. M. Morozov, "Nekotoryye voprosy mirovozzreniya i religiya," *NiR*, No. 10 (1965), p. 11.

62. Stepanov, op. cit., p. 76; A. Rogov, "Nash golos v efire," *NiR*, No. 3 (1962), pp. 10–11.

63. Rogov, op. cit., pp. 10–11.

64. Ibid.

65. S. V. Kaftanov et al. (eds.), *Radio i televideniye v SSSR* (Moscow, 1961), in JPRS No. 4,838, pp. 52–53, 74.

66. A. Shamaro, "Svet golubnogo ekrana," *NiR*, No. 3 (1962), p. 11; L. D. Glukhovskaya, "Televideniye—perspektivnaya forma ateisticheskoi propagandy," *VNA*, Vol. 9 (1970), p. 319, footnote 1.

67. V. Rudnev, "Nasha sistema antireligioznoi propagandy," *Agitator*, No. 11 (1965), pp. 42–44; B. Zaikin, "Pered samoi bolshoi auditorei," *Agitator*, No. 20 (1966), pp. 44–45; V. Komarov, "Tvorcheskaya dolzhnost," *NiR*, No. 4 (1967), p. 35.

68. Stepanov, op. cit., pp. 75–76.

69. A. Khvorostyanov and B. Borobik, "Izuver poluchil po zaslugam," *NiR*, No. 1 (1962), pp. 81–82; N. Sviridov and V. V. Talanov, "Na zemle sibirskoi . . . ," *NiR*, No. 5 (1961), pp. 72–73.

70. V. Buslinskii, "Tonkoye delo," *Agitator*, No. 7 (1961), p. 49. See also T. G. Yakovleva, *Ateisticheskaya propaganda v massovykh bibliotekakh* (Moscow, 1969), p. 41.

71. V. Uryvskii and M. Tepliakov, "Radiozhurnal 'Nauka i religiya,' " *Agitator*, No. 13 (1965), p. 33.

72. Quoted in R. Boretsky, "Problems of Television: When There Are Many Channels," *Sovetskaya kultura*, September 11, 1965, in *CDSP*, Vol. XVII, No. 39, p. 13.

73. Ibid.

74. "Ob uluchshenii sovetskogo radioveshchaniya . . . ," op. cit., p. 31.

75. N. Kozhanov and G. Kondratenko, "Monolog ili dialog?", *Pravda*, September 19, 1969, p. 2.

Chapter 6, pp. 104–118

1. K. Vimmsaare, *Kommunist Estonii*, No. 5 (1962), in JPRS No. 16,032.

2. A. V. Losev et al., *Sotsialno-ekonomicheskiye preobrazovaniya v voronezhskoi derevne* (Voronezh, 1967), p. 313.

3. See the decree of the Party Central Committee, "Ob oshibkakh v provedenii nauchno-ateisticheskoi propagandy sredi naseleniya," *Voprosy ideologicheskoi raboty* (Moscow, 1961), p. 75. See also P. N. Fedoseyev et al., *Obshchestvo i religiya* (Moscow, 1967), p. 488.

4. "Shirit i uglublyat propagandu ateizma," *Agitator*, No. 16 (1959), p. 4; "Boyevaya programma," *NiR*, No. 11 (1963), p. 5.

5. Cited in Walter Kolarz, *Religion in the Soviet Union* (New York: St. Martin's Press, 1961), p. 21.

6. I. Shatilov, "Novoye u ateistov ryazanshchiny," *NiR*, No. 3 (1968), p. 61. See also O. Severgin, "Ateizm i pechat," in I. Shatilov (ed.), *Zaboty i dela ateistov* (Moscow, 1970), p. 78.

7. Losev et al., op. cit., p. 313.

8. "Ateisticheskoye vospitaniye trudyashchikhsya," *Sovetskaya Kirgizia*, November 4, 1970, p. 1; V. Ranne, "Ateisticheskoye vospitaniye: problemy i zadachy," *Sovetskaya Estonia*, October 9, 1971, p. 3.

9. I. D. Pantskhava, *Osnovyye voprosy nauchnogo ateizma* (Moscow, 1962), p. 352.

10. V. Utkov, "Klub i veruyushchiye," *Agitator*, No. 23 (1966), p. 43.

11. A. Olshauskas, " 'Reshitelnyye mery' tseli ne dostigayut," *NiR*, No. 6 (1963), pp. 72–73. See also M. Chernov, "I umu, i serdtsu!", *Komsomolskaya pravda*, January 26, 1968, p. 4.

12. A. Osipov, "Ot serdtsa k serdtsu," *Agitator*, No. 19 (1962), p. 55. See also R. F. Filippova, "Ob effektivnosti ateisticheskogo vospitaniya uchashchikhsya," *Sovetskaya pedagogika*, No. 11 (1971), p. 18.

13. V. Chertikhin, "Ateisticheskaya beseda," *Agitator*, No. 9 (1960), p. 29.

14. "Iskat klyuch k serdtsu kazhdogo," *Sovetskaya pechat*, No. 6 (1963), p. 8. See also A. Stepanov, "Golos i zhesty oratora," *NiR*, No. 6 (1965), p. 41.

15. A. F. Okulov, "Za glubokuyu nauchnuyu razrabotku sovremennykh problem ateizma," *VNA*, Vol. 1 (1966), p. 34. See also N. Tarasenko, "My—ateisty," *Pravda*, April 2, 1972, p. 3.

16. F. G. Nikitina et al., "Formy organizatsii i opyt ateisticheskogo vospitaniya na promyshlennykh predpriyatiyakh," *VNA*, Vol. 9 (1970), p. 199; L. Antoshin, "Ateisticheskoye vospitaniye budushchikh meditsinskikh sester," in Shatilov, op. cit., pp. 173–175.

17. Yu. A. Chukovenkov, "Organizatsiya individualnoi raboty s veruyushchimi," in N. I. Gubanov et al. (eds.), *Individualnaya rabota s veruyushchimi* (Moscow, 1967), p. 22; S. V. Koltunyuk, "Dokhodit do kazhdogo—znachit uchityvat osobennosti kazhdogo," ibid., pp. 88–89.

18. M. K. Tepliakov, "Sotsialnyye issledovaniya v sisteme ateisticheskogo vospitaniya," *VNA*, No. 9 (1970), p. 118.

19. L. Bazhin, "Gotovya lektsiyu, dumai o cheloveke," *Partiinaya zhizn*, No. 11 (1963), p. 63; A. Chertkov, "Propoved i lektsiya," *NiR*, No. 8 (1965), p. 28; V. Arsyukhin, "Ravnodushiye," *Sovetskaya Rossia*, January 14, 1972, p. 3.

20. "Itogi, plany, razdumya . . . ," *NiR*, No. 6 (1962), pp. 75–76; N. P. Krasnikov, "O nekotorykh voprosakh raboty s veruyushchimi," in N. P. Krasnikov et al. (eds.), *Voprosy preodoleniya religioznykh perezhitkov v SSSR* (Moscow-Leningrad, 1966), p. 13.

21. I. Korshunov, "Umeniye ubezhdat," *Politicheskoye samoobrazovaniye*, No. 12 (1963), p. 81. See also V. Leshan, "Propaganda ateizma," *Partiinaya zhizn*, No. 8 (1972), p. 66.

22. I. Mikulovich, "Tam, gde gospodstvovala tserkov," *NiR*, No. 7 (1961), p. 82; V. A. Mezentsev (ed.), *Otvety veruyushchim*, 2nd Ed. (Moscow, 1965). The Knowledge Society also puts out a monthly journal for lecturers, *Slovo lektora*.

23. P. Klyuyev, "Bolshoye i vazhnoye delo," *Sovetskiye profsoyuzy*, No. 14 (1960), p. 39.

24. V. Surov, "Umet ubezhdat," *Agitator*, No. 17 (1963), p. 63.

25. Yu. Dmitriyev, *Kommunist Latvii*, No. 1 (1972). See also Arsyukhin, op. cit., p. 3; Klyuyev, op. cit., p. 39.

26. L. Pinchuk, "Propaganda ateizma—nasha obyazannost," *Partiinaya zhizn*, No. 5 (1960), p. 73. See also I. Zhurkin and B. Katagoshchin, "Sprashivaite—otvechayem," in Shatilov (ed.), op. cit., p. 188; B. Lobovik and B. Chudnovskii, "K voprosu ob effektivnosti ateisticheskoi propagandy," *Kommunist Ukrainy*, No. 11 (1969), p. 79.

27. Mikulovich, op. cit., p. 83.

28. N. Tarasenko and I. Shatilov, "Zaboty ateistov," *Pravda*, July 6, 1969, p. 3; Ye. Riumin, "Zhivoye slovo i glubina soderzhaniya," *Agitator*, No. 6 (1967), p. 44; Yu. D. Krasovskii and Ye. F. Riumin, "Emotsionalnost ateisticheskoi propagandy," *VNA*, No. 9 (1970), p. 132.

29. "Ob oshibkakh . . . ," op. cit., p. 72.

30. N. S. Sofronov, "Ateisticheskoye vospitaniye v selskoi mestnosti," *VNA*, No. 9 (1970), p. 244; R. Danilchenko, "Vse nachinayetsya s semi," *Uchitelskaya gazeta*, April 4, 1972, p. 2.

31. Shatilov, op. cit., p. 61.

32. Losev et al., op. cit., p. 313; G. A. Nosova, "Opyt etnograficheskogo izucheniya bytovogo pravoslaviya," *VNA*, No. 3 (1967), p. 163; Sofronov, op. cit., p. 238.

33. "Forum ateistov Srednei Azii," *NiR*, No. 5 (1964), p. 14; Chertkov, op. cit., p. 28; I. Shatilov, "Novoye u ateistov . . . ," op. cit., p. 61.

34. S. Ivanov, "How We Organize Scientific-Atheist Propaganda," *Kommunist Moldavii*, No. 7 (1961), in JPRS No. 10,899. See also Leshan, op. cit., p. 64.

35. Pantskhava, op. cit., p. 355; Mikulovich, op. cit., p. 84.

36. E. Bairamov, "Propaganda ateizma v klube," *VNA*, Vol. 9 (1970), p. 261.

37. N. Umanets, "Shapkami ne zakidayet!", *Komsomolskaya pravda*, May 29, 1965, p. 2.

38. I. P. Tsamerian et al. (eds.), *Osnovy nauchnogo ateizma*, 2nd Ed. (Moscow, 1962), pp. 382–383. See also T. G. Yakovleva, *Ateisticheskaya propaganda v massovykh bibliotekakh* (Moscow, 1969), p. 40.

39. V. Akshinskii, "U kazakhskikh ateistov," *Agitator*, No. 13 (1961), p. 50; B. Levin, "Poleznyye posobiya," *Agitator*, No. 13 (1965), pp. 34–35. See also S. V. Koltunyuk and I. G. Sidorkin, "Podgotovka kadrov—vazhnoye zveno sistemy ateisticheskogo vospitaniya," *VNA*, Vol. 9 (1970), p. 170.

40. G. Kelt, "Svyataya svyatykh—chelovek!", *Komsomolskaya pravda*, August 15, 1965, p. 4.

41. Tsamerian et al., op. cit., p. 379. See also Artem Borzenko, "Nuzhno li provodit disputy?", *NiR*, No. 2 (1960), p. 85; Artem Borzenko, "O disputakh i 'literaturnykh' sudakh," *NiR*, No. 1 (1963), p. 70.

42. Borzenko, "O disputakh . . . ," op. cit., pp. 71–72. See also V. Lentin, "Ob odnoi poleznoi forme nauchno-ateisticheskoi raboty," *V pomoshch politicheskomu samoobrazovaniyu*, No. 12 (1959), p. 83.

43. G. Zinchenko, "Neischerpayemyi rezerv," *Politicheskoye samoobrazovaniye*, No. 3 (1960), p. 127; I. Yermakov, "Zdravyi smysl i religiya," *Agitator*, No. 5 (1967), p. 48; R. Izzatullayev, "Khimiya v borbe s religiei," *Agitator*, No. 17 (1969), p. 43.

44. E. Z. Bairamov, "Osobennosti individualnoi raboty sredi posledovatelei islama," in Gubanov, op. cit., p. 117.

45. N. Serpov, "Klub ateizma," *Agitator*, No. 2 (1960), p. 54; I. Filimonov, "Selskiye ateisty," *Agitator*, No. 7 (1961), p. 51.

46. Mukvich, op. cit., pp. 56–57. See also "Teaching Methods Used to Form Firm Atheistic

Convictions in Soviet Students," *Sredneye spetsialnoye obrazovaniye*, No. 1 (1966) in JPRS No. 36,058, p. 10.

47. Pantskhava, op. cit., pp. 363–364.

48. Ibid.

49. Ibid.

50. "Eto dolzhny znat vse," *Agitator*, No. 20 (1960), p. 11. See also A. Chistov, "Agitator i gazeta," *Agitator*, No. 6 (1960), p. 35.

51. P. Sumarev, "Siloi khudozhestvennogo slova," *Agitator*, No. 12 (1966), pp. 38–40; L. Rozhenovich, "Novaya forma v deistvii," in Shatilov (ed.), op. cit., pp. 87–94.

52. A. Saar, "Ob odnom selskom raikome," *Kommunist*, No. 11 (1960), p. 58. For more enthusiastic evaluations of the practice, see M. Kurianov, "Politicheskaya agitatsiya i agitator," *Kommunist*, No. 10 (1965), pp. 45–46; M. Kaminskii, "Vystupayut politinformatory," *Kulturno-prosvetitelnaya rabota*, No. 2 (1968), p. 18.

53. Tsamerian et al., op. cit., p. 383. See also Yakovleva, op. cit., pp. 35–36.

54. "Aktivnaya rabota ateistov," *Partiinaya zhizn*, No. 14 (1961), p. 80.

55. Borzenko, "O disputakh . . . ," op. cit., p. 72. See also G. L. Andreyev et al., "Boyevoye oruzhiye ateisticheskoi propagandy," *Voprosy filosofii*, No. 7 (1964), p. 164.

56. "Itogi, plany, razdumya . . . ," op. cit., pp. 75–76; N. Teteruk, "Nastupleniye na perezhitki proshlogo," *Agitator*, No. 13 (1963), p. 42.

57. E. Bartoshevich, "O chem govoryat fakty," *NiR*, No. 5 (1963), p. 71.

58. Ivanov, op. cit. See also M. Vorotyonova, *Kazakhstanskaya pravda*, August 18, 1967.

59. Ivanov, op. cit.; A. Khvorostyanov and B. Borobik, "Izuver poluchil po zaslugam," *NiR*, No. 1 (1962).

60. A. Kozhevnikov, "Ateisticheskoye vospitaniye selskogo naseleniya v sovremennykh usloviyakh," in Shatilov (ed.), op. cit., p. 43.

61. V. Loginov, "Babka Marfa i ateisty," *Sovetskaya Rossia*, January 6, 1972, p. 3.

62. D. Sidorov, "Kto takiye iegovisty?", *Agitator*, No. 7 (1959), p. 60; V. Pivovarov and V. Smirnov, *Sovetskaya kultura*, May 11, 1972, p. 2.

63. Leonid F. Ilyichev, "Ocherednyye zadachi ideologicheskoi raboty partii," *Pravda*, June 19, 1963, p. 4.

Chapter 7, pp. 119–130

1. E. Bairamov, "Veruyushchikh nado zainteresovat," *Agitator*, No. 3 (1968), p. 54; V. G. Pivovarov and V. A. Smirnov, "Konkretnyye sotsialnyye issledovaniya na sluzhbe individualnoi raboty s veruyushchimi," in N. I. Gubanov et al. (eds.), *Individualnaya rabota s veruyushchimi* (Moscow, 1967), p. 39.

2. For a discussion of the League's efforts, see B. N. Konovalov, "Uchityvat opyt proshlogo," in Gubanov, op. cit., pp. 163–170.

3. F. Lukinskii, "Zametki o nauchno-ateisticheskoi propagande," *Kommunist*, No. 9 (1960), p. 112.

4. P. Kolonitskii, "O religioznykh predrassudkakh," *Sovetskaya Estonia*, January 6, 1971, p. 3; "Forum sovetskikh ateistov," *NiR*, No. 8 (1967), p. 11.

5. S. V. Koltunyuk, "Dokhodit do kazhdogo—znachit uchityvat osobennosti kazhdogo," in Gubanov, op. cit., p. 91.

6. Oleg Moiseyev, "Permskiye razdumya," *NiR*, No. 10 (1966), p. 4; "Aktivnyye nastupat na perezhitki proshlogo," *Agitator*, No. 15 (1963), pp. 5–6.

7. "Doiti do kazhdogo veruyushchego," *NiR*, No. 6 (1962), p. 7: "Umet ubezhdat," *Agitator*, No. 21 (1961), p. 59.

8. P. Kolonitskii, "Nekotoryye voprosy propagandy ateizma," *Politicheskoye samoobrazovaniye*, No. 4 (1963), p. 93.

9. K. Daitov, "Moi dedushka i mulla," *Agitator*, No. 4 (1962), p. 58.

10. V. Yevdokimov, "Konkretnyye sotsialnyye issledovaniya i ateizm," *NiR*, No. 1 (1968), p. 23.

11. N. Kozhanov and G. Kondratenko, "Monolog ili dialog?", *Pravda*, September 19, 1969, p. 2.

12. T. D. Gulyakevich, "Vooruzhat kadry ateistov prakticheskimi navykami raboty s veruyushchimi," in Gubanov, op. cit., p. 192.

13. Yu. A. Chukovenkov, "Organizatsiya individualnoi raboty s veruyushchimi," in Gubanov, op. cit., p. 26; Ye. A. Zavernyaeva, "Uspekh reshayut kadry," ibid., p. 182.

14. V. V. Mochalova and D. A. Varlamov, "Vovlecheniye veruyushchikh v trudovuyu i obshchestvenno-politicheskuyu deyatelnost," ibid., p. 52.

15. Chukovenkov, op. cit., p. 25.

16. Yu. P. Zuyev, "Nekotoryye rezultaty konkretnogo sotsialnogo issledovaniya opyta individualnoi ateisticheskoi raboty," in Gubanov, op. cit., pp. 157–158.

17. V. Chebulankina, "Idti k lyudyam," *Agitator*, No. 5 (1961), p. 45.

18. M. G. Pismanik, "O sostoyanii religioznosti i nekotoryykh osobennostyakh nauchno-ateisticheskogo vospitaniya sredi zhenshchin," in I. D. Pantskhava (ed.), *Konkretno-sotsiologicheskoye izucheniye sostoyaniya religioznosti i opyta ateisticheskogo vospitaniya* (Moscow, 1969), p. 230; R. K. Kozharinova and V. D. Krasitskaya, "Osobennosti individualnoi raboty s veruyushchimi zhenshchinami," in Gubanov, op. cit., pp. 127–137.

19. Chukovenkov, op. cit., p. 25.

20. E. Z. Bairamov, "Osobennosti individualnoi raboty sredi posledovatelei islama," in Gubanov, op. cit., p. 115. See also E. Bairamov, "Islam i 'natsionalnyye traditsii,'" *Agitator*, No. 24 (1966), p. 45.

21. "Borba protiv religii—borba za cheloveka," *Politicheskoye samoobrazovaniye*, No. 12 (1963), p. 75. See also A. Kurantov and P. Sumarev, "Ateisticheskaya propaganda i formirovaniye nauchnogo mirovozzreniya," *NiR*, No. 1 (1968), p. 52.

22. Ya. Aleksandrov, "Kak naiti klyuch k serdtsu cheloveka," *Agitator*, No. 4 (1960), p. 25.

23. A. Barkauskas, "Nekotoryye voprosy ateisticheskogo vospitaniya," *Partiinaya zhizn*, No. 5 (1970), p. 59.

24. S. Ivanov, "How We Organize Scientific-Atheist Propaganda," *Kommunist Moldavii*, No. 7 (1961), in JPRS No. 10,899, p. 17.

25. A. Kuzmin, "Deistvennost agitatsii," *Agitator*, No. 5 (1963), p. 33.

26. A. Pshenichnov, "Vsegda v nastuplenii," *Agitator*, No. 23 (1963), pp. 48–51. See also P. Sumarev, "Siloi khudozhestvennogo slova," *Agitator*, No. 12 (1966), p. 38.

27. Kolonitskii, "Nekotoryye voprosy . . . ," op. cit., p. 88.

28. Zuyev, op. cit., p. 161.

29. Yu. Nosikov, "Besedy s veruyushchimi," *Partiinaya zhizn*, No. 6 (1960), pp. 57–58.

30. N. K. Krupskaya, "Ob antireligioznom vospitanii v shkole," in N. K. Krupskaya, *Iz ateisticheskogo naslediya* (Moscow, 1964), pp. 129–130.

31. See, e. g., Nosikov, op. cit.

32. Chebulankina, op. cit., p. 45. See also N. A. Pashkov, "K voprosu o kharaktere obydennogo religioznogo soznaniya pravoslavnykh khristian," in Gubanov, op. cit., p. 158.

33. "Iskat klyuch k serdtsu kazhdogo," *Sovetskaya pechat*, No. 6 (1963), pp. 7–8.

34. Lukinskii, op. cit., p. 112; G. Kelt, "Svyataya svyatykh—chelovek!", *Komsomolskaya pravda*, August 15, 1964, p. 4.

35. "Iskat klyuch . . . ," op. cit., pp. 7–8; Koltunyuk, op. cit., p. 92.

36. G. I. Rubtsova, "Chutkost i zadushevnost—neobkhodimyye usloviya uspekha individualnoi raboty s veruyushchimi," in Gubanov, op. cit., p. 206.

37. M. M. Kublanov, "Protivorechiya 'svyashchennogo pisaniya' i metodika ikh raskrytiya," ibid., p. 83.

38. A Saar, "Ob odnom selskom raikome," *Kommunist*, No. 11 (1960), p. 60; "Znaniye—narodu," *NiR*, No. 7 (1967), p. 3; Ye. Riumin, "Zhivoye slovo i glubina soderzhaniya," *Agitator*,

No. 6 (1967), p. 45; N. Rodin, "Seminar na zavode," *Agitator*, No. 15 (1967), pp. 57–58; M. G. Pismanik and V. A. Cherniak, "Mesto individualnoi raboty s veruyushchimi v ateisticheskom vospitanii," in Gubanov, op. cit., p. 10.

39. A. Kostakov, "Raznoobrazit formy i metody nauchno-ateisticheskoi propagandy," *V pomoshch politicheskomu samoobrazovaniyu*, No. 11 (1959), p. 91.

40. Yu. D. Polishchuk, "Dom nauchnogo ateizma—organizator individualnoi raboty s veruyushchimi," in Gubanov, op. cit., pp. 188–189. *Agitator* is published in an edition of 1,200,000 copies, while *Nauka i religiya* is published in an edition of 350,000 copies.

41. L. Burkhanov, "Vsegda v nastuplenii," *Kommunist Tadzhikistana*, October 25, 1969, p. 2; Gulyakevich, op. cit., p. 192.

42. A. Sukhov, review of M. I. Shakhovich, *Lenin i problemy ateizma, Politicheskoye samoobrazovaniye*, No. 7 (1962), p. 135; Pismanik and Cherniak, op. cit., pp. 8–9; Chukovenkov, op. cit., p. 21.

43. M. Chernov, "I umu, i serdtsu!", *Komsomolskaya pravda*, January 26, 1968, p. 2.

44. "Umet ubezhdat," op. cit., p. 59.

45. Kostakov, op. cit., p. 91.

Chapter 8, pp. 131–158

1. A. Osipov, "Vse v rukakh tvoikh, chelovek!", *Literaturnaya gazeta*, January 30, 1962, p. 2.

2. I. Kryvelev, "Vazhnaya storona byta," *Kommunist*, No. 8 (1961), pp. 67–68. See also N. S. Kapustin, "O spetsifike nekotorykh religiozno-bytovykh perezhitkov," in I. D. Pantskhava, *Konkretno-sotsiologicheskoye izucheniye sostoyaniya religioznosti i opyta ateisticheskogo vospitaniya* (Moscow, 1969), p. 95.

3. Walter Kolarz, *Religion in the Soviet Union* (New York: St. Martin's Press, 1961), p. 2. See also Ye. Mayat, "Formirovaniye i razvitiye massogo ateizma v SSSR," *Politicheskoye samoobrazovaniye*, No. 11 (1972), p. 88; N. S. Timasheff, "Urbanization, Operation Antireligion and the Decline of Religion in the USSR," *The American Slavic and East European Review*, Vol. XIV, No. 2 (April, 1955), p. 224.

4. See Edgar H. Schein, *Coercive Persuasion* (New York: W. W. Norton and Co., 1961).

5. Paul B. Anderson, "The Orthodox Church in Soviet Russia," *Foreign Affairs*, Vol. 39, No. 2 (January, 1961), p. 299; Moshe Decter, "The Status of the Jews in the Soviet Union," *Foreign Affairs*, Vol. 41, No. 2 (January, 1963), pp. 424–425; E. I. Lisavtsev and S. I. Nikishov, "Rukovodyashchaya rol partiinykh organizatsii v sisteme ateisticheskogo vospitaniya," *VNA* No. 9 (1970), p. 98.

6. Daniel Lerner, "Effective Propaganda: Conditions and Evaluation," in Daniel Lerner (ed.), *Propaganda in War and Crisis* (New York: George W. Stewart, 1951), p. 347.

7. Quoted in V. Bazykin, "V nebesakh chelovek, a ne bog," *Sovetskiye profsoyuzy*, No. 13 (1961), p. 28.

8. D. Sidorov, "Individualnaya rabota s veruyushchimi," *Agitator*, No. 4 (1964), p. 28.

9. M. F. Zakharov, "Formirovat prochnyye ateisticheskiye ubezhdeniya," *Sredneye spetsialnoye obrazovaniye*, No. 1 (1966), p. 41.

10. M. Polkovnikov, "Lektory po razverstke," *Pravda*, November 29, 1967, p. 3; L. Krym, "Masterstvo ateisticheskogo vospitaniya," *Vechernyaya Moskva*, September 18, 1972, p. 2.

11. I. D. Pantskhava, "Vvedeniye," in Pantskhava, op. cit., p. 10. See also L. D. Adamska, *Ukrainski istorichnyi zhurnal*, No. 2 (1971), in JPRS No. 53,954, p. 77.

12. "O zadachakh partiinoi propagandy v sovremennykh usloviyakh," *Pravda*, January 10, 1960, p. 1.

13. Quoted in "Izuchat marksizm-leninizm, obladevat kommunisticheskim mirovozzreniyem," *Kommunist*, No. 13 (1960), pp. 8–9.

14. "Ateist—vsegda v nastuplenii," *Kommunist Tadzhikistana*, January 19, 1971, p. 1.

15. N. Andrianova, *Vechernyaya Moskva*, February 10, 1972, p. 2.

16. Kolarz, op. cit., p. 12; John Shelton Curtiss, *The Russian Church and the Soviet State* (Boston: Little, Brown and Co., 1953), pp. 282–283.

17. A. Okulov, "Nauchno-ateisticheskoye vospitaniye segodnya," *NiR*, No. 8 (1967), p. 17; V. I. Yevdokimov, "Ateisticheskoye vospitaniye trudyashchikhsya v protsesse stroitelstva kommunizma," *VNA* Vol. 4 (1967), p. 96, footnote 2.

18. Vladimir A. Kuroyedov, "Neskolko voprosov o religii i tserkvi," *Izvestia*, August 30, 1966, p. 4.

19. P. N. Fedoseyev et al., *Obshchestvo i religiya* (Moscow, 1967), p. 469; Yevdokimov, op. cit., p. 96, footnote 2; A. Kozhevnikov, "Ateisticheskoye vospitaniye selskogo naseleniya v sovremennykh usloviyakh," in I. Shatilov (ed.), *Zaboty i dela ateistov* (Moscow, 1970), p. 3; *Osnovy nauchnogo ateizma* (Leningrad, 1970), p. 344.

20. Okulov, op. cit., p. 16.

21. R. Baltanov, "Iz nashego opyta issledovaniya religioznosti naseleniya," *NiR*, No. 8 (1967), p. 18; N. Andrianov, "Puti k istine," *Pravda*, September 7, 1970, p. 2.

22. A. V. Losev et al., *Sotsialno-ekonomicheskiye preobrazovaniya v voronezhskoi derevne* (Voronezh, 1967), p. 303.

23. Hulusi Hako, "Communist Christianity of Khrushchevite Revisionists in the Service of the Revisionist Reaction," *Rruga e Partise*, August, 1971, in JPRS No. 54,599, pp. 7–15. Quotations on pp. 8, 15.

24. A. Mani, *Bashkimi*, February 9, 1972, in JPRS No. 55,499, pp. 10–11.

25. Hako, op. cit., p. 13.

26. I. P. Tsamerian (ed.), *Osnovy nauchnogo ateizma*, 2nd Rev. Ed. (Moscow, 1962), p. 370. See also L. Mitrokhin, "Priroda religioznogo 'utesheniya,'" *Agitator*, No. 11 (1968), pp. 56–58.

27. A. Klibanov and L. Mitrokhin, "Kommunisticheskoye vospitaniye i borba protiv religioznogo sektanstva," *Kommunist*, No. 2 (1961), p. 65.

28. See, e.g., K. Platonov, *Psikhologiya religii* (Moscow, 1967); M. A. Popova, *O psikhologii religii* (Moscow, 1969).

29. L. Ilyichev, "Formirovaniye nauchnogo mirovozzreniya i ateisticheskoye vospitaniye," *Kommunist*, No. 1 (1964), p. 41. See also M. Chernov, "I umu, i serdtsu!", *Komsomolskaya pravda*, January 26, 1968, p. 2.

30. Chernov, op. cit., p. 2.

31. Yevdokimov, op. cit., p. 107. See also N. I. Boldyrev et al., *Pedagogika* (Moscow, 1968), p. 274.

32. M. K. Tepliakov, "Pobeda ateizma v razlichnykh sotsialnykh sloyakh sovetskogo obshchestva," in *VNA*, Vol. 4 (1967), p. 139. See also Ye. Duluman, "Vospriozvodstvo religii," *NiR*, No. 7 (1968), p. 12.

33. See Vinnitsa Radio, Domestic Service, February 4, 1972, as cited in *FBIS Daily Report, Soviet Union*, March 29, 1972, p. J 10.

34. I. P. Tsamerian, "Programma KPSS i zadachi ateisticheskogo vospitaniya," *Voprosy filosofii*, No. 7 (1962), p. 3; Ts. A. Stepanian et al., *Stroitelstvo kommunizma i dukhovnyi mir cheloveka* (Moscow, 1966), p. 237.

35. V. Petrov, "Pogovorim o turizme," *Sovetskaya Rossia*, May 6, 1969, p. 2. See also Thomas E. Bird, "New Interest in Old Russian Things: Literary Ferment, Religious Perspectives, and National Self-Assertion," *Slavic Review*, Vol. 32, No. 1 (March, 1973), pp. 17–28.

36. Fedoseyev et al., op. cit., p. 485.

37. See, e.g., N. Tarasenko and I. Shatilov, "Zaboty ateistov: obzor pisem," *Pravda*, July 6, 1969, p. 3; Aleksander Motornyi, "K svedeniyu arkhieposkopa Anatoliya i dr.," *Literaturnaya gazeta*, March 12, 1969, p. 5.

38. A. Malygin, "In the Battle of Ideas There Are No Compromises," *Molodoi Kommunist*, No. 1 (1969), in *CDSP*, Vol. XXI, No. 14, p. 9.

39. Tsamerian (ed.), op. cit., p. 40; Ye. F. Muravyev and Yu. V. Dmitriyev, "O konkretnosti v izuchenii i preodolenii religioznykh perezhitkov," *Voprosy filosofii*, No. 3 (1961), p. 69; Klibanov and Mitrokhin, op. cit., p. 65.

40. V. Lazutka, "Katolitsizm i natsiya," *Sovetskaya Litva*, November 20, 1971, p. 3; A. Okulov, "Ateisticheskoye vospitaniye," *Pravda*, January 14, 1972, p. 3.

41. Muravyev and Dmitriyev, op. cit., p. 69; Stepanian et al., op. cit., p. 222.

42. Tsamerian (ed.), op. cit., p. 370.

43. Muravyev and Dmitriyev, op. cit., p. 66; V. Yevdokimov, "Konkretnyye sotsialnyye issledovaniya i ateizm," *NiR*, No. 1 (1968), p. 23.

44. A. M. Netylko, "Ob individualnom podkhode v ateisticheskom vospitanii uchashchikh-sya," *Sovetskaya pedagogika*, No. 6 (1963), pp. 31–37.

45. Yu. Mukimov and V. Tyurikov, "Trud i byt neotdelimy," *Pravda*, June 15, 1964, p. 2; Fedoseyev et al., op. cit., p. 486.

46. *Moskovskaya pravda*, October 10, 1971, p. 1.

47. V. I. Lenin, "O znachenii voinstvuyushchego materializma," *Sochineniya*, 5th Ed., Vol. 45, pp. 25–26.

48. I. Shatilov, "V sele Aleshino," in I. Shatilov, *Zaboty i dela ateistov* (Moscow, 1970), p. 96.

49. M. Mchedlov, "Nauchnyye osnovy ateisticheskoi raboty," *Kommunist*, No. 4 (1972), p. 79.

50. Alexei Sulatskov, "Chto v dosye ateista?", *Zhurnalist*, No. 11 (1971), p. 29; L. A. Filippov, "O voinstvuyushchem materializme i ateizme," *Voprosy filosofii*, No. 3 (1972), p. 72.

51. "Ateisticheskoye vospitaniye trudyashchikhsya," *Sovetskaya Kirgizia*, November 4, 1970, p. 1; N. A. Pashkov, "K voprosu o kharaktere obydennogo religioznogo soznaniya pravo-slavnykh khristian," in Pantskhava, op. cit., p. 150.

52. Ye. Zazerskii, "Rashireniye sfery politicheskogo vliyaniya," *Agitator*, No. 22 (1960), p. 52; V. Utkov, "Klub i veruyushchiye," *Agitator*, No. 23 (1966), p. 42; Ilyichev, op. cit., p. 43.

53. R. Tagiyev, "Razgovor po dusham o 'bluzhdayushchikh dushakh,' " *Trud*, August 19, 1971, p. 2.

54. See, e.g., M. G. Pismanik, "O sostoyanii religioznosti i nekotorykh osobennostyakh nauchno-ateisticheskogo vospitaniya sredi zhenshchin," in Pantskhava, op. cit., p. 226.

55. N. Obraztsova, "Ne 'rab bozhii,' a chelovek," *Kommunist Tadzhikistana*, March 23, 1972, p. 2.

56. P. Kolonitskii, "Nekotoryye voprosy propagandy ateizma," *Politicheskoye samoobrazova-niye*, No. 4 (1963), p. 89.

57. Yu. A. Chukovenkov, "Organizatsiya individualnoi raboty s veruyushchimi," in N. I. Gubanov et al. (eds.), *Individualnaya rabota s veruyushchimi* (Moscow, 1967), p. 20.

58. V. Pomerantsev, "I razum i chuvstva za nas," *NiR*, No. 2 (1962), p. 13. See also "Za deistvennost ateisticheskoi propagandy," *Pravda*, July 27, 1968, p. 1.

59. Kolonitskii, op. cit., p. 89.

60. A. I. Rogov, "Ateisticheskiye radioperedachi," in *VNA*, Vol. 9 (1970), p. 309.

61. A. F. Okulov, "Za glubokuyu nauchnuyu razrabotku sovremennykh problem ateizma," *VNA*, Vol. 1 (1966), p. 21.

62. V. Krupko, *Sovetskaya Rossia*, March 6, 1972, p. 4.

63. V. Smirnov, "Stroit rabotu differentsirovanno," *Agitator*, No. 2 (1972), p. 37.

64. See I. Brazhnik, "Ateisticheskoye vospitaniye—obshchepartiinoye delo," *Partiinaya zhizn*, No. 24 (1963), pp. 21–26; Fedoseyev et al., op. cit., p. 489; N. P. Krasnikov, "O nekotorykh voprosakh raboty s veruyushchimi," in N. P. Krasnikov et al. (eds.), *Voprosy preodoleniya religioznykh perezhitkov v SSSR* (Moscow-Leningrad, 1966), p. 7.

65. A. Okulov, "Nauchno-ateisticheskoye vospitaniye segodnya," *NiR*, No. 8 (1967), p. 17; L. Pinchuk, "Propaganda ateizma—nasha obyazannost," *Partiinaya zhizn*, No. 5 (1960), p. 74.

66. E. Lisavtsev, "Kollektiv boretsya s perezhitkami proshlogo," *Kommunist*, No. 14 (1963), p. 107; L. V. Mandrygin and N. I. Makarov, "O kharaktere i prichinakh sokhraneniya religioznykh verovanii u krestian zapadnykh oblastei Belorussii," in *VNA*, Vol. 1 (1966), p. 238. See also Bohdan Bociurkiw, "Religion and Soviet Society," *Survey*, No. 60 (July, 1966), p. 66.

67. See, e.g., "Nastupat na perezhitki proshlogo," *Turkmenskaya iskra*, September 15, 1971, p. 2; V. Loginov, "Babka Marfa i ateisty," *Sovetskaya Rossia*, January 6, 1972, p. 3.

68. N. Sokolov and S. Belous, "Chto znachit byt ateistom," *Sovetskaya Rossia*, July 6, 1966, p. 3.

69. B. Lobovik and V. Chudnovskii, "K voprosu ob effektivnosti ateisticheskoi propagandy," *Kommunist Ukrainy*, No. 11 (1969), p. 81.

70. S. Khudyakov, "Soderzhaniye i formy propagandy," *NiR*, No. 3 (1962), p. 15; "Molodezh i religiya," *NiR*, No. 8 (1962); Sokolov and Belous, op. cit., p. 3.

71. Krym, op. cit., p. 2.

72. Filippov, op. cit.

73. Dmitriyev, op. cit.

74. S. Zhmudskii, letter to the editor, *NiR*, No. 6 (1966). See also F. Sakmenov, "Nuzhna ateisticheskaya entsiklopediya," *NiR*, No. 12 (1966), p. 20.

75. See Kolarz, op. cit., pp. 94, 321, 444; Robert Conquest, *Religion in the USSR* (New York: Frederick A. Praeger, 1968), pp. 76, 108, 117; Baymirza Hayit, *Osteuropa*, February, 1972, in JPRS No. 55, 997. See also A. Kazhdan, "The Bible Means 'Book,' " *Novy mir*, No. 6 (1967), in *CDSP*, Vol. XIX, No. 38, pp. 19–20, 44; V. Basilov, "Islam i sovremennost," *Politicheskoye samoobrazovaniye*, No. 10 (1969), p. 96.

76. "O zadachakh . . . ," op. cit., p. 1.

77. A. Gaidis, *Kommunist* (Vilnius), No. 9 (1962).

78. "Zhurnalisty obsuzhdayut problemy ateizma," *NiR*, No. 5 (1963), p. 4.

79. I. Zhivoglyad, *Tselinograd Freundschaft*, March 31, 1971, in JPRS No. 53,190, p. 70.

80. Brazhnik, op. cit., p. 23. See also Tarasenko, op. cit., p. 3; Okulov, "Za glubokuyu . . . ," op. cit., p. 21.

81. Brazhnik, op. cit., p. 23.

82. B. Porshnev, "Obshchestvennaya psikhologiya i formirovaniye novogo cheloveka," *Kommunist*, No. 8 (1963), pp. 94–102; P. K. Kurochkin, *Filosofskiye nauki*, No. 1 (1972), p. 18.

83. "Teoriyu nauchnogo ateizma—na uroven sovremennykh trebovanii," *Voprosy filosofii*, No. 4 (1964), p. 11.

84. V. A. Saprykin, "Ateisticheskya rabota partiinoi organizatsii v usloviyakh goroda," *VNA*, Vol. 9 (1970), p. 226.

85. Okulov, "Za glubokuyu . . . ," op. cit., pp. 29–30; R. A. Lopatkin, "Na opornykh punktakh instituta nauchnogo ateizma," *VNA*, Vol. 5 (1968), p. 341.

86. Both polls are reported in T. Mering, "Konkretno o samom vazhnom," *NiR*, No. 3 (1969), p. 40.

87. Yevdokimov, "Konkretnyye . . . ," op. cit., p. 23. See also Tepliakov, op. cit., p. 153.

88. Losev et al., op. cit., p. 314.

89. See Joseph T. Klapper, *The Effects of Mass Communications* (Glencoe, Ill.: The Free Press, 1960).

90. V. Bukin, "Preodoleniye religioznykh chuvstv," *Kommunist*, No. 2 (1963), p. 71.

91. Herbert C. Kelman, "Processes of Opinion Change," *The Public Opinion Quarterly*, Vol. XXV, No. 1 (1961), pp. 57–58.

92. Klapper, op. cit., p. 61.

93. Gabriel A. Almond and Sidney Verba, *The Civic Culture* (Princeton: Princeton University Press, 1963), pp. 325–326, footnote 6. See also A. Shamaro, "Poyedinok," *Agitator*, No. 3 (1965), p. 45.

94. Elihu Katz and Paul F. Lazarsfeld, *Personal Influence* (Glencoe, Ill.: The Free Press, 1955), pp. 44–45.

95. Gubanov, op. cit., pp. 3–4.

96. Bernard R. Berelson et al., *Voting* (Chicago: University of Chicago Press, 1954), pp. 104, 112.

97. Stanley K. Bigman, "Prestige, Personal Influence and Opinion," in Wilbur Schramm (ed.), *The Process and Effects of Mass Communication* (Urbana, Ill.: University of Illinois Press, 1960), p. 408.

98. See Paul F. Lazarsfeld et al., *The People's Choice* (New York: Columbia University Press, 1944), pp. 152 ff. See also Marvin Karlins and Herbert I. Abelson, *Persuasion*, 2nd Ed. (New York: Springer Publishing Co., 1970).

99. Paul Hollander, *Soviet and American Society* (New York: Oxford University Press, 1973), pp. 372–373.

100. Tarasenko and Shatilov, op. cit., p. 3; A. Barkauskas, "Nekotoryye voprosy ateisticheskogo vospitaniya," *Partiinaya zhizn*, No. 5 (1970), p. 60.

101. Joan Delaney Grossman, "Leadership of Antireligious Propaganda in the Soviet Union," *Studies in Soviet Thought*, Vol. 12, No. 3 (September, 1972), p. 216.

102. Hollander, op. cit., pp. 190–193.

103. Robert V. Daniels, *The Nature of Communism* (New York: Random House, 1962), p. 328.

104. Ibid., p. 324.

105. See Richard T. DeGeorge, *Soviet Ethics and Morality* (Ann Arbor, Mich.: University of Michigan Press, 1969), pp. 83–103.

106. See Schein, op. cit., pp. 62–100.

107. Hollander, op. cit., p. 186.

108. Maurice Latey, *Patterns of Tyranny* (New York, 1969), p. 212.

109. A. G. Kharchev, *Stanovleniye lichnosti* (Moscow, 1972), p. 18; S. Golod, "Sociological Problems of Sexual Morality," in *Soviet Sociology*, Vol. VIII, No. 1 (Summer, 1969), p. 11; V. A. Mezentsev, "O sochetanii kriticheskogo i pozitivnogo v individualnoi rabote s veruyushchimi," in Gubanov, op. cit., p. 56. See also the remarks of Nadezhda Krupskaya, cited in Kolarz, op. cit., p. 28.

110. Quoted in Warren B. Walsh, *Russia and the Soviet Union* (Ann Arbor, Mich.: University of Michigan Press, 1958), pp. 427–428.

111. Raymond A. Bauer, *The "New Man" in Soviet Psychology* (Cambridge, Mass.: Harvard University Press, 1951), p. 178.

112. Gayle Durham Hollander, *Soviet Political Indoctrination* (New York: Praeger Publishers, 1972), p. 17.

113. V. I. Yevdokimov, "Mesto ateisticheskogo vospitaniya v sisteme kommunisticheskogo vospitaniya," *VNA*, Vol. 9 (1970), p. 11.

Bibliography

Western Sources

Administration of Teaching in Social Sciences in the USSR. Ann Arbor: University of Michigan, 1960.

Almond, Gabriel A., and James S. Coleman (eds.). *The Politics of the Developing Areas.* Princeton: Princeton University Press, 1960.

Almond, Gabriel A., and Sidney Verba. *The Civic Culture.* Princeton: Princeton University Press, 1963.

Anderson, Paul. *People, Church and State in Modern Russia.* New York: Macmillan, 1944.

Babitsky, Paul, and John Rimberg. *The Soviet Film Industry.* New York: Frederick A. Praeger, 1955.

Barghoorn, Frederick C. *Politics in the USSR,* 2nd Ed. Boston: Little, Brown and Co., 1972.

Baron, Salo. *The Russian Jew Under Tsars and Soviets.* New York: The Macmillan Co., 1964.

Bauer, Raymond A. *The "New Man" in Soviet Psychology.* Cambridge, Mass.: Harvard University Press, 1951.

Benningsen, Alexandre, and Chantal Lemercier-Quelquejay. *Islam in the Soviet Union.* New York: Frederick A. Praeger, 1967.

Bourdeaux, Michael. *Patriarch and Prophets.* New York: Praeger Publishers, 1970.

Bourdeaux, Michael. *Religious Ferment in Russia.* London: The Macmillan Co., 1968.

Browder, Robert Paul, and Alexander F. Kerensky (eds.). *The Russian Provisional Government, 1917.* Stanford, Calif.: Stanford University Press, 1961.

Chauncey, Henry (ed.), *Soviet Preschool Education,* 2 Vols. New York: Holt, Rinehart, and Winston, 1969.

Childs, Harwood L. (ed.). *Propaganda and Dictatorships.* Princeton: Princeton University Press, 1936.

Clarkson, Jesse D. *A History of Russia,* 2nd Ed. New York: Random House, 1969.

Conquest, Robert. *Religion in the USSR.* New York: Frederick A. Praeger, 1968.

Curtiss, John Shelton. *Church and State in Russia, 1900–1917.* New York: Columbia University Press, 1940.

Curtiss, John Shelton. *The Russian Church and the Soviet State.* Boston: Little, Brown and Co., 1953.

Daniels, Robert V. *The Nature of Communism.* New York: Random House, 1962.

Dawson, Richard E., and Kenneth Prewitt. *Political Socialization.* Boston: Little, Brown and Co., 1969.

DeGeorge, Richard T. *Soviet Ethics and Morality.* Ann Arbor: University of Michigan Press, 1969.

de Huszar, George B., et al., *Soviet Power and Policy.* New York: Crowell, 1955.

de la Saudée, J. de Bivort. *Communism and Anti-Religion.* London: Burns, Oates and Washbourne, Ltd., 1938.

Durasoff, Steve. *The Russian Protestants.* Rutherford, N.J.: Fairleigh Dickinson University Press, 1969.

Fainsod, Merle. *How Russia Is Ruled,* Rev. Ed. Cambridge, Mass.: Harvard University Press, 1963.

Fireside, Harvey. *Icon and Swastika.* Cambridge, Mass.: Harvard University Press, 1971.

Fitzsimmons, Thomas et al. *USSR.* New Haven: HRAF Press, 1960.

Fletcher, William C. *A Study in Survival.* New York: The Macmillan Co., 1965.

Fletcher, William C. *Nikolai.* New York: The Macmillan Co., 1968.

Fletcher, William C. *Religion and Soviet Foreign Policy.* New York: Oxford University Press, 1973.

Fletcher, William C. *The Russian Orthodox Church Underground, 1917–1970.* New York: Oxford University Press, 1971.

Gilboa, Yehoshua. *The Black Years of Soviet Jewry.* Boston: Little, Brown and Co., 1971.

Harper, Samuel. *Civic Training in Soviet Russia.* Chicago: University of Chicago Press, 1929.

Hayward, Max, and William C. Fletcher. *Religion and the Soviet State: A Dilemma of Power.* New York: Frederick A. Praeger, 1969.

Hollander, Gayle Durham. *Soviet Political Indoctrination.* New York: Praeger Publishers, 1972.

Hollander, Paul. *Soviet and American Society.* New York: Oxford University Press, 1973.

Hopkins, Mark. *Mass Media in the Soviet Union.* New York: Pegasus Publishers, 1970.

Huntington, Samuel P. *Political Order in Changing Societies.* New Haven: Yale University Press, 1968.

Hyman, Herbert. *Political Socialization.* Glencoe, Ill.: The Free Press, 1959.

Inkeles, Alex, and Raymond A. Bauer. *The Soviet Citizen* (Cambridge, Mass.: Harvard University Press, 1959.

Inkeles, Alex, and Kent Geiger (eds.). *Soviet Society.* Boston: Houghton Mifflin Co., 1961.

Karlins, Marvin, and Herbert I. Abelson. *Persuasion,* 2nd Ed. New York: Springer Publishing Co., 1970.

Katz, Elihu, and Paul F. Lazarsfeld. *Personal Influence.* Glencoe, Ill.: The Free Press, 1955.

Klapper, Joseph T. *The Effects of Mass Communications.* Glencoe, Ill.: The Free Press, 1960.

Kochan, Lionel (ed.). *The Jews in Soviet Russia Since 1917.* London: Oxford University Press, 1970.

Kolarz, Walter. *Religion in the Soviet Union.* New York: St. Martin's Press, 1961.

Lerner, Daniel (ed.). *Propaganda in War and Crisis.* New York: George W. Stewart, 1951.

Mackenzie, A. J. *Propaganda Boom.* London: The Right Book Club, 1938.

Marshall, Richard, Jr., et al. (eds.). *Aspects of Religion in the Soviet Union, 1917–1967.* Chicago: University of Chicago Press, 1971.

Oberlander, Erwin et al. (eds.). *Russia Enters the Twentieth Century.* New York: Schocken Books, 1971.

Park, Alexander G. *Bolshevism in Turkestan, 1917–1927.* New York: Columbia University Press, 1957.

Riasanovsky, Nicholas V. *A History of Russia.* New York: Oxford University Press, 1963.

Rickards, Maurice. *Posters of Protest and Revolution.* New York: Walker and Co., 1970.

Schapiro, Leonard, and Peter Reddaway (eds.). *Lenin: The Man, the Theorist, the Leader.* New York: Frederick A. Praeger, 1967.

Schein, Edgar H. *Coercive Persuasion.* New York: W. W. Norton and Co., 1961.

Schramm, Wilbur (ed.). *The Process and Effects of Mass Communication.* Urbana, Ill.: University of Illinois Press, 1960.

Schwarz, Solomon M. *The Jews in the Soviet Union.* Syracuse, N.Y.: Syracuse University Press, 1951.

Smith, Donald Eugene. *Religion and Political Development.* Boston: Little, Brown and Co., 1970.

Spinka, Matthew. *Christianity Confronts Communism.* New York: Harper and Brothers, 1936.

Stroyen, William B. *Communist Russia and the Russian Orthodox Church.* Washington, D.C.: Catholic University of America Press, 1967.

Struve, Nikita. *Christians in Contemporary Russia.* New York: Charles Scribner's Sons, 1967.

Szczesniak, Boleslaw (ed.). *The Russian Revolution and Religion.* Notre Dame, Ind.: University of Notre Dame Press, 1959.

Timasheff, Nicholas S. *Religion in Soviet Russia, 1917–1942.* New York: Sheed and Ward, 1942.

Treadgold, Donald W. *Twentieth Century Russia,* 2nd Ed. Chicago: Rand McNally and Co., 1964.

Trotsky, Leon. *Literature and Revolution.* Ann Arbor: University of Michigan Press, 1960.

Tucker, Robert C. *The Marxian Revolutionary Idea.* New York: W. W. Norton and Co., 1969.

Walker, Williston. *A History of the Christian Church.* New York: Charles Scribner's Sons, 1959.

Walsh, Warren B. *Russia and the Soviet Union.* Ann Arbor: University of Michigan Press, 1958.

Soviet Sources

Alekseyeva, L. *Sovremennyye prazdniki i obryady v derevne.* Moscow, 1968.

Almazov, S. F., and P. Ya. Piterskii. *Prazdniki pravoslavnoi tserkvi.* Moscow, 1962.

Balevits, Z. V. et al. (eds.). *Ateizm i religiya.* Riga, 1969.

Boldyrev, N. I. et al. *Pedagogika.* Moscow, 1968.

Bolshaya sovetskaya entsiklopediya, 2nd Ed., 51 Vols. Moscow, 1949–1958.

Brudnyi, V. I. *Obryady vchera i segodnya.* Moscow, 1968.

Butinova, M. S. and N. P. Krasnikov. *Muzei istorii religii i ateizma.* Moscow-Leningrad, 1965.

Fedoseyev, P. N. et al. *Obshchestvo i religiya.* Moscow, 1967.

Filatov, A. *O novykh i starykh obryadakh.* Moscow, 1967.

200 BIBLIOGRAPHY

Garkavenko, F. (ed.). *O religii i tserkvi.* Moscow, 1965.

Gubanov, N. I. et al. (eds.), *Individualnaya rabota s veruyushchimi.* Moscow, 1967.

Kaftanov, S. V. et al. (eds.). *Radio i televideniye v SSSR.* Moscow, 1961. Translated in JPRS No. 4,838.

Kampars, P. P., and N. M. Zakovich. *Sovetskaya grazhdanskaya obryadnost.* Moscow, 1967.

Kharchev, A. G. *Stanovleniye lichnosti.* Moscow, 1972.

Kichko, Trofim. *Iudaism bez prikras.* Kiev, 1963.

Klimovich, L. I. *Islam.* Moscow, 1965.

KPSS v resolyutsiyakh i resheniyakh Sezdov, konferentsii i plenumov TsK, 7th Ed., 4 Vols. Moscow, 1954–1960.

Krasnikov, N. P. et al. (eds.). *Po etapam razvitiya ateizma v SSSR.* Leningrad, 1967.

Krasnikov, N. P. et al. (eds.). *Voprosy preodoleniya religioznykh perezhitkov v SSSR.* Moscow-Leningrad, 1966.

Kratkii nauchno-ateisticheskii slovar. Moscow, 1964.

Krupskaya, N. K. *Iz ateisticheskogo naslediya.* Moscow, 1964.

Kryvelev, I. A. *Lenin o religii.* Moscow, 1960.

Lenin, V. I. *Polnoye sobraniye sochineniya,* 5th Ed., 55 Vols. Moscow, 1958–1965.

Lenin, V. I. *Sochineniya,* 4th Ed., 39 Vols. Moscow, 1941–1960.

Losev, A. V. et al. *Sotsialno-ekonomicheskoye preobrazovaniye v voronezhskoi derevne.* Voronezh, 1967.

Marx, K., and F. Engels, *On Religion.* Moscow, n.d.

Merkurov, G. *Mass Organizations in the USSR.* Moscow, n.d.

Mezentsev, V. A. (ed.). *Otvety veruyushchim.* 2nd Ed. Moscow, 1965.

Okulov, A. F. et al. (eds.). *Voprosy nauchnogo ateizma,* 12 Vols. Moscow, 1966–

Osipov, A. *Katekhizis bez prikras.* Moscow, 1963.

Palgunov, Nikolai G. *Osnovy informatsii v gazetakh.* Moscow, 1956.

Pantskhava, I. D. (ed.). *Konkretno-sotsiologicheskoye izucheniye sostoyaniya religioznosti i opyta ateisticheskogo vospitaniya.* Moscow, 1969.

Pantskhava, I. D. (ed.). *Osnovyye voprosy nauchnogo ateizma.* Moscow, 1962.

Persits, M. M. (ed.). *Kritika iudeiskoi religii,* 2nd Ed. Moscow, 1964.

Platonov, K. *Psikhologiya religii.* Moscow, 1967.

Popova, M. A. *O psikhologii religii.* Moscow, 1969.

Ramm, B. Ya. et al. (eds.). *Religiya i ateizm na zapade.* Moscow-Leningrad, 1965.

Shatilov, I. (ed.). *Zaboty i dela ateistov.* Moscow, 1970.

Skazkin, S. D. et al. *Nastolnaya kniga ateista.* Moscow, 1968.

Slovar ateista. Moscow, 1964.

Smirnov, N. A. *Ocherki istorii izucheniya islama v SSSR.* Moscow, 1954.

Spravochnik propagandista i agitatora, 1966. Moscow, 1966.

Sputnik ateista, 2nd Ed. Moscow, 1961.

Sputnik komsomolskogo aktivista. Moscow, 1962.

Stalin, I. V. *Sochineniya,* 13 Vols. Moscow, 1946–1955.

Stepanian, Ts. A. et al., *Stroitelstvo kommunizma i dukhovnyi mir cheloveka.* Moscow, 1966.

Torzhestvenno, krasivo, pamyatno! . . . Moscow, 1966.

Tsamerian, I. P. *Osnovy nauchnogo ateizma,* 2nd Ed. Moscow, 1962.

Ugolovnyi kodeks RSFSR. Moscow, 1966.

Voprosy ideologicheskoi raboty. Moscow, 1961.

Vorontsov, G. V. *Marksistskii ateizm i yego sovremennyye falsifikatory.* Moscow, 1972.

Vorontsov, G. *O propagande ateizma.* Leningrad, 1959.

Yakovleva, T. G. *Ateisticheskaya propaganda v massovykh bibliotekakh.* Moscow, 1969.

Yemelyanova, K. L. *Pervyi v strane.* Leningrad, 1964.

Yezhegodnik muzeya istorii religii i ateizma, 7 Vols. Moscow-Leningrad, 1958–1964.

Index